Of Thee,
Nevertheless,
I Sing

Other books by William Lee Miller

Piety Along the Potomac

The 15th Ward and the Great Society

Of Thee, Nevertheless, I Sing

An Essay on American Political Values

WILLIAM LEE MILLER

HARCOURT BRACE JOVANOVICH

NEW YORK AND LONDON

Printed in the United States of America

The quotations on pages 177 and 178 from
"The Slippery Slope" by Robert Smith, © 1973
by The New York Times Company, are reprinted by permission.

Library of Congress Cataloging in Publication Data

Miller, William Lee.
Of thee, nevertheless, I sing.

Includes index.
1.   United States—Politics and government—
1945–   2.   Political ethics.   3.   National characteristics, American.   I.   Title.
E743.M56   320.9′73′092   75-2009
ISBN 0-15-167986-X

First edition

B C D E

To my mother and father

Contents

Of Thee, Nevertheless, I Sing

On Certain Difficulties
in Being an
American Democrat

"For all I know," wrote H. L. Mencken, the most entertaining of our home-grown critics, "democracy is a self-limiting disease. . . . There are thumping paradoxes in its philosophy, and some of them have a suicidal smack." Mencken, the Baltimore Nietzsche, did not assess these "thumping paradoxes" in the way a democrat would do, nor did he take a position with respect to them that could be accepted by many other Americans: he flatly maintained that what this amusing but dreadful country needed was an aristocracy. He further seemed to say that the extraordinary civic virtue to be found in such an aristocracy would coincide exactly with the most refined taste in wine, literature, German music, and Chesapeake Bay seafood. Not many of the rest of us would expect that the social order would ever arrange itself to bring together all of those excellences in quite that way.

Nevertheless, Mencken saw something that our sentimental democratic materials and 200th-birthday celebrations may obscure—namely, that this American democracy makes severe requirements of a citizen, requires in fact a subtle set of values, and is quite a complicated and demanding social arrangement. Whether or not it contains thumping paradoxes or any suicidal smack, at least it is not easy. We can see this now more clearly than anyone could in Mencken's day. He wrote his antidemocratic prejudices and his jibes against America long before "this Republic" reached its present level of power, complication, importance, accomplishment, and disarray.

In particular he missed the spectacle that came to be called, in

3

the curious way that public discourse works, by the name of a luxury apartment complex in Washington. When I imagine Mencken being alive to watch the Watergate epic, with its endless subplots, each with its new cast of moral cripples, I am reminded of a story told by Mencken's English counterpart and superior, George Bernard Shaw. It seems, wrote Shaw, that a man famous throughout many counties for his mighty oaths and the power and beauty of his swearing watched all of his worldly goods spill out of a runaway wagon bumping down a hill into a river. Surveying the resulting scene this champion of cursing quietly remarked, after a pause, "I cannot do justice to this situation." So I imagine Mencken, the amused critic of American democracy, watching Watergate.

He also did not live to see this democracy, with all its warts and thumps and paradoxes, serving as the mightiest nation in all the world. He saw the beginnings in the forties, but he did not see the debacle of Vietnam. Back in 1926, when he wrote *Notes on Democracy*, it did not matter nearly so much to the world how what he called "this Republic" comported itself. There were not then the immensely powerful instruments for carrying out the Republic's purposes all over the globe: there were no B-52's to drop bombs on peasants in Southeast Asia, no Polaris missiles, no SEATO or NATO, no Coca-Cola in Mozambique, no "pattern of world responsibility" plus thermonuclear weapons. The utterances of committees in Washington did not, in those days, reverberate so loudly around the world.

There was no possibility of an appeal to the "national security" of the world's most powerful nation, equipped with weapons that could incinerate mankind. There was no cadre of spies from the OSS and the CIA who could bring their talents home from clandestine missions abroad to serve now in domestic partisan politics. There were zero television sets instead of 85 million, and no expectation that the face of the president himself would appear in one's living room, with earnest full-color appeals to "my fellow Americans." The presidency was a less weighty institution; one can scarcely imagine entreaties to spare Warren Harding in order to save "the Presidency."

The chief of the thumping paradoxes, in Mencken's view, was

this. Every American is enjoined—virtually required—to try to "get ahead" individually, on the one side, and then, on the other side, his egalitarian and "democratic" fellow citizens attack and envy him, and try to pull him down, if he *does* get ahead. Mencken, complacently smoking his cigar far above the sweating masses down below, was cheerfully contemptuous of both parts of this paradox, but he reserved his most stinging disdain for the envy and incomprehension that the "boobs" feel for any man of genuine distinction.

The present book—an examination of American political values—has quite a different point of view from that of H. L. Mencken. In the view to be presented here, the United States is not the scandal and farce he saw it to be, nor is democracy a ridiculous impossibility. These pages will not recommend that we try at this late date to procure some aristocrats, nor will they suggest that we see in our countrymen Mencken's great mythic character the American boob. The writer of this book has a respect for citizens of Laramie, Wyoming, and for Eagle Scouts in the Southwest Kansas Council of the Boy Scouts of America, and for voters on both sides of Orange Street in the old fifteenth ward of New Haven, Connecticut (not to mention for senators, mayors, and assistant secretaries of state), of a kind that Mencken would never for a moment have entertained. Edmund Wilson wrote that Mencken's *Notes on Democracy* was "a sort of obverse of *Leaves of Grass*," a reversal of Walt Whitman's sentimental embrace of every man, the common man, democratic man. If one were forced to choose, it would be better to take Whitman's view than Mencken's, although it should also be said that there are realistic democratic philosophies—Abraham Lincoln's and Reinhold Niebuhr's come to mind—superior to either.

But for all that, one can agree with Mencken that this American "democracy" is much more demanding and complicated than its celebrants have ordinarily seen it to be; that it requires of its citizens civic virtue of a superior order, not altogether unlike what Mencken attributed to his aristocrats; and that by the measure of these severe requirements this Republic has a defective political culture. Our recent history is a series of object lessons on that point.

/

I say, "by the measure of these severe requirements." I intend to examine those defects, but it should be said before that is done that the standards by which the defects are discovered are quite demanding. If you start with something less than the American democratic expectations, then you may arrive at quite another assessment. If this free people were snuggled in the Alps or arrested forever in the eighteenth century, with no world-encircling powers, then one might tolerate our shortcomings with comparative equanimity. In easier circumstances and by other, lesser standards the judgment might be different.

One may formulate our national defects into something close to paradoxes, whether or not they thump. As the angry unsilent majority of the early seventies showed once again, the United States of America can be a conservative country that has sought to conserve, beyond the time of its proper application, an unconservative liberalism, resisting social progress in the name of the progressivism of another era (*classical* liberalism: celebration of private interest; automatic opposition to government; defense of the unbridled free market). As many observers have seen and many residents of American small towns have testified, this country can be conformist in its "individualist" creed, coercive in its nominal libertarianism ("In this country a man is free to do what he wants and if he doesn't, by God, we will force him to"). We have preached as an international creed a peculiar nationalism ("Americanism") very much dependent upon our own particular circumstances and national good fortune, and have from time to time exhibited annoyance that other peoples, with their different histories, have not sprung forward with sufficient alacrity to embrace that creed. Because we are, in our own national self-estimation, "innocent" of any desire to dominate others or harm them, we can allow ourselves to do rather unconcernedly what would appear to be quite uninnocent deeds: Hiroshima and Nagasaki; the My Lai massacre; the secret bombing in Cambodia; the whole Vietnam episode.

In our social arrangements at home, the complexity of the relationships between freedom and equality goes well beyond the feature that entertained Mencken. Seen favorably, the United States has developed a remarkable solution to the perennial conflict between those two great values, which in Europe often stood in opposition to each other. We combined them in our guiding principle of "equality of opportunity": men have, or are supposed to have, an equal "start" in an economic and social "race." But as the struggles over blacks and whites and poor people in the sixties made clear, that familiar ideal of equality of opportunity is neither as easy to accomplish nor so complete a solution to the eternal problem of men living together as Americans sometimes seem to have thought. President Lyndon Johnson's speech at Howard University in June 1965—which, although we did not know it then, was to be the high point of the development of official American doctrine on race and poverty—quite poignantly described the environing and subjective ingredients of a child's life, and an adult's life, that make for unequal opportunity—the influences of neighborhood, school, and family. If one includes the environing circumstance, then "equal opportunity" is not an ideal to be proclaimed glibly, given what Johnson called the "gateless poverty" of America's slums. And even if there were, as there is not, equality of opportunity in the United States, society would still not have reached its final glory: "equal" opportunity is used by opportunists to consolidate unequal advantages, and "winning" an economic "race" is scarcely the highest of human objectives. Although one rejects the complacent Menckenesque disregard for the economic condition of the poor, one may join him and his aristocrats in disdaining the vulgarity of a culture built around the idea of "getting ahead" and "making it."

The ideal of "equality" itself, proclaimed from time to time in heart-felt slogans by all of us who are democrats, is not, as we know in our more sober moments, so easy either of definition or of achievement. The multitude of different meanings of the great egalitarian ideal has been lovingly explored by social philosophers. Does one mean equal pay for equal product, or equal pay for equal time at work, or equal pay for equal need, or equality in something beyond mere payment—satisfaction, respect, moral stature in the eyes of God? Every equality by one test means inequality by another. Aristotle wrote that the Just is a form of the Equal, but the Equal in one respect is interwoven with the unequal in some other respect. More recently political practitioners have been encountering and describing these difficulties more concretely. In the United States since about the time of Johnson's Howard speech there has grown a great muddle and murk around the ideal: Equality of *results?* of *groups?* Equality sought by quotas or by "affirmative action"? A rueful literature since the middle sixties has made the complexity of the practical meaning of equality even clearer than it needs to be.

The national contradictions of central interest to the present book lie, I believe, at the root of these other perplexities. They are the following: that democracy requires one set of values, and American culture teaches another; that modern life requires a moral clarity that its own machinery inhibits; that twentieth-century American democracy requires a civic responsibility that its own characteristics discourage.

Our theme, in other words—to have done for the moment with paradoxes—is the cultural undergirding of American public life.

The word "cultural" here is used in the broad sense that the anthropologist uses it, distinguishing the fabric of human effort from "nature": the bare baby and his wail and what is wiped off him is "nature"; but everything that is put on him, fed to him, rattled at him, tossed in his crib, and (in particular) said to him, is "culture." What is now said to him in this national culture falls short of the needs of our free institutions.

The binding threads of a culture are its values—particularly, because of our history and our heterogeneity, in this culture. And if a young ruler in a monarchy needs careful nurture in order when grown to rule honorably, so in his different mode does the citizen under a republican form of government like this one. He, too, requires from his culture instruction in his duties and formation of his values; he requires nurture when young and a supporting ethos throughout his life. I need scarcely add the conclusion, after the events of the years just past: We are in this regard visibly delinquent.

One can predict with assurance the wary response of an American reader to what has just been written: Who is to proclaim these "duties"? What authority is to do this shaping and forming of values, this nurturing, this talking to bare babies about their civic virtue? Who decides? Any modern American worth his pinch of salt fills the air with clouds of relativism and doubt at any suggestion that somebody might know what is just or virtuous or right: who are you to say? He responds on cue with instant accusations against anyone in whom he discerns a trace of the notion that he might "know what's good for you." I suggest that he is fighting a battle that has long since been won, and producing, as battlers fighting ancient wars often do, new damage in another direction. Or perhaps I mean it is a battle on several fronts.

Which was the defect in John Ehrlichman, H. R. Haldeman, and their group?

—That they were moral absolutists, fanatics, running over grandmothers because they were sure that they were right? (See Ehrlichman's excursus on the unreported moral lapses of liberal senators, repeated references to Righteousness and Absolute Loyalty, or that straight arrow pointed in the wrong direction, Egil Krogh.)

—Or that they were cynics, children of darkness, men who knew no law save their own self-interest?

For the most part one would choose the second of these, but the simultaneous plausibility of the first suggests the complexity, that they may flow into one another. As with the Nixon White House, so with American culture. Dogmatism is not the world's only danger; a moral vacuum is a danger, too, and a more pertinent one today, and curiously can turn into its apparent opposite.

To answer the skeptic's questions:

Who are you to say what is Just? You. You are a "moral agent," as the textbooks used to say, and that is an essential foundation for free government.

Aren't there 118 different ideas about what is Just, and who's to choose? Not that many, and you choose.

If I know what is Good or Right, won't I force it on others? No, you will enter your convictions in the conversation of democracy . . . in the forming of a culture. And that culture will be improved thereby. The cycle otherwise is downward.

This democratic social order, in which "We, the People" discuss, decide, and act, must be a collaborative undertaking; the culture's billboards proclaim instead an uncollaborative careerism, competitive and self-seeking to the farthest private swimming pool.

It must assume a citizenry able to conceive a general welfare; the culture has instead encouraged the citizen to look at the great public issues from the angle of his private gain; more recently, many of its teachers have assured him such a general welfare does not exist.

This democratic arrangement, if it is not indeed to require for its guidance Mencken's aristocrats, if it is instead to rest upon "the consent of the governed," must arrange to have the capacity for rational consent spread widely among those who are to be governed. The governing of a free people is a work of deliberation, of conversation, of discussion, of debate and argument, and even persuasion. That assumes that citizens can speak and listen and think and sometimes be persuaded. It is not fashionable to say so, but it is nevertheless true that despite all the irrationality and self-interest in it, it rests at last upon the reason and the conscience of citizens, upon a "public" that develops a mind and a will. It presupposes, therefore, a citizen who is the bearer not only of a private interest, of his chunk of a group interest, but also of some capacity for justice.

Collaborative, democratic government requires a recognition of the principle of government, and of the principle of the public good. American political culture has been strongly imbued with the opposites of these qualities: a considerable anarchistic feeling, although it has never been called that (that government is best that governs least); and an excessive trust that pursuit of private interest will serve the common good.

I exaggerate somewhat, to be sure; in fact, this culture has in it many values. Those I have mentioned and will anatomize further are, although strong, only one part of the story. This book is not to be one of those unremitting attacks upon the United States with which Americans periodically and masochistically entertain themselves.

The nation has recently been well supplied with material for such masochism. The malaise at the time this is written, not long before the bicentennial, is at least superficially the result of a series of stunning blows: the fear of nuclear war in 1961–62; the assassinations; the strange and terrible war in Southeast Asia that Americans could neither win nor agree about; the riots in the cities, the protests, the youth revolt, with a first faint whiff of anarchy; the hardhatted recoil against all of that, and the sense that the nation was unraveling; the glimpse of a possible economic future different from the long expansion we have known; and Watergate.

The chapters that follow will touch on some of these matters, especially the last. They will deal rather selectively with some of the cast of characters, and political points of view—liberal, radical, conservative—as these have taken their turn on the national stage.

3

The polity itself, as I have said, is both internally complicated and morally exacting. Combining minority rights and protected individual liberties, on the one side, with majority rule and popular sovereignty, on the other, is a good deal more intricate than we have ordinarily seen it to be. Each part of this combination has its own hazards; putting them together increases the difficulty.

There are libertarians from the continent who do not share our transatlantic devotion to "democracy." You will find a passage in F. A. Hayek's widely read book of 1944, *The Road to Serfdom*, in which Hayek, Austrian by birth, wrote this:

We have no intention . . . of making a fetish of democracy. It may well be true that our generation talks and thinks too much of democracy and too little of the values which it serves. It cannot be said of democracy, as Lord Acton truly said of liberty, that "it is not a means to a higher political end. It is itself the highest political end. . . ." Democracy is essentially a means, a utilitarian device for safeguarding internal peace and individual freedom. As such it is by no means infallible or certain. Nor must we forget that there has often been much more cultural and spiritual freedom under an autocratic rule as under some democracies. . . .

The plain inference is that in such a case one is to choose the autocratic rule. It is a passage that few Americans would have written. For us, the value of democracy has bitten deep enough to be no instrument of another, higher end, but itself an intrinsic value, or a symbol of the intrinsic value of the human person without regard to station.

Each part of this American combination, as I say, makes its own claims, and together they require both conviction and self-restraint: not easy to put together.

Majority rule, or rule of the demos, the people, in our liberal democratic and constitutional setup is by no means absolute. It is limited by the protection of the minorities who disagree, and of individual freedoms protected no matter who is majority or minority. Our polity is not only a rule by the majority; it is a rule by a majority within limits—the majority cannot vote a "mandate" to send the "plumbers" on their expeditions, or to persecute the Washington *Post*, or to use the Internal Revenue Service for partisan vengeance. The limitations upon today's majority include the protection of the conditions under which the minority may overthrow it tomorrow—the right to express its point of view, to organize, to agitate, to produce newspaper articles the majority does not like, and to seek to become itself a new majority.

We are by no means a polity with a simple "popular sovereignty" or simple rule of numbers. We grant authority to popular majorities only when they have achieved their support under the conditions of liberty, and continue to observe its limitations. Any momentary "majority" has moral dignity, in other words, only when it has achieved its position under conditions of freedom and fair play—conditions that allow the other fellows continually to oppose it and next time maybe to defeat it.

This combination, carried out amid the passions of politics in a heterogeneous society, requires a high level of self-restraint. A rather difficult set of rules has to be written on the conscience of the democrat. It is really rather a remarkable development, in the history of mankind's effort to live together, that now, in the parliamentary democracies, the defeated side, after the votes are counted, acquieses in its defeat and yields power gracefully, or at any rate peacefully, to the winners. It does so even where the stakes are high and the feelings strong. It is no small accomplishment, as these things go. A citizen of a working liberal democracy is trained from childhood in accepting votes, abiding by the majority, and respecting the process of its rule.

Many countries of the world even yet do not have any such set of popular habits: defeated parties reach for their guns or head for the hills. In a South American country during the 1948 election in the United States of America, a native was reported to be shocked by the concession speech Governor Thomas Dewey made after Harry Truman had won: how could Dewey so demean himself, after all Truman and he had said about each other? How could he support the winner and call upon his supporters to do the same? How unmanly, thus to crawl! Happily our own measure of machismo and absolutism has been tempered by decades of democratic experience.

There are obligations and self-restraints required of each of the factions and parties in the democratic order. Our history is instructive not only in the degree to which we have been able to inculcate those restraints but also in the degree to which we have not, as two pungent recent examples with a slightly different shape remind us: the rejection of merely procedural restraints by the most militant of the radicals in 1965–70, and that rich vein of object lessons in undemocratic behavior, the Watergate affair.

Both these recent collections of experiences show the inadequacy of our democratic nurture. The young revolutionaries regarded the evils of American society as so severe and so obvious as to make legitimate a violent attack upon them: shouting so that Dean Rusk could not speak, invading the International Affairs Center so that it could not do its work, trying to "shut down"

Washington, planting a bomb in a university building. That their sneering rejection of merely procedural restraints influenced for a time so wide a section of the young and of the intelligentsia shows how weak our training in the democratic ethos can be. Those in the penumbra around the radicals, in the days of their notoriety, were not well equipped in their political-moral training to resist the fad of the moment. They got over it not so much through better understanding (though historical events played an instructive role), as through a change in the fad.

When the Watergate cynics followed them on the national stage, the grossest ignorance of the duties of a citizen appeared in the nation's highest offices. Let us content ourselves here with just one of the hundreds of cautionary tales from the vast Watergate literature.

Senator Talmadge: Am I to understand from your response that you placed the expediency of the next election above your responsibilities . . . to advise the President of the peril that surrounded him? Here was the deputy campaign director involved, here were his two closest associates in his office involved, all around him were people involved in crime . . . and you deliberately refused to tell him that. Would you state that the expediency of the election was more important than that?

Former Attorney General Mitchell: Senator, I think you have put it exactly correct. In my mind, the re-election of Richard Nixon, compared with what was available on the other side, was so much more important that I put it in just that context.

More important than the checks and balances of separated powers is the balance between representatives of different interests, values, parties, and philosophies. The two-party system and the seeking of a majority under conditions of freedom—conditions that allow that majority to be overthrown—have their internal moral logic. The Watergaters demonstrated again and again that they did not understand it—they did not comprehend their moral obligation to their adversary in a democratic system. They did not understand that they owed something to those who oppose them, and should continually learn something from the opposition.

4

At the same time that American democracy puts all these claims and restraints upon a citizen's individual conviction and interest— he must allow others to speak, compromise, acquiesce when the vote goes against him—it also does require (as does any polity, but for additional reasons of its own) that there be leaders. And it requires moreover that ordinary citizens have convictions (non-majority convictions, unordinary convictions) and express them, and act in their behalf, in order that there be a public will.

This does not mean that American democracy needs aristo-crats, supermen, or multiples of H. L. Mencken. It does mean that this polity needs citizens who combine in themselves its dou-ble (or multiple) discipline, its complicated moral pattern, includ-ing having convictions about the public good. Democracy requires both self-limitation—an openness and toleration and ac-quiescence in the people's decision (where such decision is appro-priate)—and an inclusive respect for all men, including men of the humblest station, of a sort that Mencken would have found ridic-ulous; and, at the same time it does indeed require something not altogether unlike the assurance and clarity and independence of moral judgment that Mencken assigns to his aristocrats.

American democracy is threatened in one direction, as is well known, by absolutists and fanatics who jam the works with their refusal to bend. But American democracy is also threatened in the other direction, as is not quite so well known, by hollowness, by manipulative public-relations people and hucksters, by dema-goguery and the rootless mass that responds to demagoguery, by that parade of hollow men and team players from the White House horrors team; by amoral technicians. As often happens in these cases, the threat of one of these evils has encouraged men in reaction to embrace another. And as also often happens, two evils that appear at first to be opposites turn out in the end to be much alike.

The American democrat, seen critically, may then be like Mar-tin Luther's drunken peasant: put back on his donkey after falling off on one side, he proceeds to fall off the other.

And the ground to which he falls is the same from whichever side he tumbles—an irresponsibility that endangers the social arrangement he is supposed to embody.

5

Mencken, as I said, thought the solution to American democracy's manifest contradictions was that there be aristocrats. The solution, really, is the more likely, but also in some ways harder, one that there be democrats. By a "democrat" I mean a bearer of the fragile ethos that makes this internally complex arrangement serve its humane purposes. That is a more exacting task than aristocratic single-mindedness.

Mencken rather grandly names the virtues a true aristocracy would possess, which, he says, the plutocratic pseudo aristocracy of the United States totally lacks: "A clean tradition, culture, public spirit, honesty, honor, courage—above all, courage." (An interesting list, from a man continually mocking the YMCA and the Boy Scouts.) Whatever reaction against the plutocratic ideal one can find in the United States, he said, it lacks nevertheless "aristocratic disinterestedness, born of aristocratic security." Those of us who disagree with Mencken have the hope and expectation that there can be in the American democracy a secure and disinterested citizen (let us not say a social class, as Mencken did, or an "elite," in the present language of the social sciences) who is the bearer not only of the virtues of Mencken's gentlemen but also of some others, and who lacks the sense of superiority, disdain, and self-satisfied separation from the masses that rises like an odor from every page of Mencken's amusing prose.

What additional virtues? Self-restraint is certainly one . . . the self-restraint that another man's liberties require. Self-criticism is another . . . a kind of *social* self-criticism or humility: openness to other views and a willingness, within limits, to compromise. One may quote from President Gerald Ford an alliteration that is more appealing than some we heard at an earlier time: "communication, conciliation, compromise, and co-operation." What I represent, politically, socially, economically, what I understand, out of my experience and social location, is not final, complete, absolute—and I know it is not. Other men have experiences and interests and values that I do not know about, but need to: in the process of democracy I learn. But I (I, the citizen of a free country) do not come to this learning as a blank sheet of paper. I come not only with experiences and interests of my own, but also with a mind and conscience that responds and judges. If my culture from the crib onward teaches me that there are no standards by which to judge, but only interest and opinion, then I am a defective democrat.

Writings sometimes appear, springing apparently from exasperation with absolutists and fanatics, that insist that the very *essence* of American democracy is "compromise." But of course it is not. Compromise and adjustment are usually desirable, but there must be an antecedent moral substance on the foundation of which one may, to a degree, accommodate: one compromises from a position. And on some few foundational matters one does not.

There is Mencken's vision of an aristocrat, disdainful of democracy. There are people-flattering demagogues—some, it is possible to believe, at "the very highest levels" in our recent past. There are proud absolutists—many visible on the public scene in recent years. And there is the democratic statesman. Those of us who do not share Mencken's view can say at least this: that the difficult combination of virtues the latter requires is not altogether unknown, and that this Republic with all its faults can find in itself the resources to make them increase.

6

I promised earlier that this book would not be one of those unremitting attacks upon the United States. In partial fulfillment of that promise I now risk one last paradox, more amiable than those that have gone before: this Republic is better than it seems, better than it sounds, certainly better than it has sometimes behaved. A free people can from time to time surprise itself with an Abraham

Lincoln, after a string of James Buchanans. Such a nation, democratic, energetic, and diverse, can produce something more
worthy than (measured by its culture) it "intends," perhaps than
it "deserves": the Constitution; the New Deal; the Marshall Plan;
the civil-rights movement; the exposure of the Nixon scandals.
The naturalized citizen who was once my boss, Max Ascoli, of
the *Reporter*, delivered at Marquette University, in Wisconsin, in
the days of Senator Joseph McCarthy, an address in which he
paid testimony to merits of his adopted country that are less visible than the shortcomings exemplified by McCarthy and ridiculed
by H. L. Mencken; he called it "The Hidden America."

Reinhold Niebuhr wrote a chapter in his moderately severe
1952 assessment of this country, *The Irony of American History*, in
which he explained that "Experience" had triumphed over
"Dogma": in the New Deal this country had achieved a nearer
approach to social justice than our individualistic language might
have led one to expect. In the late forties I heard Niebuhr, at a
meeting in New York, rise to defend this nation's virtues against
Paul Tillich and another German refugee, who were mercilessly
applying to this vulnerable nation their ferocious European
theories about a grindingly impersonal "mass society" manipulated by "elites," in which society not only the working class but
also almost everyone is in a "proletarian situation": they do not
control their own lives. Niebuhr, despite the remnants in him of
his youthful radical attacks upon our bourgeois culture, rose to
speak "just one nationalist word" against these "damned Conti-
nentals." For all that you can criticize in America, he said, still
that truck driver you see there on the sidewalk has his self-
respect, and that is something.

One needs to point out that this nation has the moral resources
to do what it needs to do, in order to encourage its being done. It
is not impossible, as even our recent troubled history, by a realistic test, has shown.

In the years since World War II, and especially since the assassination of John F. Kennedy, this American political culture has
already undergone that test. That it has in some sense passed it is
to its credit; and shows powers of continuity and resilience and
accomplishment that those fierce and terrible attacks on

"Amerika" read and written a few years ago by my younger colleagues did not comprehend. They did not assess either the qualities of our nation or the somber complexities of politics from a sufficiently realistic perspective. Not every nation, inexperienced, could rise from unprepared isolation to unprecedented world power and responsibility as swiftly, as ably, as beneficiently, and, on the whole, as honorably as did the United States in the forties. Not every nation, as Churchill's gracious comment implied, could have found within itself the resources to propose and to carry out that "most unsordid act in history," the Marshall Plan. Not every society, locked in a balance of nuclear terror, could survive the shock of the assassination of its young leader, and pass that enormous power into other hands, as smoothly as did the United States in 1963. Not every nation could itself create, out of its own internal moral chemistry, the civil-rights movement and the turning around of the whole history of a caste system written into law and custom, as did the United States in 1954–68. Not many societies could find resources within their other institutions to counteract the immensely powerful machinery concentrated at the top and peacefully, lawfully, honorably force a resistant and imperious chief of state to abdicate, as the United States did in the months from March 1973 to August 1974. I shall not attempt the favorable interpretation of the Vietnam war, since to do that is to sound like some of the speeches of President Lyndon Johnson that are best left unremembered, but one may at least mumble in passing that even that disaster is capable of an interpretation not altogether discreditable to the United States. Each of the shocks and miseries, as well as the accomplishments, of the recent period is capable of such an interpretation.

What is one's standard of judgment, after all? Where in the history of man's struggle to live together is the perfection implied by the more simplistic and unyielding condemnations of the "Corporate State," and "Sick Society," the Imperialistic Arrogance of Power? It is not to be found in either the deeds or the ideas of those who make such condemnations. Judged by a realistic and historical standard, the United States is an impressive accomplishment.

But having said that much one must stop. It is not the intention of this book to obey the injunction to "Speak Up for America," or to reiterate that "the system" works. I shall not say what is GOOD about America or celebrate this "Great" country. The greatness of America is present in times and places in which nobody is talking about the "greatness of America"; "the system" works well when no one is defensively insisting that it does. America's faults and vices are so closely related to her virtues, accomplishments, and beneficent possibilities as to require careful discrimination . . . discrimination of the sort that either defensively "Speaking Up for America" or sweepingly condemning the "Corporate State" prevents one from making. One wants no part either of the embarrassing boosterism of the early seventies or of the immature radicalism of the late sixties, those mutually reinforcing twin simplisms, each pointing to the other to justify its own exaggerations. No serious person wants to be so presumptuous as to give the United States of America a grade—A+, C−, or F. What is to be done, rather, is to examine, with an unending series of discriminate judgments, the characteristics of our political culture, as they serve and fail to serve its own high purposes.

Part One

Some Movements,
Men,
and Events

On Moral Crusades
and Also on a
Really Realistic Realism

(with Ike as an Example)

Some veterans back from Vietnam would sit in the back row of the classroom wearing their boots and listening with a certain silent circumspection to wordy discussions of the "Just War," the morality of the use of force, and the terribly hard choices that "policy makers" had to face. Sometimes, during one's lecture, making points one, two, three more or less in sympathy with those policy makers, one would remember a sentence from Ernest Hemingway, written in the disillusion from another war . . . a sentence reflecting as it may be the perception by these silent ones in their boots of those policy makers, the sting of whose "hard choices" they themselves had actually felt in the most personal way. Perhaps it might also reflect their back-row view of a discussion of such matters in a secluded classroom. Hemingway wrote in *A Farewell to Arms,* about the Italian Battle Police catching deserters behind the lines in World War I, that they "had that beautiful detachment and devotion to stern justice of men dealing in death without being in any danger of it." So, at a further remove, it may be with the "policy makers" and their "hard choices," except that the object of beautifully detached devotion recently has been the National Interest. Hemingway's sentence is the sort of ironic *ad hominem* that often appeals to a man—a young one in particular—who is not on the making end but on the receiving end of great national policies.

Nevertheless, as Hemingway's generation of Americans was to

have all too much opportunity to learn, someone must form the policies and make the decisions. Hemingway's sentence, and a more famous passage from the same book that I will quote in a moment, serve the purpose of this chapter, to make both more sober and more complex the criticism of the familiar ways that Americans moralize politics. These are to be rejected not only for the mischief they themselves cause, but also for the mischief done in reaction against them—cynical and disillusioned reactions among the common folk; "tough-minded" and "hard-boiled" reactions among political professionals; positivistic—"scientific"—reactions among the intelligentsia; above all, the reactions of withdrawal and distaste among sensitive people like Hemingway. One must, in other words, criticize yet one more time American moralism and sentimentality not in the service of cynicism, but in the attempt to encourage the persistent civic virtue for which the simpler views are a counterfeit. Neither our older moral idealism nor the characteristic reactions against it represent the political nurture this Republic's condition calls for.

The Battle Police and the National Security Council, and the courts and the secretaries of state and the makers of many policies high and low do have to make decisions, and the gravest of these do "deal in death," and that death does not ordinarily include their own: what is one's conclusion? One wants them to know what they are doing—to be aware of its seriousness. One wants them to speak about these matters not as Woodrow Wilson did but also not as the writers of memos about "options" did in the Pentagon Papers, or as the writer on military strategy Herman Kahn does, jauntily dispatching continents in a cloud of jargon. As to style, one would prefer that of George Kennan, in which the care and humane reflectiveness show that he is not unaware that he may be "dealing in death." One wants such men to make "good" and "just" decisions, whatever that may mean, without such a beautiful detachment as never to comprehend what their decisions mean to others.

But at the same time one wants the citizenry to know that such decisions must be made by someone, and that that often is not so easy either intellectually or morally. If both leaders and citizens in this "great power" need a more humane and a more profound political culture, it is not clear that the ironic stroke of Hemingway, or his anti-intellectual taciturnity, or his antisocial withdrawal and individual stoicism, gracefully expressed though they be, will lead to that result. Not everyone can make a Separate Peace, nor is humankind best served by those who yearn for one.

The other quotation from Hemingway is the well-known passage in which the narrator Frederic Henry—plainly equipped with the author's own sensibility—hears a passionate young Italian patriot say that the sacrifices of the brave men shall not have been in vain. Frederic Henry remarks:

"I was always embarrassed by the words sacred, glorious, and sacrifice and the expression in vain. We had heard them, sometimes standing in the rain almost out of earshot, so that only the shouted words came through, and had read them, on proclamations that were slapped up by billposters over other proclamations, now for a long time, and I had seen nothing sacred, and things that were glorious had no glory and the sacrifices were like the stockyards at Chicago if nothing were done with the meat except to bury it. There were many words that you could not stand to hear and finally only the names of places had dignity. . . . Abstract words such as glory, honor, courage, or hallow were obscene beside the concrete names of villages, the numbers of roads, the names of rivers, the numbers of regiments and the dates."

One can understand that response. Men feel that way about hortatory and allegedly uplifting abstractions that stand in contrast with the realities they have seen. It is a response that applies to modern warfare, and to the catastrophes of the twentieth century following upon the promises of the nineteenth. It applies in particular to World War I, about which Hemingway was writing, and to the primary abstract uplifter Woodrow Wilson, one of the chief Americans to give moral idealism a bad name.

Hemingway's paragraph reflects a sensibility and a discipline that are not only temperamental and aesthetic but also moral. These qualities are expressed also in many other passages in which the insensitive behavior and the flabby overuse and misuse of weighty words are undercut by a sharp ironic juxtaposition with a contrasting reality. The English guide in "The Short Happy Life of Francis Macomber" says explicitly that there is "no pleasure in anything if you mouth it too much." In *Death in the*

Afternoon Hemingway says that for Americans (in contrast to Spaniards) "all our words from loose using have lost their edge."

That distaste for the overstatements of World War I reflects the sensibility of a writer and a particular kind of writer—an American writer put off by a flabby American talkative idealism and hypocrisy; an American ex-newspaperman imbued with the priority of the concrete—dates, names, particulars, because they carry meaning to readers, because they are real, because they are not, as Holden Caulfield later would put it, phony. "Abstract" is a bad word. Hemingway had, and yet did not really have, the older American newspaperman's anti-intellectualism; he was, we may say, a pseudo anti-intellectual. The rejecting of abstractions, of intellectualism, of general ideas and mouthing things too much applies pointedly to social ideals and to conduct—to morals—and especially where there is life and death and serious consequence: the beautiful detachment and devotion to stern justice of men dealing in death without being in any danger of it. Hemingway in this regard epitomized a sensibility of many of the best of Americans reacting against their national environment, and, of his generation, reacting against their time.

Very well. But now look back at that quotation from Frederic Henry, the famous paragraph about his embarrassment at obscene abstractions. Notice that Henry (Hemingway) himself uses the word "dignity" at the end of the third sentence. Is that not an abstract word? Is that not one of those words that appears in proclamations slapped up by billposters on top of other proclamations? Is that not a word much like those (honor, courage, glory) that he found obscene, when placed alongside the names of specific rivers and regiments? Hemingway as much as Woodrow Wilson must on occasion use such an "abstraction."

On fewer occasions, to be sure. Whereas Wilson mouthed such words too much, and they lost their edge, Hemingway was sparing in such use, with a writer's care. That is itself a testimony to a moral as well as to an aesthetic sense.

As many commentators have said, Hemingway's work (laconic, concrete) was shot through with ethical preoccupation: how properly to live. There is a code to be maintained even if the chattering folk in the café, or the crowd at the bullfight, fail to comprehend it. There is an early appreciation by Edmund Wilson, called "Hemingway: Gauge of Morale," that comes close to presenting Hemingway at his best and truest not only as a gauge of changing attitudes but also as an implicit moral guide who will straighten those attitudes. We, too, in whatever our work may be, have had our defeats, and our opportunities not to be defeated in defeat, as has the old bullfighter in *The Undefeated,* and we may learn something for edification in our town trials from Hemingway's story.

Hemingway wanted to do something well, and did, and he wanted to express something serious about how life is and should be, and he did. Some of his readers, thirty years and several wars later, carrying their copies of the Scribner paperback of his short stories on the subways and around the campuses want to do that, too. Most of these people will not be bullfighters or fishermen. Most will not be men at war; some of those who have been will then return and sit with their boots in the back rows of the classroom. It is too bad no Hemingway has done what he did for men at war, bullfighters, and fishermen for precinct committeemen, presidents, division managers, secretaries of state, and judges sitting on courts dealing in death without being in any danger of it. Institutional life, political life also pose questions, going beyond those posed to bullfighters, about how properly to live and what purposes to serve.

1

With World War I, the United States joined modern history, if one may put it that way, and, as a thousand writers have indeed put it, "lost her innocence." But the skepticism and disillusion and withdrawal of all the Frederic Henrys, after the war, did not make an end to the moralistic strain, and the utopian strain, in American politics. They had, of course, a long history.

An American sociologist has written,

Authoritative observers from De Tocqueville, through Bryce, Siegfried and others, down to such recent studies as those of Vernon L. Parrington, Margaret Mead, Gunnar Myrdal, and Harold Laski, have agreed on at least one point: Americans tend to "see the world in moral terms."

It is a constant theme. For just one of a multitude of examples, when Margaret Mead wrote about the American character, in the later World War, she said in her introduction:

As America has a moral culture—that is, a culture which accepts right and wrong as important—any discussion of Americans must simply bristle with words like *good* and *bad*. Any discussion of Samoans would bristle with terms for awkward and graceful. . . . If I were writing about the way in which the Germans or the Japanese, the Burmese or the Javanese would have to act if they were to win the war, I would not need to use so many moral terms. For none of these peoples think of life in habitually moral terms as do Americans.

It may be wryly remarked in the wake of the moral idiocy and cynicism of Watergate that excessive moralism can scarcely be said just now to be our foremost problem. And yet it is a problem still, linked to the warp in American political culture that helped to produce Watergate. Self-righteousness was not altogether missing from that set of adventures, and may be ready to make its appearance within another cast of characters in its aftermath. And the fanaticism of those whatever-it-takes Nixon loyalists was one particularly blatant form of the simplification and black-white absolutism that regularly appears in the moralizing mentality.

Meg Greenfield wrote wisely in *Newsweek* for June 10, 1974 that the sanctimony of Mr. Spiro Agnew and of others in the Nixon circle, so admonitory about law, order, and other people's morals, should have been a signal. She asked herself what former Vice President Agnew could have felt inwardly when, after lecturing the public about the need for higher moral standards and the evils of permissiveness, he would then accept in secret an envelope filled with cash. Did he chortle cynically? Probably not. More likely he made no connection between his words on the platform and his own deeds. Evil deeds were done by somebody else—radiclibs, protesters, criminals—not by people like himself.

One of the more revealing moments in the Watergate morality play—I expand now on Ms. Greenfield's point—was the response of Ronald Reagan to the first reports: these men may have made errors but they are not *criminals*. It was quite evident that "criminals" were to him by definition a different sort of person from his friends and associates, persons like himself, who did the deeds of Watergate. Some of this would be a matter of social class, and even of race—thus a kind of sociological self-righteousness. Mixed with it there was the blinding individual self-righteousness, self-protectiveness, to which all men are tempted. Sanctimonious and moralistic attitudes often reinforce this vice: Evil is located elsewhere, over there, with them, those others, those bad people different from me. Evil is represented by permissive judges, Daniel Ellsberg, and the young militants who proposed to shut down Washington—not by the solid citizens and bright young men of the White House, the Attorney General's office, and the Committee to Re-elect the President.

Greenfield gave this matter another turn: she noted that "many of those who were most affronted by the moralizing and ball-and-chain wielding of the Nixon administration . . . are now coming on all aquiver with fury at the least consequential Watergate infractions . . . and calling for everything but electrocution in the streets." It was a point well made. We anti-Nixonians were fully capable of constructing a self-justifying demonology of our own, loading all the nation's evils on that Watergate group, sometimes with a trace of self-praise. For all one's respect for the role of the Washington *Post*, it does make one a little uneasy when in Woodward and Bernstein's *All the President's Men* Benjamin Bradlee, the *Post* editor, gleefully exclaims in victory "The White Hats win!" Watch out for all people who regard themselves as the white hats.

The moralism of these American colonies has been criticized a hundred thousand times since Cotton Mather's day, or Roger Williams' day, but it is necessary in these pages to condemn it once again. It keeps reappearing in ever new forms. Just when one believes that it must have been battered beyond recovery by a swarm of pragmatists and sociologists, skewered by some laconic phrases from Hemingway and by cocky laughter from Mencken, punctured fatally by a well-known paragraph from George Kennan, evaporated in the hot sun of modern scientific amoralism, buried under a thousand articles by Reinhold Niebuhr, "there it comes again," like the deathless and fast-growing vine in the old George Price *New Yorker* cartoon, energetically rounding the corner of the house once more just as the desperate householder cuts away the last round with his shears.

When one argues that American democracy requires some solid ethical stuff in the citizenry, then it is necessary, in order not to be misunderstood, explicitly to repudiate the familiar American politics (or antipolitics) of Righteousness, the oversimple "mouthing too much" about these matters, the often self-vindicating division of the world absolutely into Good and Evil, "Right" and Wrong. What is needed is not the outlook of John Brown, or of William Jennings Bryan, or of McKinley's way of discovering God's convenient will for the United States in the Philippines, or of Teddy Roosevelt in his bully pulpit aspect or standing at Armageddon, or of Woodrow Wilson speaking the glorious hallowed sacred words that Frederic Henry found, by contrast to the battles he fought, obscene, or of John Foster Dulles, or of Dwight Eisenhower either, or of a hundred others out of the rich and variegated but dubious American tradition of moralistically "crusading," politics, right, left, and center.

The United States, puritan in some of its beginnings, evangelistic and revivalist in important nineteenth-century influence, liberal and individualist and voluntarist in politics and economics (these qualities reinforcing the moralism from the religious source) has produced a whole series of "crusades," of a widely varying social value, from campaigns against Demon Rum and Sunday mail to campaigns against slavery.

Those "crusades" have characteristically been passionate, zealous, full of fervor. They have been surcharged with emotion and filled with the drama of conversion and revival. Although, to be sure, there is a place for zeal in politics, this single-minded crusading kind is inappropriate and misleading because it cannot last, and because it is doomed to disillusion. The underlying expectation is that a sufficiently dramatic rousing of energies will resolve the dilemmas of history, which in fact it will not. The discussion of public affairs regularly features an underlying impatience with the mixed and problematical, and yearns instead for a show of proclamatory fervor . . . a politics of high and pure and uncomplicated causes that is dissatisfied with a treatment that is not rousing and final. It is not the style of political wisdom.

The crusade is the march of the pure against an evil. It pretends to look down upon the world of power and conflict from a realm of moral perfection above it; it puts forth its aggressive effort to make over or eliminate the evil, by crusaders who still in their own view of themselves retain their purity. That, too, is not the style of political wisdom.

The subordinate layer of pugnacity underneath the surface may break through when the exhortations fail and conflicts of interest are made plain. The outlook we have described is philosophically unprepared for such conflicts. When confronted with them, it tends to fall back upon sharp moral distinctions, finding the cause not in social arrangements or inevitable differences of perspective, but in the evil will of some particular persons, who refuse to have a change of heart and be good men, who are on the wrong side of a moral issue, and who therefore are fit objects for the crusader's wrath.

All of this has been criticized before, and one would have thought it would have vanished. But it has not. The reaction against its evident shortcomings, perhaps like the reaction of Hemingway's hero to the large Wilsonian vibrations, is itself defective and too evidently a reaction: not yet political wisdom. So then, in an ethos in which the roots of such wisdom are not as deep as they need to be, there comes a reaction to the reaction. There comes a new explosion of Righteous politics, fueled by historical evils to which the spirit of debunking and withdrawal and matter-of-factness seems to a new generation to be a quite inadequate response.

Recent American political history provides an instance of the whole sequence. When the Eisenhower years came to an end and a very different and much younger man was president of the United States, a no-nonsense "operational" atmosphere established itself in Washington, in sharp contrast to assorted moralizings of Ike and Dulles. This atmosphere was parallel to a positivistic atmosphere in universities, and to the "end of Ideology" perceived by political writers and commentators. Perhaps also there was a parallel to those so-called existentialist ideas (a long way from Kierkegaard) in which one "created new values every day" and to that "situational" ethics, rejecting general principles, that was seized upon with such gleeful eagerness by the young, especially as it applied to sexual behavior.

Then came the Vietnam war. More references to honor, glory, sacrifice, and "not in vain"; more Frederic Henrys embarrassed to hear them. There was Peace with Honor, and the Free World fighting Aggression, together with many bombings and shootings and even torturing and assassinations, and certainly confusion. The Vietnam issues were intense; the American intellectual atmosphere into which those weighty issues were projected had been uncritically nationalistic and instrumentalist (among intellectuals in one way; among men of the world in another). To the young and the sensitive in the late sixties there was available no widely understood tradition of ethical discrimination with which to interpret the war, to resist their nation's policy and yet remain loyal to the nation. Along with the war came weighty issues about blacks and the poor and the manifold defects of American society. There was nothing there with which to calibrate ethical judgment—nothing to do but crank up again out of American culture another sudden and mindless politics of Righteousness. And so there appeared once more a moral absolutism of the sort we had thought to be dead. It was resurrected in all its righteous armor in the antiwar and young left movements of the late sixties, *Right* from the Start.

Here is this, as it used to be called "innocent," country, this once puritan country choked with moral intentions, this democratic country in which policy is made with an eye to the simplifications of the hustings, trying to cope since December 1941, or August 1945, with a political task that would have made the darkest European practitioners of *Realpolitik* turn pale. It goes without saying that we have not begun to develop the depth of thought, of language, or of moral understanding to match the nation's role.

Oversimple moralizing and ideal expectations encourage then a disgusted, even a cynical, reaction in the disillusioned aftermath. Sets of attitudes that are apparent opposites tend to come in pairs within a culture—in the United States, moralism and a positivism that thinks the facts speak for themselves; utopianism and a cynicism that says the world is a jungle; evangelical conversionism and a sociological determinism that sees everything done by social forces and the environment untouched by human hands.

One may observe these attitudes not only following and reinforcing each other but also sometimes coexisting. Among one's students there is a recurrent type, cynical about politics (about human society, really) because his expectations are too high—or, rather, too naïve—or "pure" or uninformed. On Tuesday such a student has the rosiest expectations; on Wednesday a snarl for the world that has not met them; sometimes he has both on the same day.

One can observe also among one's fellow professors a kind of arrested development, as they become stuck in place at the annual relativistic and skeptical assault upon the freshmen. Among writers for a broad audience and among eggheads generally there is something of the same: a permanent Menckenesque condescension toward the struggles of ordinary mortals with the issues of purpose and principle. Mass democracy in a scientific age in once puritan America seems to keep most of the visible intelligentsia locked into that first stage of criticism of the most popular errors.

The presidents of the United States often do seem to reflect the characteristics of the period in which they hold office, going beyond the activities of government. Of no president is this truer than of Dwight D. Eisenhower. He was the Good Man Above Politics whom a certain kind of nonpolitical American has regularly looked for, and looked for particularly in the fifties as a respite from the relentless exactions of all the disturbing history after October 1929. After the end of the Korean war and of Joseph McCarthy's exploits, and after the death of Stalin, there came that curious period of complacent nostalgia and materialism, of piety and empty "righteousness," a pause in the day's occupation that was known as the Eisenhower.

Of Thee, Nevertheless, I Sing

Ike was "above politics." He was "not a politician." In his first campaign he named what he was doing a "moral crusade": not an ordinary political campaign, like others, but something higher, something better. Ike himself embodied the cluster of old "American" values many of his countrymen wanted to see vindicated, against the terrible changes of the twentieth century: simplicity, friendliness, "sincerity," down-to-earth practicality; "spiritual values" without much unpleasant specificity, "morality" (clear, uncomplicated, possibly even "absolute"). He represented all these things while being at the same time a tremendous war hero—a successful man in the most unequivocally practical of businesses. His war role gave him a universal and suprapartisan appeal. He was in the eyes of much of the public a great man, matched to the size of the world's problems.

Now, after the long agony of the Vietnam war and after Watergate and after second thought about the "strong" presidents, Eisenhower, golf club in hand, has risen calmly to a higher place in critical esteem than he held when he was in office. His caution and his military authority could keep the American nation from military involvement in Asia; his comparative indolence, with all of its accompanying jokes ("what if Sherman Adams should die and Ike should become president?"), did not appear in 1973 and 1974 to be as undesirable as it had in the fifties. But if the critics of Eisenhower at that time overdid it, the reaction was overdone, too. That era did represent all too well a central core of attitudes which are not harmless.

The pejorative term "moralism," as we used it particularly in the fifties, covered diverse sins. One was simplism, perhaps the thread running throughout: a vast and complicated political world is tidied into a simple two-sided black-white right-wrong picture (Dulles: "Neutralism is immoral") that eliminates qualification, variety of circumstance, and change, and thus falsifies a complex world. Another, perhaps almost identical, is absolutism: he who crams the real world's political complexity into the two-sided popular sort of moral language (the language of Principle, of Right and Wrong, of Moral and Immoral) may cast it into an unyielding mold inappropriate to day-to-day politics. Woodrow Wilson, the common theory goes, should not have put the issues

34

of postwar collective security into so absolute a form as to make compromise with the Republican senators impossible.

At the heart of these matters there is the self-righteousness, individual and/or collective, to which we alluded earlier. The simplified picture of the world often turns out to have the man drawing the picture unequivocally on the side of goodness and right. In a much celebrated modern discussion of ethics and politics, the essay by the great German sociologist Max Weber that is called *Politics As a Vocation* and is well known to all graduate students, there is only a brief dismissive introductory reference to this phenomenon—much briefer than its place in the world would merit. Weber wrote about "a quite trivial falsification" in which "ethics may . . . appear in a morally highly compromised role," as when a man justifies his turning from one woman to another with "reasons," or as when a victorious or vanquished nation after a war legitimates the outcome with moralizings about postwar guilt. Weber concludes: "If anything is 'vulgar,' then, this . . . this fashion of exploiting 'ethics' as a means of 'being in the right.' " But it is no mere fashion, or a minor matter, but a powerful human current, the undertow of self-justification. It is significant enough in individuals; in the collective units that make up politics it is pervasive. Collective man continually interprets the world in such a way as to put himself "in the right."

Many articulate Americans reacted in the fifties against individualistic moralism of the Eisenhower sort, and legalistic moralism of the Dulles sort, in somewhat the way the fictional Frederic Henry had reacted to the idealistic moralism of Woodrow Wilson. They may have overdone it in somewhat the way that Henry (or Hemingway) did: to define their understanding too much by that negation.

We may pair the unharmless attitudes of that time with the opposites to which they gave perverse encouragement.

"Dirty Politics"—"Politics" as Panacea. The symbolic Eisenhower

was the epitome of American deprecation of politics as such, the deprecation reflected in the derogatory flavor of the word and of its cognates "politician" and "political," an attitude already strong before Watergate. This disdain implies that politics itself is an unnecessary intrusion into the harmonies of life, an intrusion that is evil in its essence. "Politics," said those of us who argued against these "unpolitical" attitudes, is looked upon as bad and unnecessary, because it is the realm in which conflict, the collective base of life, the grip of self-interest, and the pervasiveness of power, all come out into the open. In fact, we said, these are "realities": constant and omnipresent. But for many, many Americans whose philosophy does not accommodate these pervasive "realities," "politics" appears as a separate, negative realm, which one can evade and repudiate by an act of will. "Politician" is for such people an invidious term, because the man engaged in that activity is peculiarly prone to compromise moral ideals, and to create conflict, because of his traffic with a "dirty" part of life. To be "political" is to be self-promoting, power-seeking, and compromising; it is a pejorative. For an American political candidate to be able to say, as Eisenhower could, "I am not a politician" does not hurt him in American politics; on the contrary, it helps him. The belief in an unsullied and accessible realm "above" politics reflects the culture's voluntaristic and idealistic ingredient, which looks upon all activity touched by the factional contention over power as unnecessary and nasty; it believes that there is an achievable realm of universal harmony above and apart from all that nastiness. Voluntary associations for persuasion and co-operation are desirable, in this view, but political parties are suspect, and alliances and pacts are dubious. Charity and humanitarian action should be pure and separated from political action.

The domain of moral ideals "above politics" is inhabited by the "good man"; one of the main ways one may rise "above politics" is to look, not at factions and their interests, but at an individual and his character. The cliché "I vote for the *man*, not the party," we said, is a reflection of this treatment of politics in personal and "moral" terms; it contains the plain implication that looking at politics in this way is morally superior to the views that deal in groups, parties, interests, and policies. A great deal of the feeling that being an "independent" is more praiseworthy than being a party man roots in this conviction that the solution to political problems is to get "good" men in office, men of character and "integrity." ("Integrity to *what?*" we would ask.) "Good" men—we would say—may reflect the uncriticized interests and limitations of their group as clearly as "bad" men do; "good" individuals can do evil politically, and vice versa. We would say with Max Weber: Whoever does not know good men can do evil, and evil men do good, is politically an infant.

Against those middle-class Americans who say with self-congratulation "I vote for the man, not the party," we developed a celebration of the political party, the "responsible" two-party system. Against the common American disinclination to recognize the differences of interest, and the pervasiveness of power in its many forms, we elaborated alternatives, in which the "realities" of the group, of power, and of interest were given central place. Against the standard American disapproval of "politics" and "politicians," we celebrated the political arts—and not in that denatured middle-class unpolitical way, by baptizing them as "public service," but by embracing the gritty core of compromise, adjustment, being a broker of interests, as a central value. (It is indeed a value, but not the highest, and only when its necessary work is exercised in the frame of purposes one can respect.) A thousand writings attacked "antipolitical" attitudes and celebrated "politics" itself as essential to democracy. "Schools" of "pluralism" and "realism" developed, and a theory about the "group basis of politics." The congressmen and aldermen and mayors and city chairmen whom we knew conveyed to us a definite endorsement, in the teeth of the culture's prejudice, of "politics," understood in the narrow modern sense, as a positive good.

But "politics" did not need endorsement and defense so much as it needed a deeper understanding. "Power" is a central and perennial theme, to be sure; but simply because a culture like ours has not comprehended that does not mean that we should, turning the coin, make it the primary theme. (Justice should be the primary theme.) "Groups" and their "interests" are basic political facts, and it is foolish not to know that. Nevertheless, there is more to politics than they account for. Among those voters who (to our dismay) voted for Ike, there were many who thought they were doing the best they could for their country.

We "realists" were prone to say, without originality, that politics is the art of the possible. There are, to be sure, impossiblists against whom such a point, expressed perhaps in fresher language, still needs to be made. In the daily work of politics one must take as given the condition of the people, and the arrangement of power: they provide the stuff and the limitation for political action. But that is only a part of the story. The other and more important part is the purposes men bring to that given reality, and the conceptions by which they seek to shape and to alter it.

High politics is not the art of the possible; it is the art of enlarging what is possible, and of making what had hereto been impossible come in the range of what can be considered.

4

Moralized Economics—the Economy as a "Preference"-granting Machine
Ike believed that the law of supply and demand was, as he said in his first State of the Union message, "natural"; that to interfere with it is perverse; that an annually balanced federal budget is a moral imperative; that "Keynesian" economists are wicked. He held, far more than most of his associates did, the image of classically proper fiscal behavior filled with moral content: certain "natural laws" of the economics of the free market were a reflection of an immutable moral order. He believed, and encouraged much of the public to continue to believe, in an older, simpler moralistic conception rooted in an individualistic picture of society. The symbol of probity was: the Balanced Budget.

A highly moralized attachment to that symbol of rectitude was part of Eisenhower's legacy. At one point in his second term he encouraged Congress to reduce the budget he himself had proposed—that is, the executive branch had proposed.

Americans loaded with Benjamin Franklin admonitions to Thrift and Work and Frugality in personal dealings had difficulty conceiving the distinctive characteristics of the national economy, and the role of government, in terms that differed from their personal economic life. Ike encouraged them not to try. He would repeatedly say that the national economy and the economy of the household are bound by the same rules. He gave encouragement to those stern-faced ladies who stiffen indignantly at the notion—pernicious to them—that the nation could "spend its way into prosperity."

By the time Eisenhower's vice president had made his way, by a bumpy road, to the White House, it was widely said that "we are all Keynesians now," and Nixon himself was to offer a "full employment balanced budget" . . . a federal budget that *would be* balanced were the economy to be operating at full employment, an "expansionary" balanced budget in which the central government's expenditures were deliberately intended to stimulate the economy. But Nixon would reinforce another piece of the moralized economics of the older individualist sort, the "work ethic," so-called (applied to the other fellow), that is grudging, suspicious, antagonistic to the poor, the hang-over of puritanism at its worst, which is dreadfully afraid that somebody somewhere is getting something for nothing, a "handout" indeed, and would rather let people starve than risk supporting "welfare chiselers."

The United States has been the world's foremost example not only of capitalism but also, in the past, of the ethic that is supposed to be linked to it. In his famous essay about Protestantism and the spirit of capitalism, Max Weber used an American classic, Benjamin Franklin's autobiography, to exemplify that spirit: "time is money." But in the last half of the twentieth century we rounded the corner into a new economics and a new economy that appeared to be at odds with that sturdy underpinning of the nation. Spending and saving; consumption, thrift, frugality, and debt; scarcity and abundance; perhaps even work seemed to take on a different valuation.

Back before inflation became the primary problem, the textbooks would tell the modern Benjamin Franklins about the "paradox of thrift": if too many are too thrifty, the penny saved is not a worthy act of penny-earning but an antisocial reduction in the healthy employment-producing flow of pennies. The "demand-creating" engines of advertising and the consumer economy joined their more potent urgings, in song and story, to whatever one learned from textbooks.

The older economics dealt with the individual consumer's choice in the marketplace, but assumed that the over-all state of an entire national economy was an automatic thing governed by immutable laws. But the new economics following John Maynard Keynes had long since challenged that assumption. The cycle of boom and bust should no longer be regarded as an uncontrollable given, like hurricanes and sunny days. It is affected by the flow of spending and of saving, which is not automatic, not "natural," but cultural. Men in key places can change it, move it, decide about it. The over-all economy should no longer be regarded as an untouchable machine that is inherently self-correcting. It does not automatically use the society's full resources. On the contrary: left to itself, it can muddle along indefinitely at a level far below its potential, with men and factories idle, as, indeed, the United States did from 1929 until World War II. But Keynes's analysis showed that that can be prevented, by deliberate social action (largely, by implication, governmental action). History had already proved this outlook by not only the experience of the United States during World War II, but also subsequent European economic miracles in peacetime.

At first glance this new economics appeared to bring a complete revaluation in economic attitudes. As far as government is concerned, the complete revaluation may hold at second glance, too. But what we did not make clear—to ourselves even—is that the new economics need not be so revolutionary for individual values. Personally one can still be hard-working and sober, enterprising and frugal—possibly even brave, clean, and reverent—without thereby endangering the nation's collective well-being. Under the right circumstances or the right definition, one can even be thrifty. It would have been well had that been kept more clearly in mind by those of us who, though "progressive" in economics, are conservative in culture.

The Keynesians on principle "as economists" had nothing to say about the composition of the rising gross national product their analysis recommended: ships were as good as sealing wax, pushpin the same as poetry, all goods and services in the national product. The implicit message was that MORE was better, and that it did not much matter what it was. Those of us who were taught by them therefore did not make clear enough that nothing really required that we give our approval to supersonic aircraft, redundant gas stations, yearly auto models, electric drink-mixers, and beer cans that fling themselves open at the approach of a customer. There was no necessary connection between the new economics and the soft hedonism of a prosperous and materialistic society, or with Britain's sinking giggling into the sea. We did not make sufficiently clear that with the new economics, even more than with the old, the culture we shape depends upon our values. We had been taught to resist the old ethic of thrift, and to endorse MORE and spending and the bigger pie and the rising GNP; we were therefore not in particularly good shape to cope with a worldwide inflation and an energy crisis.

"Moral" Purpose in World Politics—"Realism" about the "National Interest"   In world politics it was not so much Eisenhower as his secretary of state, John Foster Dulles, who served as the negative pole for the Frederic Henrys of the fifties. During World War I, or afterward, the Hemingways who had been in the trenches or in the ambulances, reacted against the soaring proclamations of Woodrow Wilson. In the fifties the objectionably moralistic world interpretation was not soaring and visionary but legalistic and prosaic; it did not proclaim the coming of a beneficent new world arrangement but insisted on the preservation of this one. But the moral absolutes remained, prominent and simple, in these two Presbyterian minister's sons (Wilson and Dulles). And a whole body of thought, a large cluster of writers, gathered around the repudiation of the views symbolized by the two of them: views that were legalistic, perhaps (that German submarine warfare had violated international law), utopian-idealist, perhaps (the people of world, who want peace, will build on the ashes of war a Collective Security system that will make an end to war), but moral-

istic certainly. There had developed already in the interwar period a "realism" in the interpretation of world affairs for which Woodrow Wilson's abstract idealism—proclamations put on walls on top of other proclamations—was the bête noir. This outlook on world politics was given a tremendous new strength by the internationalist-isolationist debate of 1936–41 in which the most eminent of the realists ("interventionists" then), shaping their collaborative purpose in the Century Club, engaged in an unmistakably meritorious campaign of public education. And then with the apparent revelations about Soviet intentions after the war, "realism" hardened into place. The attack upon what George Kennan called, in some famous paragraphs, the "legalistic-moralistic" strand in American attitudes toward international politics became almost as familiar as the phenomenon against which it was directed. So did the parallel attack on "utopianism" and "idealism."

Perhaps, as I say, it became almost too familiar. This "realism" should not have become the whole of a political outlook; it was and is only one necessary part. The political realism that developed in the United States may have become overly emphatic, partly because it was overreacting to the American atmosphere. It represented a kind of a first lesson in politics. But a first lesson is not an entire position, and especially not when it is chiefly a polemical reaction against a broad public attitude. And perhaps it was not the most essential first lesson. The chief failing of American political culture is not the inadequate comprehension of "power" (although that is a failing), but the inadequate understanding of human community and interdependence.

The "realists," perhaps I should explain, included the most distinguished political thinkers of the last generation: in addition to Kennan and Dean Acheson, this group included Hans Morgenthau, Reinhold Niebuhr, one side of many-sided Walter Lippmann, at least in an earlier phase, William Y. Elliot and his prize student at Harvard, Henry Kissinger, and many other influential diplomatists and teachers of international relations, together with many political writers and teachers and journalists and, especially, practitioners. They taught the "hazards" and "perils," the "dilemmas" and "tragic choices," with which political life on the great stage of history inevitably is filled. They taught in par-

ticular the Balance of Power: Kissinger came to high office pas-
sionately defending that central idea. Many of us who came of age
politically at the time of World War II accepted something of this
outlook. But I think we should have been clearer about the subordinate place of this "realism."

It is important to be "realistic," but it is even more important to
know what purposes one's "realism" serves. The late Reinhold
Niebuhr, intellectually perhaps the most influential of the realists
(Kennan, speaking of a whole group of political thinkers, called
him "the father of us all"), once defined political realism in this
way: "the disposition to take into account all factors in a social
and political situation which offer resistance to established norms,
particularly the factors of self-interest and power." Very well.
There is this resistance—self-interest and power—which must be
taken into account. But what then are these "established norms"
that they resist? Are these norms really so well established? Are
those babies in their cribs talked to properly now, to "establish"
those "norms"? Niebuhr himself came out of the background of a
"social" Christianity of which he was at once (with appropriate
paradox) the most eminent representative and the most trenchant
critic. That social Christianity had as its chief "norm" a "social
justice" that was by no means fully "established" either in religious circles or in America at large. It still is not. Although it
has some strong roots in American culture, it must fight a running battle all the time with another "norm" with (perhaps) even
stronger roots, that of competitive individualism and private gain.
And a "realistic" outlook, by itself, does not necessarily lead to
the one norm rather than the other. Every American has heard
the familiar defense of competitive individualism—the American
appropriation or misappropriation of Adam Smith and Herbert
Spencer, with a dash of Andrew Carnegie—that through all these
decades now has justified unfettered capitalism and hardheart-
edness toward its victims exactly in "realistic terms": "self-interest" makes the economy productive through "incentive" and
"enterprise."

In an opposite political direction "realism" alone does not protect against the ruthlessness of the authoritarian left; misunderstood, it may encourage it. This "realism" said that men are self-

ish, especially in the large lumps that carry on politics; that conflicts among group interests are to be expected; that the thread of power runs all the way through society, with invisible manifestations in the board room, the bank account, and the country-club lunch as well as such obvious forms as guns, barricades, strikes, armies, stock sales, and the ownership of television stations. In other words, the realists taught that exhortation and persuasion did not reach very far; that reason and conscience were weak where strong self-interests were at stake; and that a harmony among men was not a likely achievement, nor a surface, apparent harmony necessarily desirable ("Justice is more desirable than peace"—Reinhold Niebuhr). The revolutionary radicals characteristically have accepted all that, quadrupled. They have said a sharp line of conflict does, or should, run clear through society down to the bottom; that the New Left of the late sixties claimed that only confrontation with physical power, probably violent power, will bring the fundamental changes that this (in their view) essentially "sick" or evil society requires. "Realism" indeed! At the height of the late sixties' radicalism, the students who came reeling from the class of a young black instructor in the law school—POWER! DEMANDS! MILITANCE! SICK SOCIETY!—to a seminar on ethics found the latter tame and pallid by comparison, although they did find themes in the quasi-Marxist Niebuhr books of the early thirties compatible with the outlook they were discovering.

In international politics, to recommend "the national interest" as a guide, and the balance of power as a necessity, is by no means to settle all questions. The still-larger question is the moral content of that "interest," of the "nation" that protects its "interest": how much that "nation" with its "interest" has a decent respect for the opinions of mankind, for the "interests" of other nations. Unless there are men within the nation who have higher values than "the national interest," that interest will be defined in the lowest and most exclusive way.

I think that we overdid it. We did not make clear enough the subordinate place of this "realism" and therefore we did not sufficiently distinguish a realism that serves humane ends from one that does not.

On Changing Hearts and "Consciousnesses"

(with Race as an Example)

Once upon a time white Americans in their dining rooms and barbershops would speak about what they would call, if not something worse, the "Negro Problem." Then, back in the early years of World War II, the Swedish sociologist Gunnar Myrdal produced for the Carnegie Corporation the extraordinary volume (*An American Dilemma*) that might have been called "The White Problem," because Myrdal explained that the true location of this "problem" was in "the heart of the white man." In that important organ, he said, there was a moral "dilemma" between the nation's egalitarian Creed and the severe prejudice of color caste against the Negro.

Not so! said many of us at the time. Don't locate the problem in the white man's heart; to do that is to give aid and comfort to an all too familiar enemy . . . it is to encourage the view President Eisenhower was later, to our great chagrin, to articulate, that the solution to America's problem of race had to wait upon some alteration of the insides of America's white persons. Racial injustice, we said, is not primarily an internal, psychological, attitudinal, "educational," or "moral" matter; instead, it is located out there in the political and economic structure of society: in real-estate boards, in segregated schools, in discrimination in the jobs in the factory.

We feared that those who snatched at Myrdal's phrase without reading his book would assimilate it to the most insidious of all the American moralistic themes, the evangelistic idea of an inner moral turnabout by every individual, "one by one." Politics, ac-

45

cording to that view, is "dirty" because it deals with the sordid outer world of powers and interests, leaving the inward man untouched. The good man (like Eisenhower) is the answer to the problems of the world, because it is only from within a good man that goodness can come. The issues that deserve to be treated are the *moral* issues, because they lay a claim upon the moral sense within; and the way to deal with the social order is through a call to the heart of men: "Changed individuals will change society." If we begin with the transformed individual, then social problems—in a phrase we were to hear again and again—"will take care of themselves." Change in racial relations must come through "a slow process of education," rather than by the force of law or by political action. The change must be voluntary and inward. "What I'm working for here," President Eisenhower said, in the middle of the Little Rock crisis in 1957, "is a change of heart."

Actually, we responded, he was not "working" for anyone's change of heart. Although he said hearts should be changed, he did nothing himself to change them; rather, the opposite. He spoke of "education" and "moral" suasion, but he himself did no educating or persuading and gave no moral testimony. On the contrary; he said the word "slow," which is what much of white America always wants to hear. The president of the United States in the historic moment in 1954 when the Supreme Court declared segregation unconstitutional did not give it his own support, and confirmed instead the misleading pious individualism that unwittingly or wittingly served the cause of segregation and inequality.

There were the semiracist folk, who insisted the "race problem" was "moral," internal, and individual exactly because they did not want anything to be done about it. There were the naïve ones who made the same insistence because that was the way they looked at society. These latter had brotherhood weeks and they exhorted people and made appeals and they said how nasty it was to have "prejudice" and they put posters in streetcars. Those of us who disagreed with them noticed that the darker faces in the streetcar posters were carefully accommodated to white standards of beauty, and we did not think the brotherhood approach was very effective.

And so in the forties and fifties it was necessary to attack all that, concentrated as it was on the "heart" and on "prejudice" and on "attitudes." The real home address of the problem was *not* the inward parts of the white man. It was—society. It was *structure*. It was the objective pattern of segregated and discriminating housing, employment, and schooling. Segregation must go! Racial segregation and discrimination form a systematic pattern of unjust treatment, and it is that *pattern* that must be destroyed. So we said in those days, in the late forties and early fifties.

And we insisted that *law* was the primary way to do it. One of the reasons we resisted the notion that the racial problem is located in anybody's "heart" is that that notion was closely allied to the merely hortatory methods of attack upon it, methods usually set over against the resort to law and coercion. "You can't change hearts by law!" was one of those completely predictable responses, repeated and repeated and repeated, that reveal something unmistakable about a culture. "You cannot legislate morals" was another version, this one equipped with a standard illustration: Prohibition. As we all had to have ready our answers to questions about the marriage of our daughter, at one level, so at another level we had to be ready to answer these arguments against *laws* in the "moral" field of Negro rights. Laws are not necessarily intended to change "hearts," we said; they are intended to affect actions. And then, we added, the changed conditions that result from those changed actions will (on the second round, so to speak) have an effect on attitudes, on "hearts," if you will, after all. We used to cite the evidence of those integrated sections of Detroit where blacks and whites living side by side did not participate in the 1943 Detroit race riots; we used to cite the evidence of changed attitudes in the experience of integrated work teams. The way to change attitudes and "hearts," we said, was to establish a national Fair Employment Practices Committee.

We had many other arguments in favor of the use of law against racial discrimination: the patterns of segregation and discrimination had been created in part by law, and could therefore be undone by law.

Because this earlier debate had been so much against a naïvely individualistic opposition to the role of law, it developed in many of us of that generation a considerable wariness about "education" and moral appeals and the merely "attitudinal" aspect of "race relations."

Then the laws were passed. Beginning in 1954, the courts and legislative bodies fundamentally altered the American body of law on race. Between 1954 and 1968 the law was turned around. In 1964 and 1965 alone there was enacted a group of laws far surpassing what the Truman Civil Rights Commission, for example, had even thought to propose. These court decisions and civil-rights laws had a much greater effect than the widespread and disdainful criticism, in the late sixties, would admit. Still, the effects were more uneven and slower and more complicated than those of us who had grown up endorsing an FEPC had argued they would be. This body of law did not transform American race relations to the degree that many of us in that generation—naïvely now, perhaps, in our turn—may have expected.

And meanwhile there were other influences beyond the decisions of courts and legislatures.

1

In June of 1966, as the great days of the civil-rights movement were coming to an end, the president of the United States, trailing Secret Service men, strode suddenly into a conference on civil rights at the Shoreham Hotel in Washington, and did an unusual deed of the sort his successor might have called a "historic first": he did not serve, as he always does in such a case, as the speaker of the evening; instead, he introduced the speaker of the evening, Thurgood Marshall. Lyndon Johnson spoke, and Thurgood Marshall spoke, celebrating the victories won in the courts and legislatures. Seated listening, meanwhile, unintroduced and unreferred to at the head table, disturbed, it was later reported, by the evening's emphases and omissions, was the principal symbol of another facet of the movement, Martin Luther King, Jr. The law was not the only way the national culture was altered to the subject of race. There was also, as it was called, "direct action."

It is instructive on that matter to look back now at something Niebuhr wrote more than forty years ago, in an atmosphere very different from either 1966 or today. This is from *Moral Man and Immoral Society,* a book that holds up better than do most political volumes published as long ago as 1932. Niebuhr was arguing against his usual enemies, the naïve social idealists who were not willing to stain themselves by using power in the interests of justice, and who did not fully grasp the ideological distortion of every group's reasoning about society. In one of the later chapters, after he has his main thesis laid out, he discusses violence and nonviolence, resistance and nonresistance, with Gandhi as his chief example. Gandhi's so-called soul-force, he said, was often assigned a moral superiority it did not deserve: nonviolent resistance is, after all, a form of *resistance.* "A negative form of resistance does not achieve spirituality simply because it is negative." Nevertheless, where it is appropriate "non-violent resistance" can be a useful strategy. One place in which it is appropriate is in the efforts of the black man to achieve justice in America.

It is hopeless for the Negro to expect complete emancipation from the menial social and economic position into which the white man has forced him, merely by trusting in the moral sense of the white race. It is equally hopeless to attempt emancipation through violent rebellion.

There are moral and rational forces at work for the improvement of relations between whites and Negroes. . . . But these educational and conciliatory enterprises have the limitations which all such purely rational and moral efforts reveal. They operate within a given system of injustice. . . . However large the number of individual white men who do and who will identify themselves completely with the Negro cause, the white race in America will not admit the Negro to equal rights if it is not forced to do so. Upon that point one may speak with a dogmatism which all history justifies.

On the other hand, any effort at violent revolution on the part of the Negro will accentuate the animosities and prejudices of his oppressors. Since they outnumber him hopelessly, any appeal to arms must inevitably result in a terrible social catastrophe. Social ignorance and economic interest are arrayed against him. If the social ignorance is challenged by ordinary coercive weapons it will bring forth the most violent passions of which ignorant men are capable. Even if there were more social intelligence, economic interest would offer stubborn resistance to his claims.

The technique of non-violence will not eliminate all these perils. But it will reduce them. It will, if persisted in with the same patience and discipline attained by Mr. Gandhi and his followers, achieve a degree of justice which neither pure moral suasion nor violence could gain.

Niebuhr goes on to name some of the specific strategies an American Negroes' campaign of nonviolent resistance might employ. The reader is reminded that the following paragraphs were written when Martin Luther King, Jr., was four years old.

Boycotts against banks which discriminate against Negroes in granting credit, against stores which refuse to employ Negroes while serving Negro trade, and against public service corporations which practice racial discrimination, would undoubtedly be crowned with some measure of success. . . .

It is an extraordinary series of paragraphs to read now, striking in their prescience. Nevertheless, with hindsight one may note the absence of any reference to the law: to the courts, to legislative bodies, to the franchise. Niebuhr was right about the limits of purely moral suasion, and about the necessity for organized black pressure. But as the story developed in the decades that followed, there was a more central role for the principal legal institutions—the courts at first, and later the president, and then Congress—than his analysis would have allowed. And in the contrapuntal development of law, power, and suasion, the culture of the white man did undergo at last a greater change than, in those years, one would have predicted.

A decade after Niebuhr's book there was Myrdal's giant volume. It was of course much more complicated and satisfactory than our fears about his locating the trouble in the white man's "heart" implied. He had a famous theory about the "vicious circle" of prejudice causing the discriminations in society which furnished grounds for prejudice; Shaw had put the point succinctly when he wrote that the great American nation forces the Negro to shine its shoes and then despises him for being a bootblack. Myrdal explained the interrelatedness of the many parts of circles of segregation, discrimination, and prejudice, in a pattern of "cumulative causation," from jobs to housing to education to health and so on around again. The sheer piling up of material about every part of Negro life in the very big book helped drive home the accumulation of causes.

But the circles were not necessarily always vicious, in his view. There could also be cumulative causes set to work in a positive direction. And one of the points of beginning about which he was more hopeful than many was education.

There is a passage in Myrdal about an "educational offensive" against racism that one may look at again now, after thirty years, with a certain curiosity. It follows his discussion of "the convenience of ignorance" to the white American.

. . . The Northerners want to hear as little as possible about the Negroes, both in the South and in the North, and they have, of course, good reasons for that. The result is an astonishing ignorance about the Negro on the part of the white public in the North. White Southerners, too, are ignorant of many phases of the Negro's life, but their ignorance has not such a simple and unemotional character as that in the North. There are many educated Northerners who are well informed about foreign problems but almost absolutely ignorant about Negro conditions both in their own city and in the nation as a whole.

. . . The average Northerner does not understand the reality and the effects of such discriminations as those in which he himself is taking part in his routine of life. . . .

He then ends a chapter with this implied exhortation, in which the italics are his:

. . . We do not share the skepticism against education as a means of mitigating racial intolerance which recently has spread among American sociologists as a reaction against an important doctrine in the American Creed. *The simple fact is that an educational offensive against racial intolerance, going deeper than the reiteration of the "glittering generalities" in the nation's political creed, has never seriously been attempted in America.*

. . .

51

What followed, of course, was a good deal more complicated than an "educational offensive." A unanimous decision by the United States Supreme Court that segregated schools are inherently unequal has a powerful educational effect, but it is also law—it has its educational effect because it is law, and law from the final and most prestigious source. The judges themselves had been "educated" about race by the culture's conversation in the decade before their decision.

A Montgomery bus boycott is educational in a sense, but education mixed with that necessary ingredient of forceful resistance that Niebuhr mentioned. Ten years later at Selma when an angry white man asked a marching white nun what she was trying to do to the white race, she replied, "Educate it."

Plainly the effort to affect attitudes by means of persuasion and education, direct and indirect, would not by itself have been enough. There had also to be the immensely powerful effect of the court and the Constitution. There had to be direct nonviolent resistance. There had to be, ten years after the court's segregation decision, the most intricate politics in the Senate to enact cloture on a civil-rights bill. And that intricate politics within the Senate required an intricate politics between the Senate and its constituencies.

There must also be, as we learned to say, objective change in the patterning of race in society, not only for the primary reason—justice for racial minorities—but also for the secondary but deeply important reason that this patterning is a chief teacher to our "attitudes." It is not the only one, though, and the picture of the "structure" of society we used to have was too narrow: jobs, housing, lunch counters, racial enrollments in schools. The complex of ideas and attitudes by which this "structure" was interpreted, the *culture* of race, was even more important.

The marked improvement in American white racial attitudes since World War II does not go deep, perhaps; it certainly does not reach the point of persuading many whites to make sacrifices, or what appear to be sacrifices, to rectify this ancient injustice. The nation in the late sixties passed into a period of anti-antiracism, of which the passionate opposition to "forced busing"

people now take black class presidents, integration, interracial dating matter-of-factly. In tests of the difference in response between older and younger Americans to pictures of interracial couples, the older ones, shown a white-black couple after a series of racially homogeneous ones, register agitation; younger persons have much less of a response. That seems the most hopeful kind of development: a change not in will or intellect alone but in the emotional responses and expectations built into persons by their culture.

The circular relationships that Myrdal describes can be affected at any point, as he said; one may try to change culture and "attitudes" as well as social arrangements.

Educational influences that are serious and of the right kind, reinforced by the cultural surroundings, can have an effect. Presumably the content of the college atmosphere specifically on race has some part in making more liberal the racial attitudes of those with more education. Nevertheless, the specific and explicit teaching about race must have made a considerable difference. Did a college education liberalize racial attitudes before the forties? One thinks of the older University Club bigots. It is to be doubted that Yale men became racial equalizers under the teachings of William Graham Sumner; rather, the opposite. It is to be doubted that the students in Middle Western universities in the twenties, when the appealingly iconoclastic professors were readers of H. L. Mencken, had any notion that the intelligent white man necessarily worked for racial equality; Mencken certainly did not. White men who were young in those days sometimes say a little plaintively that all this about race, the Negro, and so on just wasn't talked about when they were in college.

One must of course be as careful to avoid complacency in discussing improved white attitudes as in discussing the growing black middle class and the improved black economic position. As the latter means a widening gulf between the middle class and the remaining poor, so the former may mask many subtle new forms of racism and of other ills (a stereotyped contempt for "redneck" lower middle-class "racists" that is itself much like the evil it pretends to condemn, for one important example).

Nevertheless, there is progress. It is important to see in an overview that this is so: that this whole turnabout has been an instructive story. It represents the kind of persistent American democratic reform, mixing politics, law, and education, that one wants to see done also in other fields.

2

An American who has spent many hours of his youth contending with the idea of a "Change of Heart" dear to his countrymen may then be startled to read the same theme defended by European writers he respects. Perhaps they spent their early years arguing against a different kind of opponent.

Karl Jaspers wrote that there must be an "inner" "ethical" change, like a wave, or else mankind will blow itself to pieces with nuclear weapons. "It is not enough to find new institutions," he wrote in a powerful book published in English in 1961 under the title *The Future of Mankind.* "We must change ourselves, our characters, our moral-political wills." The novel situation created by nuclear weapons, that man now has the capacity to destroy human life, requires a "new man," "a change in man," a "new way of thinking." To an American this sounded suspiciously like the point of view I have described. Jaspers did not, however, use this theme to resist changes in laws and institutions or to avoid or neglect politics: he dealt with political problems in intelligent detail.

An American reader nevertheless found his overarching theme misleading. One would welcome, of course, sweeping ethical changes in the make-up of mankind, assuming them to be changes of the right kind, but in politics one has to deal not with men as we "would wish them to be" but with old, real, present, unchanged men. One may doubt, furthermore, that widespread inward transformations are brought about by such direct and general exhortation; such inward changing as we do undergo comes about instead through the alteration of our specific loyalties and the enlarging of our specific commitments.

We very much want the collective egotism of nations to diminish, in a period of proliferating nuclear weapons. That diminution will not come overnight, sweeping like a wave across mankind, nor will it come about in response to Jaspers' sober book or to thundering editorials calling out for "Two Billion Angry Persons" (all the people of the earth, telling their leaders they don't want war: that is a false separation of "leaders" and "people." It won't happen that way, since "peoples" often want something that leads to war at least as much as their "leaders." And 2 billion angry human beings is rather a frightening conception. So, it may be, is a single world-wide sweeping wave of inner moral alteration. Which implies the point: the ethical changes that count most for politics are those that come not in a wave but in the accumulations of a culture and the altering social habits of institutions).

Since Jaspers wrote, the nations of the world have been through some precarious moments, including a nuclear crisis, without any sweeping inner ethical changes. In the Cuba missile encounter the decisive virtue had nothing to do with the moral state of mankind in general, but was, rather, a limited kind of prudence on the part of two sets of world leaders. A thin reed, you may say, and risky next time. What, then, do you want in its place? Institutions of some kind and a balance of power, in addition to whatever there may be of universal moral regeneration. It is mostly in these institutions that hope must be found: in strategic arms limitation talks, the test-ban treaty, nuclear non-proliferation agreements, détente perhaps, tacit as well as formal understandings among the nations. We develop these institutions—while men's hearts may or may not change a little toward a less suspicious and jingoistic attitude.

George Orwell is perhaps the political writer of the recent period whom one would most admire, so that it is a little unsettling for an American reader to find in him a sentence like this: "If man would behave decently, the world would be decent, is not such a platitude as it sounds." To our ears it is indeed such a platitude, unless one fills the word "decent" with more political content than it usually has been thought to carry.

This sentence appears in Orwell's essay on Charles Dickens.

It seems that in every attack Dickens makes upon society he is always pointing to a change of spirit rather than a change of structure. . . . His approach is always along the moral plane. . . .

. . . Useless to change institutions without a "change of heart"—that, essentially, is what he is always saying.

If that were all, he might be no more than a cheer-up writer, a reactionary humbug. A "change of heart" is in fact *the* alibi of people who do not wish to endanger the *status quo*. But Dickens is not a humbug, except in minor matters, and the strongest single impression one carries away from his books is that of a hatred of tyranny. . . .

Orwell half accepts the merely "moral" radicalism in Dickens:

. . . Dickens is not *in the accepted sense* a revolutionary writer. But it is not at all certain that a merely moral criticism of society may not be just as "revolutionary"—and revolution, after all, means turning things upside down—as the politico-economic criticism which is fashionable at this moment. . . . Two viewpoints are always tenable. The one, how can you improve human nature until you have changed the system? The other, what is the use of changing the system before you have improved human nature?

One might suggest that changing either of these—"human nature" or the system—is rather a larger project than one wants, or needs, to undertake. Change the culture; reform the institutions; that should be enough for now.

The moralist and the revolutionary are constantly undermining one another. Marx exploded a hundred tons of dynamite beneath the moralist position, and we are still living in the echo of that tremendous crash. But already, somewhere or other, the sappers are at work and fresh dynamite is being tamped in place to blow Marx at the moon. . . .

The United States, perhaps the least "Marxist" of major Western nations, and the most susceptible to the "moralist," has a role to play in this explosion. But to do it we cannot go back to that older individualist moralism. In the United States the "if men would be decent" sort of thing is still common, and not merely among "reactionary humbugs" and "cheer-up writers," although we have certainly had our full quota at least of the latter. In the United States that view has not been confined to reactionary humbugs. Here a political naïveté, and a stronger pious and moralistic individualism even than England's, have brought many unwittingly to the support of such a view who were not necessarily reactionary or privileged, or humbugs either.

We have had a considerable spirit of generosity in this country, and of humane feeling, as many observers from other countries have said. Myrdal, for example, remarked that perhaps no other country has as many "cheerful givers" as America. But this cheerful giving and humane feeling diminish markedly at the boundaries of politics and of serious social and economic rearrangement: charity, yes; social justice, maybe. This generosity is deflected not only by vested interest (although, to be sure, that is a major fact) but also by a faulty collection of social ideas, of which the individualism reflected in those slogans about changes of heart is one of the most important.

What we need are hearts changed to include more adequate understanding of men in society than the idea of changing hearts one by one provides for. Or a notion of "decency" that includes a decent relation to the shaping of public life. Or a collaborative and democratic moralist, rather than the older private and individualistic sort. And the American moralist who might be tamping the dynamite for Marx should not be as anti-institutional as Charles Dickens was.

Bertrand de Juvenel, the contemporary French political thinker, wrote a passage in his book entitled *Sovereignty* arguing against a modern inclination (I picture him in debate with French Marxists) to see justice not as a virtue but, rather, as an arrangement of society. "The logical end of the illusions now in vogue," he wrote, "is the quite absurd one, of a society in which everything would be arranged justly and no one would have to be just." Some good students in one's class nod soberly in agreement with that sentence. Juvenel, to the further approval of such students, condemns the "barren and lazy thinking" that pictures distributive justice as the work of a "supreme legislator." "Rather," he wrote, "it is the duty of each single person . . . what we should be concerned with is that the whole ceaseless process of change should be increasingly permeated by the quality of justice in our own individual wills." That sentence hits the familiar spot in the American psyche: our own wills; each single person; every one do his part; conversion; volunteer; each individual; change your heart; self-reliance; you can do your part.

Any American knows from the long struggle over race the pernicious result of a view that amputates a real or alleged individual goodness from social arrangements. It is of course true that each individual has his duties. Each white American has claims of "commutative"and "distributive" justice that arise from his station in life: each white schoolteacher to the black kids in the class; each white judge to the black persons brought before the court, often by white policemen, who have their duty, too, to render justice; each white homeowner, to neighbors "regardless of race, creed, or color," as we Americans used to say. One may indeed run through American social order up and down and sidewise from banks to churches to grocery stores to automobile companies to loan sharks in the ghetto and find at every spot a claim of white man's obligations to justice to black men (to other men, too). It is furthermore true that "social" justice will not be achieved without virtue in those individual men: that law alone, or government policy alone, cannot overcome the "One Huge Wrong," or any other wrong, of American society. Racial conservatives borrowed from that truth (that law alone cannot achieve justice or utterly transform recalcitrant humanity) to construct one major rationalization for a monstrous error and injustice, America's racial system. They resisted changes by law, and left matters to changes of "heart," which at the same time many of them did not encourage or represent in their own persons—which in fact the resistance to change in the law helped to prevent, because law and custom, and law and conscience, function with a complicated reciprocity.

Justice is and must be both a virtue and a social arrangement, neither of which can take the place of the other. And one does not fully possess the *virtue* in the modern democratic world unless one is, as individual moral agent, properly related—"justly" related—to making just social arrangements.

"Virtuous" white men battered their consciences year after year against institutionalized injustices—slavery, Jim Crow law, a systematic pattern of racial discrimination—that were formidable *structures* ("social arrangements") independent of their individual "disposition to give each man his due." Much greater numbers of individual white men of no great moral distinction one way or another, gas-station owners, real-estate brokers, policemen, or loan officers in a bank, were caught up in a pattern, larger than themselves, that, as they would protest from time to time, they did not make: I just work here. Not only the black American but also in his different way the white American was caught in a powerful social complex that was beyond his making and beyond his undoing, by any individual acts of distributive or commutative justice or love or charity. It was there. If you are going to be fully a good man, a just man, then do not choose to be born a white American, in 1880 or 1900 or 1920, because that is the wrong place to start: you are in the wrong by definition, given that collective historical identification. Each alternative moral choice for you individually is fouled by the pre-existent collective reality; the nastiness of radicals and some blacks about "white liberals" in the sixties was one symbol of that.

In the late forties I was told about an honorable white man (a "just" man, one supposes, after the model of Juvencl's paragraph, with a remarkable disposition to give each man his due) who traveled through the South making a point of calling every black man he met "Mister." (Black men were called "Boy" or "George" even if they were sixty years old, and never "Mister Jones"; one memorable touch in James Baldwin's great paragraph in *The Fire Next Time* about black soldiers coming "Home!" from World War II is his reference to signs in railroad stations that said "white *ladies*" and "colored *women*"). Now, what does one make of this little anecdote, this mild version of an early freedom rider? One might say it is nothing or it is everything—it is everything whether persons are respected as persons and equals; it is nothing that one white man blowing into the hurricane tries to do this little duty to justice. A whole structure of injustice built into every part of collective life, and embedded in a thousand pieces of culture, folklore, and custom stood in immense resistance untouched by his gesture.

One thing needed was exactly what Juvenel decries: an alteration in social arrangements, independent of whether men individually were "just" or not.

Now to make the proper contrast to these others one may refer to another non-American writer, one who comes onstage from quite a different direction: George Bernard Shaw. There are many other and more recent socialist writers but none, so far as I know, that one reads with one-fifteenth as much pleasure. (All socialist writings are boring, but Shaw's are less boring than others.)

When Shaw had finished his jaunty exposition of socialism in the first part of *The Intelligent Woman's Guide to Socialism and Capitalism*, he stopped and took a chapter to lecture his intelligent woman about the dangers of taking what he had said personally. He warned her against, as his chapter title put it, a merely "personal righteousness." English people, "especially English ladies," he wrote, "are so individualistically brought up that the moment they are convinced that anything is right they are apt to announce that they are going to begin practicing it at once, and to order their children and servants to do the same." (Shaw assumed that his intelligent Englishwoman would have servants.) "When they became convinced of the righteousness of quality, they proceeded to do ridiculous things like commanding their servants to take their meals with the family (forgetting that the servants had not bargained for their intimacy and might strongly object to it), with Heaven knows what other foolishness, until the servants gave notice, and their husbands threatened to run away, and sometimes even did." Put away that sort of individualist naïveté, says Shaw, and support socialism, which is not at all a matter of individual acts of charity toward the poor, but of *Justice* in society brought about by *law*. "Socialism abhors poverty and would abolish the poor." In this chapter, as in his plays, Shaw tries to make the point shocking:

A hearty dislike and disapproval of poor people as such is the first qualification of a good Equalizer. Under Socialism people would be prosecuted for being poor as they now are for being naked. Socialism loaths almsgiving, not only sentimentally, because it fills the paupers with humiliation, the patrons with evil pride, and both with hatred, but because in a country justly and providently managed there could be neither excuse for it on the pauper's part nor occasion for it on the patron's. Those who like playing the good Samaritan should remember that you cannot have good Samaritans without thieves.

So, by law, says Shaw the Fabian socialist, make a society "justly and providently managed"—which means socialism, which 'means equality of income—and there will no longer be either thieves or good samaritans.

Shaw does not quite say it will no longer be necessary in the glorious day when all that is brought about for individual men (and women) to be "just" or personally righteous. He does say there will still be room for "kindness" in any society—but plainly for him the social rearrangement is all-important. The "just" social arrangement for him is simply stated (equality of income) and, by implication, capable of some sort of final realization. This Shavian outlook is one version of the sociologism and utopianism that others, particularly on the left, reproduce in other forms: alter the SYSTEM, change the human environment radically, produce thereby a New Man, a New Humanity—and all is solved.

Well, it isn't. It will not be. No altering of the social "system"—to equality of income (even assuming one could attain it, which one cannot) or to anything else—solves the endless problem of justice, of men living together with other men on this earth. There is indeed always and endlessly, as Juvenel said, the necessity for "each man" in his own relations to be just. It is necessary in face-to-face dealings with other persons, which no social restructuring takes care of for us. Many have noted that one type (not the only type) of radical and of liberal social reformer is notably callous and indifferent to the *merely* individual needs of those around him, especially if those needs and those individuals fall outside the categories that his ideology instructs him to favor: to encounter in person the sizzling illiberality of many liberals and radicals toward working-class whites, in the middle of battles over racial issues, was an instructive experience. In some cases the individual whom it is not necessary to notice when one is overturning systems and achieving social justice may even be a member of the oppressed group on whose behalf one is alleged to be fighting: it is not rare to encounter radicals (white and black) whose understanding of the evils of the racial system has "progressed" far beyond mere liberal kindness, to the point where he is particularly contemptuous of individual black persons.

The disdain of a certain kind of socialist and communist for a merely individual human being of the "working class," of the proletariat, is a thread running back, I believe, to Karl Marx himself. There are some rather amusing notes in Edmund Wilson's *To the Finland Station* in which he reproves Marx for his shoddy individual conduct—toward his wife, Jenny, toward Engels, and toward actual workingmen who had the presumption to have their own ideas about Marxism. As Reinhold Niebuhr wrote, "The highest achievements of social good will and human kindness can be guaranteed by no political system"; "No system of justice established by the political, economic, and social coercion in the political order is perfect enough to dispense with the refinements which voluntary and uncoerced human kindness and tenderness between individuals add to it."

Few would quarrel with that. The larger issue has to do not merely with "refinements" that are "added"—with Karl Marx as an individual behaving decently to the librarians at the British Museum. It has to do, rather, with this: the way one thinks and behaves in the continuing work of making, upholding, and remaking social institutions. That is now itself also a part of one's role as a moral agent. A just man participates in the making, and continuing, of a just society. So it is now in a modern democracy, with the consenting of the governed.

It is a mistake to separate either institutions and social forces from the free human beings who carry them forward, or individuals from the environing institutions that make them what they are.

If an American considers the tortured history of race in his country, he knows he wants there to be, exactly, a "just" social arrangement that does not depend upon the moral quality of individual men. There have been honorable and just white Americans throughout American national and colonial history: Quakers, preachers, abolitionists, antislavery leagues, philanthropists, advancers of colored people—more than the recent fierce criticism of America's "racism" and white deviltry would admit. But formidable institutions of slavery, Jim Crow law, and the caste system of segregation and discrimination remained a powerful social structure, independent of the goodness and badness of the human beings, white and black. Conversely, as the Supreme Court in 1954 made its decision, and the sequence of changes in culture and law and in politics and economics is set in motion—as the "social arrangements" become more just—multitudes of whites behave more justly toward blacks even though they are in a sense no "better" individually considered.

Justice is both a virtue and a social arrangement, to a degree independently, and neither of its aspects is a substitute for the other. One does indeed want a just social arrangement independent of the quality of individual men. And justice as virtue is incomplete now, for a citizen of modern democracy, unless it includes "social" justice . . . for an American democrat this will mean that what is "just" should include the "disposition to give what is due" through the patterning of society—to serve justice, that is, by relating oneself properly as citizen to the fulfilling and the shaping of the social order. One's will and disposition should include, along with those Aristotelian kinds of justice, exactly the category of "*social* justice." For a modern man, and for a citizen of democracy, the quality of justice "in our wills" necessarily includes the disposition to give what is due to groups of people, and to present to one's conscience the pattern of the social order, with its nests of injustice. There is a vast intellectual difference between the classical and high medieval worlds of Aristotle and St. Thomas and this modern world; we are now able to present in the conversation of democracy the forms of our social order to our minds as amenable to change. And the ordinary citizen has now his duty to appraise them and his role in changing them.

A Note on Humor and
on Self-Criticism and
on Assorted Semiheroes

(with Adlai Stevenson Among the Examples)

The sordid events of Mr. Nixon's Watergate, following upon the unpopularity of Lyndon Johnson, brought the upgrading of a number of other, contrasting, high officials, past and present, by a kind of compensatory mechanism in public feeling. The updraft of Eisenhower has already been noted. The immense esteem for Henry Kissinger rests on a solid foundation in his abilities and in his accomplishments, but that esteem has had a boost from the contrast Kissinger represented to the president who first appointed him. There were moments in the last throes of the removal of Nixon when that president's supporters (for example, Joseph Maraziti, of New Jersey, on the House Judiciary Committee) seemed to be arguing that Nixon should be retained in office because Dr. Henry Kissinger had such a high regard for him.

One of those polls that regularly asks which American is most admired found in the last months of Nixon that first place did not go to the president, as it usually does, or to Billy Graham, but to Henry Kissinger. On the whole one may be pleased by that result. Nevertheless, if it should be that Kissinger, the former professor now a political leader, combines the vanity that Max Weber rightly notes as the occupational disease of professors with the love of power that is endemic to politicians, then perhaps our admiration should be mixed with a trace of wariness. Kissinger has had what a labor leader might call a sweetheart contract with the press, and also the high regard simultaneously of the intellectuals and of the citizenry at large; it is in some ways like the situation of John F. Kennedy at the height of Camelot. It would be better if we did not have this voguish celebrity-making overpraise, on the one hand, followed at an interval by a wave of "revisionist" articles and books and attitudes. One may predict that the latter will one day come for Henry Kissinger.

President Gerald Ford was another beneficiary of the compensatory mechanism, and in the first days of his presidency he responded to its opportunities. The normal flow of public admiration toward the president had been blocked by Watergate, and had sought other outlets: hence the extra element in the response to Kissinger; hence a quite favorable public appraisal of Ford even when he was vice president. When he became president, the frustrated public esteem came flooding back to the White House in tidal waves.

This mechanism of public opinion not only seeks out someone to admire; it also seeks out symbols of the specific qualities that it needs to admire and remember because at that moment they are missing in the major figures of public life. Harry Truman came back into public esteem in the Watergate period in part, one may safely infer, because he symbolized qualities then missing in the occupant of the White House, and missing also to some degree in the other occupants in the years between Truman and Nixon. A best-selling book by Merle Miller, *Plain Speaking*, represented, beginning with its title, a clearly implied contrast to these other men who held, as Truman typically put it, that job in the White House: no vanity and no pretense, but self-confidence all the same; roots in the common folk but much historical knowledge; decisive leadership without grandiloquence; "plain speaking." In the era of Nixon's tax-supported palaces in the sun there was obvious appeal in the now classic story about Truman's reply to the question put by Ray Scherer, of NBC, about what he did the first day after he became president: "I took the luggage up to the attic." Although we Americans have developed an unfortunate instinct for royalty, for making celebrities and symbols out of presidents and their families, we also still can respond to a story like that one. We like Lincoln's reply when the visitor exclaimed, "Mr. President, you are shining your own shoes!" "Whose do you

67

shine?" We also like it when historians tell us, as they did repeatedly during the events of the recent past, that Thomas Jefferson after being inaugurated as president waited for the second seating at the lodginghouse where he was eating. President Ford, retrieving his Washington *Post* in his bathrobe from the front porch of his Alexandria home, responded well in the first days to these and other sound desires of the American public: "Truth is the glue that holds government together, not only our government but civilization itself." "Here the people rule." "It is good to be back in the people's house" (the House of Representatives). "There will be no illegal tapings, eavesdroppings, buggings, or break-ins by my administration." The press response was so euphoric that one could anticipate the "revisionists" to come.

If we look for men to symbolize desirable qualities in the democratic statesman, there would not be many recent candidates of high visibility superior to the foreign-policy group in President Truman's administration. In particular one remembers the relationship between Truman and Dean Acheson, and between the two of them and General George C. Marshall, whom they both deeply respected. Acheson's graceful tribute to General Marshall in *Sketches from Life* strikes a note of honor and of disinterested patriotic service, both in the subject and by inference in the writer, that is all too rare in American politics. It is a nice scene, of President Truman telling General Marshall that the Marshall Plan will go down in history with his name on it, and dismissing all objection with a commander in chief's order. Though they may have had a narrowness of focus about foreign policy, as it seems to us now, and may have seen excessive merit in sheer decisiveness (doubtless Truman should have lost some sleep after deciding to use the atomic bomb on Hiroshima), still one wishes for their equal again, and with domestic social reform as much in view as they had world politics in view.

Perhaps it is appropriate now, in the aftermath of Richard Nixon, to quote Acheson's account of another familiar story:

Excerpt from the transcript of press and radio news conference of January 25, 1950:

Q: Mr. Secretary, have you any comment on the Alger Hiss Case?

A: Mr. Hiss's case is before the courts and I think that it would be highly improper for me to discuss the legal aspects of the case or the evidence or anything to do with the case.

I take it the purpose of your question was to bring something other than that out of me. I should like to make it clear to you that whatever the outcome of any appeal which Mr. Hiss or his lawyers may take in this case I do not intend to turn my back on Alger Hiss. I think every person who has known Alger Hiss or has served with him at any time has upon his conscience the very serious task of deciding what his attitude is and what his conduct should be. That must be done by each person in the light of his own standards and his own principles. For me, there is very little doubt about those standards or those principles. I think they were stated for us a very long time ago. They were stated on the Mount of Olives and if you are interested in seeing them you will find them in the 25th Chapter of the Gospel according to St. Matthew beginning with verse 34.

Have you any other questions?

After the press conference was over, Mick McDermott, Special Assistant for Press, who had served secretaries since Mr. Hull, walked with me in silence to my door. "I am going to ask a favor of the Secretary of State," he said, "which I have asked only once before in my service. May I shake your hand?"

I may suggest now a certain restrained revival of interest in another and rather different model out of our recent political past, Adlai Stevenson. He does have in his favor the apparent fact that Nixon despised him; Stevenson certainly would not have insisted on the importance of being "Number One," "hanging tough," "stonewalling," and the like. He came reeling and wounded to Santa Barbara from the 1960 Los Angeles Democratic convention, stunned by the "toughness" of Kennedy's fight for the nomination, which was still a long distance from the world of H. R. Haldeman. The Kennedy brothers came to have severe reservations about Stevenson, in part because of his long state of semidecision about whether to run in 1960. Truman, an original Stevenson sponsor in January of 1952, when he was president, came to be disillusioned: Stevenson became "that fella" who can't make up his mind whether he wants to go to the bathroom. Acheson in his memoirs dismisses Stevenson with the back of his hand: "a good staff officer but without the stuff of command," and spoke disparagingly of him at other times. Governor Stevenson did have the personal characteristics (defects, if they are defects) that began to be communicated to his following after the flush of the 1952 enthusiasm wore off: as a Democratic mayor whose city he visited remarked, where Stevenson sat was not necessarily the head of the table. Much was made, at first sub rosa and later in public, in criticism of Stevenson that he had trouble making up his mind ("the Hamlet thing") and lacked executive force.

No doubt Adlai Stevenson was not everything that we Stevensonians thought him to be in 1952. We idealized him. As the years went by those of us who were his enthusiastic supporters came to learn he had grave limitations as a political leader.

But some of the most severe criticisms of Stevenson we may be allowed somewhat to discount. The judgments of Truman, Acheson, and the Kennedys were all forged in the heat of political battle. And those judgments reflected the styles of those doing the judging, which styles themselves may not be the world's only way of carrying on politics. One might retort about Acheson, with his long Washington years of peremptory and dismissive judgments, that he was overstuffed with the stuff of command. Stevenson, with his faults, had been a successful governor of Illinois, had shown a rare grace in giving expression to the ideals of a public of which Acheson was inclined to be disdainful. And he was definitely not a tough guy seeking power.

Stevenson became, in a way unmatched in recent American political history, what Jimmy Durante spoke of in another connection as "duh toast of duh intellectuals." He was certainly called by that name many times (the party boss of Jersey City once introduced him flatly, and in that setting ambiguously, as "the greatest intellectual in the world"). But he was not an "intellectual" in any serious sense. Rather, he was an appreciator of intellectuals. He was not a philosopher-king, but a "king" who admired, spoke for, listened to, and borrowed from "philosophers." Carl McGowan said generously at his funeral, he was "a completely civilized man." (Most "intellectuals," in this age of specialization, are incompletely civilized.) Stevenson valued a kind of generalized elevation and "idealism" (with all its ambiguities), for which he himself became the symbol and spokesman in the politics of his time. He was a politician of the Higher Plane, the companion and then successor in that role to his great friend Eleanor Roosevelt.

All over the world there are people who were first brought into politics because they were moved by Adlai Stevenson. The touching moments of the politics of the fifties were almost all his: the speech as governor welcoming the 1952 Democratic convention to Illinois, when he first stepped onto the stage of history; his celebrated acceptance speech; the gracious concession with the little story from Lincoln: "I am too big to cry, but it hurts too much to laugh." At the 1960 Democratic convention, at which Stevenson's own role was not particularly a happy one, even persons fully committed intellectually to Kennedy found themselves suddenly moved, as nothing the efficient Kennedys did could move them, by Senator Eugene McCarthy's extraordinary speech in behalf of Adlai Stevenson.

Although Stevenson never again rose to the height of his 1952 campaign, there was a certain gallantry in the way he tried through the years thereafter to live up to the expectations of all the eggheads around the world who believed in him far more than he believed in himself.

Stevenson was the most eloquent recent spokesman ("eloquent" ranked just behind "witty" and "urbane" in the eulogists' adjectives for him) for an American social idealism, a kind of self-critical Woodrow Wilson with a sense of humor. The self-criticism and the humor made his idealism much different from that of Wilson, taking the bane of self-righteousness from it.

He was able to criticize himself; and his party, and his nation. "Self-criticism is the secret weapon of democracy, and candor and confession are good for the political soul." These characteristic words of Stevenson stood in contrast not only to Nixon's sharply different view, and to the sentiment on the subject of contrition of the unspeakable Ronald Ziegler; they stood in some contrast also to the far more honorable attitude of Truman and Acheson. I suggest that these two worthies could have used a dash or two of this quality of Stevenson's.

Stevenson's humor was not a minor decorative matter. He told partisan gags and after-dinner jokes which were like those of other politicians, except funnier and more sophisticated. Yet he went beyond that to generate a spirit of which humor was an essential part. His wit and humorous remarks were not just audience-warmers preceding the serious business of the evening. They were part of the essence of his approach.

It is not quite true, as James Reston, of the New York *Times*, was to write in the summer of 1972, that the "country hasn't had a good giggle or a vivid line from any prominent politician since Adlai Stevenson." Even the Nixon cabinet, which one would assume could not be confused with the Algonquin Round Table, produced one good joke. This had to do with the aforementioned Kissinger, and his alleged toughness. His predecessor as secretary of state, William Rogers, said that when they asked Henry what he thought of the Indianapolis 500 he replied, "They're all guilty."

A great many prominent politicians have a supply of jokes, like the story that Senator Edmund Muskie tells about the Texan who tried to impress a Maine farmer with the size of his ranch. "I can get in my car and drive all day and still not leave my own spread." "I had a car like that once."

Of course many prominent politicians have gags written for them, to warm the audience at the start of the speech. The Kennedy brothers had the money and connections to obtain good gags of this sort. But the two older brothers began toward the end of their lives to reveal something a lot more interesting, a distinct humorous ingredient in their own personalities. Robert Kennedy, the short, silent young man with the tousled hair who rode the Stevenson staff bus briefly in 1956, and kept to himself, seemed a very sober and unfunny fellow. (In addition, his reputation was suspect for his having worked on the McCarthy committee staff). He seemed all sobriety and deadly earnestness in his early years pursuing Jimmy Hoffa. But he began at the end of his life to show a nice unruthless impishness. I like to believe it is true that his well-known remark about George McGovern came as a correction to someone who quoted him as saying that McGovern was *one of* the most decent men in the Senate. "What I said was that George McGovern is the *only* decent man in the Senate."

In the days of the television program called "Get Smart" and the "would you believe . . ." jokes, Robert Kennedy responded to the hoots of a crowd at his description of his humble birthplace: "Would you believe a small mansion?"

A rare and dry sort of detached humor appeared in John Kennedy once he became president. (It had not been apparent before, perhaps in part because Stevenson's humor had not been a political asset.) One appreciated JFK's admonition to John Kenneth Galbraith, "I don't want to hear about agricultural economics from anybody but you, Ken. And I don't want to hear about it from you, either."

And there was his response to some programmatic request: "I agree. But will the United States government agree?"

I believe the highest and most original humor from major figures in American politics came from that odd combination of Pied Piper, Don Quixote, St. Francis, and the Lone Ranger, Eugene McCarthy. He had an irresponsible whimsy that no one else could risk. He said he thought he might speak in the debate on the platform at the 1972 convention. On what subject? "Well, what do you have going about twelve o'clock?" His political world seems to have ended not with a bang or a whimper but with a stifled yawn.

McCarthy's humor was as good as Stevenson's, but it was a different kind. Although Stevenson came from Illinois, his humor partook less of Mark Twain and robust masculine frontier blasts than of the sensitive, Benchleyesque verbal and whimsical humor of New York and Harvard in the twenties, flavored with North Shore after-dinner-speech "levity," as he once called it himself. It featured a deflating of overserious purposes, and, above all, self-mockery. The joker and his work were the regular butt of the joke, which very much confused the sobersided people. This "eloquent" speechmaker kept joking about speechmaking:

"I have one point to make tonight. That's not many, but it is more than can be found in some speeches—including a few I've made myself."

"I suppose I must talk and you must listen. I do hope that we both finish our work at about the same time."

In McCarthy's case, on the other hand, although on one of his many sides he could be even excessively humble, the humor certainly did not feature self-mockery. On the day in February 1968 when Robert Kennedy declared his presidential candidacy, McCarthy wryly remarked: "I still believe I am the best potential president in the field, even after today's announcement."

In the campaign that was to follow he would say, "I am beginning to look better as a candidate as the country has time to look at the others that are left over."

Earlier, in the fall of 1967, when he announced his candidacy, he was asked whether he would withdraw if Robert Kennedy entered the race. "Well, it might not be as voluntary as that" was one thing he said. But to the idea that he was a "stalking horse" for Kennedy, he said something else. "You know the story about the time at the Kentucky Derby when Coaltown was supposed to be the stalking horse for Citation," he said, "but then Coaltown just kept on running."

McCarthy's humor was sardonic, pointed, often erudite and wasted on an audience that did not understand. It was a world apart from those professionally produced gags in processed Kennedy speeches (about "greasy kid stuff," for example) that assume that the only shared culture available for politicians' humor is the world of popular entertainment. McCarthy remarked, just before he announced his candidacy in the Lyndon Johnson days of 1967, that whereas some of his fellow Democrats attacked him angrily for splitting the party, others came to him "like Nicodemus" to urge him to run. Not many people these days could pick up that allusion to the Pharisee who, according to the Fourth Gospel, stealthily "came to Jesus by night." He unkindly dismissed the state of Indiana as a place where when you say "the poet" they think you mean James Whitcomb Riley. He remarked to a university audience that Arthur Schlesinger, Jr., sometimes wrote history *before* the event, "and that can ruin a discipline."

Eugene McCarthy's humor reflected his peculiar detachment and nonchalance, and perhaps one may also say his moral and intellectual and even "spiritual" snobbery, his sense of superiority.

Stevenson was not like that, though there were people who thought he was, and his humor was not like that. In Stevenson's humor there was a constant self-deprecation rarely found in McCarthy's.

A continuing spirit of humor like Stevenson's does not reflect fundamental frivolity, as the plodding one-dimensional sobersides who dislike it think, but a high and complex, and ultimately serious, double vision, a two-level perspective, which is rare in politics but very desirable. At the same time that one pursues one's purpose earnestly one can let in glimpses of a larger perspective which transcends and qualifies it. Thus Stevenson's high humor was linked to his objectivity and his humility. "*Who* leads us," he said, in his famous welcoming address to the 1952 convention, "is less important than *what* leads us—what convictions, what courage, what faith—win or lose." I suppose it is conceivable that some other major politician would utter such a sentence, but not that any other would really have believed it.

After Stevenson's death, James Reston revealed that in a long interview in January 1952, immediately after President Truman had called Stevenson to the White House and asked him to run for the presidential nomination, he had reflectively stated not only that General Eisenhower would get the Republican nomination and win the presidency, but also that, perhaps, for the health of the parties, he should win. On reading this one asks oneself this: What other active politician, having just been offered by the president of the United States a chance to run for that office himself, would have talked about it in so detached a manner?

Characteristically, Stevenson made himself the first target of his humor.

Less than six weeks before his death, he made an informal and nonpolitical visit to an American college of which he had been made a fellow, and charmed the faculty there as almost no other politician of our time could have done. In a pleasant moment after dinner, he told a story, typically on himself, about the time some years ago when he was made a fellow of a college at Oxford or Cambridge (I can't remember which). The convivial evening wound happily along until the moment when Stevenson, completely unprepared, had to rise at the table and make a response.

Wondering what to say, he picked up the menu as he rose. On one page of the menu had been printed the names of other guests honored at the dinner, men from Oxbridge colleges, listed by their formal title only. "My greeting into politics has led to a surprising association with the great of the world," Stevenson reported having said, "but I never in my wildest imaginings expected that I ever would be sharing the platform with"—and here he read from the menu—"the Warden of All Souls and the Master of Jesus."

This man who never expected to be a fellow with the "Master of Jesus" told jokes deflating himself continually—too much so, according to even friendly critics.

Stevenson's humor was a product, too, of the same spirit—critical and aspiring—which made him avoid clichés, and make a particular point to tell people what they wanted to hear, "talk sense to the American people."

"Let's tell the truth, that there are no gains without pains, that we are now on the eve of great decisions like resistance when you are attacked, but a long, patient, costly struggle. . . ." By 1956 some Stevenson advisers wanted to ditch this tell-them-about-the-pain theme; one dismissively called it "Calvinistic." But Stevenson himself did not want to abandon it, and in his 1956 campaign, which otherwise was not distinguished, he insisted upon talking, against all political advice, about an end to H-bomb tests.

Stevenson's career was not that of a man seeking power to make a bright name for himself, or to exercise his ego, or to enjoy pushing the world around. It was, rather, that of a man fulfilling honorably and gracefully, but reluctantly and with self-doubt, responsibilities thrust upon him.

In his last years a double obligation pulled on him. He was constrained to defend in the United Nations the policy of the United States government—policy he did not make and of which he was apparently not even accurately informed on some occasions—and at the same time to serve the many citizens not only of this country but throughout the world for whom Adlai Stevenson was no ordinary diplomat. He was not impressive in those years. But when he died, one remembered what he had meant in the fifties.

I suppose if it comes down to a choice one would prefer that the more direct and self-possessed John Kennedy be president rather than Adlai Stevenson; at least that had come to be the clear choice, partly out of considerations of political appeal, by the spring of 1960. Conceivably one would have to agree to the choice of the doughty and plain-spoken Truman over Stevenson, although in 1952 many of us would never have believed that. Dean Acheson, "present at the creation" of postwar foreign policy and magisterially advising about and commenting on American policy from the time he left the Department of State until he died, had no doubt much greater respect among knowledgeable political people than did Stevenson. Stevenson's bosses in those last years, John Kennedy and Lyndon Johnson, who showed once they got to the White House some qualities not so apparent during their rise to power, had the iron and ruthlessness and also the luck to reach office that he never attained.

Still, one may be grateful that these men are not the only political models for the nation: there is also a Stevenson. At the time of his death, in August 1965, one overstated it a little sentimentally this way: Against the day when every American politician is a realist, a "pragmatist," a tough guy who does not finish last, a hawk, a calculating poll taker with an instinct for the jugular and a manual for going directly after power, an operator who can put his youthful idealism into escrow until he reaches the top, there stands in the pages of American history, with a hole in his shoe, the "Governor." He stubbed his toe on the way to the White House and he did not in his later career live up to his promise. Nevertheless, in his own moment on the stage he did show to the world the better side of America.

On the Limitations of
Tough-minded, Technical,
Realistic, Hard-nosed,
Pragmatic Liberalism

(with John F. Kennedy as an Example)

The commencement address on the old campus of Yale on a
pleasant June day in 1962 was a good one judged by many of the
criteria appropriate to the occasion: it was important; it was well
written; it was crisply delivered; it was short; and it had a sufficient supply of the standard witticisms about the host institution
("It might be said now that I have the best of both worlds . . . a
Harvard education and a Yale degree"). It may also have been a
satisfactory speech if one judged it by the political criterion of the
moment: the distinguished speaker extended an olive branch,
halfway at least, toward a business community that was just then
in its Union League Clubs telling rancorous stories about him.
The previous April there had been a fierce and memorable controversy over steel prices, which controversy had produced a
famous story about the president's attitude toward big-steel men:
"My father always told me they were sons of bitches. I never really believed him until now." At Yale in June, President John
Kennedy tried to mend fences with these sons of bitches and to
state his own position fully: there need be no renewal of the old
hostility between the business community and a Democratic administration. They had common goals. The ideological warfare of
the past was over. The problems now were of a different and
more complicated sort from those of the past. And the "myths"
about economic policy that Americans used to believe should now

be set aside. The address served the young president's immediate purpose well enough.

But as one sat there in a borrowed academic gown, a member presumably of that community of scholars committed to (what was the phrase Kennedy borrowed from Yale's president?) "liberal learning," one found in the speech a theoretical backbone that was unsettling. This president of the United States, with his Harvard education and his Yale degree, this liberal Democrat and heir to a long tradition of progressives, this leader of the most powerful nation in the West, gave his wholehearted and explicit endorsement to the view that the nation's problems now required, not "political" or "philosophical" answers (his words) but, rather, "technical" ones.

The "technical" and "sophisticated" solutions that he urged us to seek were set in contrast not only to the "myths," "clichés" and "illusions" of the past, but also to the "ideological" and "philosophical" and even "political" approaches that once may have been relevant, but were no more. In the time of John C. Calhoun (Yale, 1804), said President Kennedy, and also in that of William Howard Taft (Yale, 1878), there were relatively "dramatic," "sweeping," and "simple" issues, which today had largely disappeared.

The central issues of our time are more subtle. . . . They relate not to basic clashes of philosophy or ideology, but to ways and means of reaching common goals—to research for sophisticated solutions to complex and obstinate issues.

What is at stake in our economic decisions today is not some grand warfare of rival ideologies which will sweep the country with passion but the practical management of a modern economy. What we need are not labels and clichés but more basic discussion of the sophisticated and technical questions involved in keeping a great economic machinery moving ahead.

One asked oneself: Is that right? It is true, of course, that we never need "clichés," but is the alternative just "technical sophistication" and "practical management"? That is the way it appears to the machinists of the "great economic machinery," to be sure, but should the president of the United States have adopted their view?

Was it wise and right for such a leader to suggest that the problems of an earlier day (of 1860? of 1933? of 1945–46?) were "simpler" and less "subtle" than those of his own—and yet at the same time indicate that the allegedly more difficult problems of this day were soluble by technique alone?

What did the president say to the Yale men, as he exhorted them—as commencement speakers do—to go out and take their part in the great world? What vision did he hold before them, as their president and their commencement speaker? He said: "You are a part of the world, and you must participate . . . in the solution of the problems that pour upon us, requiring the most sophisticated and technical judgment."

It was scarcely an exhortation that would make the human heart miss its beat. The entire address might have been written by a member of the Yale economics department. Perhaps, indeed, it was.

It was not difficult to formulate the argument against its theme. The specialists who write such speeches and who are produced by the ethos such speeches encourage do not always know where their "sophisticated and technical judgment" should leave off, and a larger judgment—about fundamental values—should begin. But should not presidents know about that? And, for that matter, college seniors?

The "operational" fellow, the expert, the man who possesses what Kennedy called "sophisticated and technical judgment" isolated one particular field or activity, in order to concentrate upon the procedure within it. In order for his work to proceed, he must assume the worth of the end to which his work is addressed. In order to get on to his own question—how?—he must assume that the end he is serving has an assured value that he does not, himself, examine. As a cobbler cannot continually be asking himself whether shoes as such are a good, so an economist cannot continually ask himself whether "productivity" or "consumer satisfaction" or (we may add, portentously, in the fifties and sixties) "economic growth" is a good; he must take that for granted, and get on to his job. Where the end to be achieved is simple, discrete, unambiguous, and noncontroversial, such a technical approach raises no problems: find the One Best Way, the best technique, to make shoes, and make them. But in social policy the ends to be served admit of no such simple description: one objective (controlling inflation) conflicts with another (government spending for social welfare)—or, rather, with many others. The ends that are served are not unambiguously good: "consumer satisfaction" and "economic growth," apparent goods, are subtly intertwined with assorted evils, and are not as simply defined as at first appears—or as the economist, that high-level technician, wants and requires. In social policy the ends to be served have shifting and complicated meanings; it is of the very essence of politics that men differ about their meaning and their worth.

The ends of politics, moreover, are not neatly separable from the "means" the technical man thinks he deals with exclusively; usually he bootlegs in some assumptions about ends in his work on the means. One might argue that political leadership, which must interpret the historical situation, and fit together the several and conflicting ends, is pre-eminently the activity that cannot properly be reduced to sheer technique.

But the technical man will tend to regard all "generalities," good ones and bad ones, as airy, empty, and misleading. He will believe, as President Kennedy said in New Haven explicitly, that the "declaration of the objective" is "easy," while only the attainment is really difficult, requiring "hard thought." One form of the warfare among the specializations, of course, is the dismissing of some endeavor different from one's own (especially that of one's natural enemies) as "easy," whereas one's own line of work is difficult, sophisticated, requires hard thought. Those other fellows don't know what it is like because they've never met our payroll.

The specialist wants to deal with problems only case by case, or, as the president said, to treat each case "on its own merits," without much regard for—indeed, with some resistance to—an over-all conception. Most of all, technicians will dismiss consideration of the moral ends their technique serves; these are already agreed upon, or are impossible to deal with, or are somebody else's job, or, anyway, something not to talk about. Let us talk instead, they will say, about "ways and means," about how to do it, about "sophisticated solutions."

Kennedy said that, in contrast to the problems of the thirties, the fiscal and monetary problems of the sixties demanded "technical answers, not political answers." Earlier he had said, in a similar context, that "this is basically an administrative or executive problem." Surely that was wrong, or at least a bad way for a political leader to put his point. By rejecting "political" answers, he meant to put aside predictably partisan or well-labeled approaches; he meant to tell businessmen, frightened by his treatment of Roger Blough and Big Steel, that he did not intend to revive the New Deal's conflict with the Economic Royalists. But he seemed to say something more than that, and something that needed to be questioned more than it was.

Policy on taxes and spending and interest rates and economic growth involves—along with much economic fact—a whole nest of inexact judgments—really, ethical judgments—about values and interests. Though these judgments may be complicated, and in some cases require expert economic knowledge, and though they may not sort out neatly under existing political labels, still they are not "technical." They are not "administrative" or "executive." If we could just get enough moral juice back into the word, we could say they are, exactly, "political." "Politics," or, rather, "policy," is the meeting point between technical considerations (how does the thing work) and ethical considerations (what is good), and neither part should be left unexamined.

The political leader's job, surely, is to articulate an interpretation of these larger-than-technical choices. Of the "Leader of the Free World" (as we were saying back then) this should be preeminently true.

Kennedy's prime purpose in the speech, to be sure, was not to deal with these theoretical matters. He was trying to get the current economic discussion onto relevant issues, and to counteract a stereotyped conservative view. To do that he fell back, not on a fully articulated alternative view, but simply on an assertion of the complexity of problems, and of the need for know-how. For the moment, in this "know-how" country, that may have been an effective tactic. But what would it mean in the long run? What would it leave as the intellectual deposit of the Kennedy administration? Who would it allow to define the philosophical issues?

. . .

On Limitations of Pragmatic Liberalism

When in 1962 I gave the academic gown back to its owners and gathered my uneasiness about that theme in Kennedy's speech into a magazine article, the result was mixed reviews. Usually articles in magazines of a political character and a limited circulation elicit, if anything, favorable comment, because a certain fit between the writer's ideas and the readers' has been prearranged. But this article split the readers of a liberal magazine, split the members of the intelligentsia who read it, divided even the editors. The favorable reaction of some readers seemed more intense than usual. The grumpily negative reactions of others were a surprise, although the popularity of Kennedy among "intellectuals" was plain enough.

It is no longer news that there were flaws in the John F. Kennedy version of American liberalism. The word has gone forth, from that time and place, to friend and foe alike. It is also not news any more that there were defects in the broader tradition of liberalism that Kennedy inherited (in Ted Sorensen it was a birthright; in John Kennedy it was an acquisition in adult life). This was the "tough" and nationalistic liberalism, the "pragmatic" liberalism, of the generations of the time of Franklin D. Roosevelt and World War II—a liberalism that had been accustomed to power and to supporting national policy. And it is obvious enough that the compounded shortcomings of liberalism in a measure helped cause the sequence of recent troubles. The Nixon scandals grew in some part from an ignorant but genuine recoil against the militant protests of the late sixties; those protests, in turn, grew in some part from deficiencies in modern American liberalism.

And those deficiencies were not confined to liberals: they could almost be summarized in this way: modern American liberalism too much reflected the intellectual and moral shortcomings of American political culture as a whole.

So Kennedy serves here as a symbol for cultural inclinations much larger than his own or his family's characteristics. These paragraphs are not intended to be part of the "revisionist" literature of disparagement of the Kennedys. The late president, who was exalted beyond his deserts by some citizens during his short administration, and by many more in the yearning for Camelot's return after his death, is now, more than ten years later, in quite another phase of the cycle of public appraisal; the downturn, like the celebration that preceded it, is overdone. Although there were faults chargeable to the peculiarities of the particular man, as to any man, and in his case in an unusual degree also to the family ethos and paternal influence, still many of the Kennedy shortcomings that are now rather suddenly becoming commonplaces of political discussion belong in fact to a much wider set of people than this one man, or this one family or this one administration. These shortcomings sprang from the positivistic-plus-romantic American liberalism of that time (of the wartime and postwar generations); and from the politics of mass communication and celebrity, which is going to be with us in the future, and from the values of the country as a whole in all its phases.

To appraise one particular thread in American politics, the characteristics that distinguish the Kennedy family and JFK's administration must be set aside, and what Kennedy shared and exemplified must be looked at instead.

He exemplified a great deal, about his time, about liberalism, about America itself. In some of his characteristics he was almost as "American" as his predecessor. Like Eisenhower—and perhaps unlike the previous liberal hero, Adlai Stevenson—he reflected in his public person certain broadly popular American traits.

In this country that celebrates the "young man going places," he was young, and even though he had a million dollars at the start, which is not the way it used to be done, he nevertheless was "going places" indeed.

He was the youngest man elected president of the United States, the youngest of all except the equally vigorous Theodore Roosevelt to hold the office. It was a staple of commentary at the time, that the two men who "rode together down Pennsylvania Avenue," as the saying goes, represented the oldest president in office (Eisenhower was then seventy) and almost the youngest, two widely separated generations.

And the young twentieth-century president represented activity, energy, movement. The Boston way he pronounced the often-repeated word "vigah," became a rather affectionate national joke. He was going to "get the country moving again." If there was any place that Eisenhower's public person could be criticized, effectively, to a broad American public, it would be just there: he seemed a static figure; he did not display vigorous activity and practical knowledge of his work. (Incidentally, the recent crop of Kennedy critics has seemed to neglect this: the degree to which characteristics of the JFK administration were a conscious, though of course not explicit, contrast to that of Ike.) Toward the end of Eisenhower's presidency, after the 1958 recession, after Sputnik and the U-2 affair, even his supporters acknowledged sadly that he was not as energetic as they might like.

The active, "dynamic" American youth, moving upward in the world, is not to be empty-headed: he is to have the high intelligence required for successful performance of his job. Nixon once used, against Stevenson, a verbal contrast that appears repeatedly in many American connections, between being "intelligent" (which is a word of praise) and being "intellectual" (which is not). One is to be "smart," and "quick," able, as the popular self-help books put it, to "think straight"—but not to be talky, reflective, literary, speculative. Kennedy had the desirable American kind of "smartness": practical, "intelligent" straight thinking. Although he read lots of books, he read them *fast*.

And he knew facts. To be smart is to be able to win prizes on a quiz show: if you're so smart, why aren't you rich? Your smartness should *produce*—produce quick answers, immediately tangible results, displays of memory, tangible items in the Gross National Product; fourteen good ideas, sixteen correct answers. Kennedy in this regard, again, was quite unlike his predecessor. The previous president had had the faults of an older American moralism, inclined to approach political questions from above, with a simple, general moral principle or two, lots of trust in good will, and a loose grip on facts. He regularly confessed, in press conferences, that he was being told something he had not heard before, and often appeared not even to know what a conscientious newspaper reader would know. His successor, by total contrast, knew things it is to be doubted a president should know. In the famous first debate with Nixon—in all the debates, actually— Kennedy put himself on a par with the then vice president of the United States in stature, and ahead of him in debating smartness, by rapid-fire ticking off of factual material. In the televised press conferences after he became president—that immensely effective medium for him—he continued the display of factual knowledge begun in the debates. He knew, and cited, the exact latitude and longitude of a Portuguese ship; and the exact amount of the imports of Cuban sugar. Eugene McCarthy, sitting calmly in his Senate office, talking reflectively as long as one wanted to talk—no rush on his part to be anywhere else to learn some facts, to *do* something—remarked wryly that these were scarcely the sorts of facts a president ought to know or to cite.

Over against Eisenhower's sojourn on the "Green Fairways of Indifference," Kennedy represented action. His language was masculine, activist, dynamic: move, act, do, begin. He announced, "I run for the Presidency . . ." not "I shall run," or "I propose to run" (Robert Kennedy's announcement, more than eight years later, took the same form). His style in the presidency was direct, energetic, active, a clear contrast to the Eisenhower days. The hard-working administration, with much late burning of lights, was commented upon at the time.

People working for him were hardly ever home until eleven, or if home for dinner, then a hundred calls had still to be made. And often they stayed up all night, and they were proud of it. Henry Fairlie remarks, in *The Kennedy Promise*, "It is sometimes hard to avoid the impression that the Kennedy brothers, and those they gathered to their service, thought that something was amiss if they were able to enjoy an unbroken night's sleep."

In their first vigorous year in office the president's brother, the Attorney General, congratulated the Justice Department employees who were discovered by a license-plate check to have come in voluntarily to work on Washington's birthday.

W. Willard Wirtz, before he became secretary of labor, had a humorous section in a speech giving rules for "New Frontiersmanship": get to the office first, depart last, and when you go home leave the lights on; telephone officials before they arrive in the morning; train your secretary to say when you are out that you have just left for the White House.

Tocqueville's paragraphs about American activism attribute this quality to sheer necessity and lack of time. Americans, he wrote, "have little time"; they "lack leisure"; they are busy "subduing a continent"; therefore, they do not reflect or speculate or think deeply—as, he implies, they would otherwise do. But even with a continent subdued, we Americans still believe activity to be worth-while for its own sake; we do not know any other way to be. Doing, as such, is a prime value for us.

So in this regard Kennedy was American indeed—too much so. The style, not of the president alone, but of the administration was active, energetic, presumably invigorating. One young New Frontiersman—newly risen to great power, a man who helped to choose the others—remarked in the early days of the administration, as he moved briskly across the lobby of the Shoreham Hotel, each of his strides an important act, that the word that best described the new administration, he felt, was the word "athletic." This rather Hemingwayesque administration was to have the grace and timing and courage of athletes—but not at all mindless brawn. The leader was quick, bright, smart; the followers were to be quick, bright, smart . . . the brightest and the best, as David Halberstam should have ordered the words in his book title, ten years later.

John Kennedy himself embodied the virtues respected by many great American journalists (they loved him; they were his friends; he was one of them), and also by the rigorous, modern operating professionals of Washington, the think tanks, and the universities. He wanted to go into particular subjects in detail, one by one, case by case; he did not appear to be much interested in "ideology"; he understood the need to turn to specialists.

Back in the years from 1956 to 1959, when he was a senator thinking about being a presidential candidate, academic specialists who visted him came away glowing with appreciation of his knowledge of the particulars of their field. After he became president, the policy people in each area, by and large, were happy with appointments he made.

In Kennedy himself, and in the people upon whom he drew, there was a firm respect for facts, an ability to make precise discriminations, an inclination toward the analytic operation of the mind, a lawyerlike, or perhaps legislatorlike, case-by-case argument-by-argument approach—together with a lack of interest in traditional "philosophical" matters.

Kennedy was at one with the experts dealing with questions of public policy. Like them, he would not settle for a vague and general view. Like them, he understood the need to turn to men who have knowledge in special fields. Like them, he respected hard facts. He was interested in "ideas," but more in the practical ideas of the economist, policy planner, and specialist than in the theoretical ideas of the philosopher, the speculations of the theologian, the abstractions of a nonscientific political thinker.

Ted Sorensen turned to me once in the late fifties, when he was scrambling daily to help his young senator become president, and asked which professors at Yale had "ideas" that "the Senator" might want to know about. A confusing discussion ensued. "Ideas" to him were not what "ideas" were to me. He meant specific programs and proposals: Yale economics professor James Tobin's later proposals for a guaranteed annual income would have been an "idea"; Harvard economist Seymour Harris' proposals for the succor of New England industry at about that time were, indeed, "ideas," and he used them. I had another, older, idea of "ideas."

Kennedy represented not only perennial American traits, but also the development of those traits in a modern outlook, and the attachment of that outlook to American liberalism.

The refrain of the Yale speech echoed the view promulgated in the social-science seminars of the graduate school for a decade and more before Kennedy gave it: the view that the Great Issues of historic political philosophy are dead, and good riddance; the view that all that was worth learning about society was technique, method, fact (especially a fact that one could count). It was a constricted outlook, with which American liberalism had come to be too closely allied.

One need not search far in the troubled political history of the sixties for object lessons in the shortcomings of a merely "technical" outlook, or of the activist and "tough-minded" attitude. The most serious was to be found in the terrible storm of American policy in Southeast Asia.

"Technical and sophisticated management" comes to be embodied, in the new way, in whiz kids who have tamed the bureaucracy, and, in the old way, in the lumbering bureaucracies the Robert MacNamaras try to tame. These human organizations develop an inertia of their own, and roll unstoppably down their track. In the first spring of the Kennedy administration, there was an example in the Bay of Pigs fiasco.

One of the books about that disaster, *The Cuban Invasion*, by Tad Szulc and Karl Meyer, came in the end to a central villain: "the insulated rationalism of a sheltered bureaucracy," that "hulking, stubborn giant that seemingly can only look where it has been and not whither it is tending." "Experts," cloaking their work in secrecy, were able to derail even the policy of their putative superiors as "the occasional ideas of a dilettante."

. . . a segment of the powerful bureaucracy committed itself to a specific approach to a particular problem. Its money, its prestige, its esprit de corps were enrolled in a project the bureaucratic experts judged to be sound . . . it swept along an entire government behind a plan that rested on the secret knowledge of those who were steering in darkness.

The whole project seemed to move mysteriously and inexorably toward execution without the President being able either to obtain a firm grip on it or reverse it. Under both Eisenhower and Kennedy it grew, changed and forced decisions without any clear statement of policy or procedure.

Sorensen's excessively favorable book about the administration in which he served at least does not mitigate the disaster of the Bay of Pigs; he confirms essentially what the other commentators have said. He has set forth, characteristically in a series of numbered lists (five errors in the decision-making process, five fundamental gaps between what the president actually approved and what he thought he was approving, three sources of these gaps, and a partridge in a pear tree) the multiple causes of this fiasco, but comes in the end to the same point as Szulc and Meyer.

The whole project seemed to move mysteriously and inexorably toward execution without the President being able either to obtain a firm grip on it or reverse it.

Instead of the President telling the bureaucracy that action was necessary and that they should devise certain means, the bureaucracy was

89

telling the President that action was necessary and that the means were already fashioned—and making his approval, moreover, appear to be a test of his mettle.

One might say they were giving him their "sophisticated and technical judgments."

It is not necessary in these pages to add to the mass of words already written about the war in Vietnam, which mass of words has long since surpassed in tonnage all the bombs dropped in World War II. But if we nonradicals deny that the Vietnam war exhibited a "sickness" of our society, a necessary outcome of a systematic and fundamental evil in America itself, at the same time we can scarcely put it in brackets and pretend that it was purely an aberration. We cannot isolate it from what we are and believe—as Americans, as members of the World War II generation, and as liberals. It was not a "liberals' war," as the radicals charged for a time, as part of their attack on liberalism. But it was a war that some liberals helped to initiate, to which for varying lengths of time many others of us acquiesced. It was a gross mistake, which grew in some part from the alliance between liberalism and a cold-war outlook held too long, and a realistic endorsement of the "national interest" held too uncritically. And those alliances, in turn, reflected the link to "technical and sophisticated judgments."

John F. Kennedy was not exactly born and raised with such a world view. His father, by all reports, was a tough guy and a "practical" American indeed, who made millions of dollars (our test of practicality, even of manhood) in his own lifetime. But there was another world of thought available to Kennedy, with rather different tests. It is a little surprising how this subject has vanished from view today, considering how prominent it was in 1956–60. Fairlie wrote 346 pages about the Kennedys without mentioning it; other critics, and defenders, too, now do the same. I suppose it has something to do with what is considered good taste, but even more with what is considered important and unimportant. The point is this: John F. Kennedy was the first president of the United States to be a member of the Roman Catholic church. There was a time when that would have mattered a great deal. I want to exhume that buried subject to provide both an illustration and a conclusion to this chapter's point.

In the perspective of history, having a Roman Catholic president of the United States was no small matter. Not long ago, the nation could have been described as Protestant in its foundations and in its ethos—and Protestant of the left, of dissent and individualism. The United States also to a quite unusual degree, among the nations of the West, has been shaped by modern ideas ("liberal" in the older sense) of the free individual and of challenge to authority and to tradition. The great polar opposite position to dissenting Protestantism and liberal individualism has been the Roman Catholic church.

For this country of dissent and of classical individualism now to have elected a Roman Catholic as president—given what the presidency means for Americans, given their religious and intellectual heritage—ought to have been significant.

But it turned out instead to be an event covered with ironies. One of them was to be expected, for reasons of political necessity: when this once very Protestant country did elect a Roman Catholic to its highest office, he turned out to be a supporter of the strictest separation of church and state; the joke was that he turned out to be our first Southern Baptist president—one, that is, who defended a thoroughgoing separation more characteristic of that group than of his own church.

There was also a more subtle and far more important irony, which had to do with philosophy and temper of mind. The first member of the church of Rome, the intellectual bastion of the perennial philosophy of Natural Law and the major institutional opponent of the skeptical, reductionist, and relativist philosophies of modernity, turned out to be in fact the first man of a thoroughly modern temper to occupy the White House.

In the content of his presidency it was far more significant that he was a young man born in the twentieth century and educated by twentieth-century social scientists (his Harvard education and Yale degree) than that he was a Roman Catholic. Even the content of the remarks at his funeral mass reflected the work of his Unitarian speech writer.

It need hardly be said that he was not an expert in theological and ecclesiastical matters. Eugene McCarthy—no fan of John Kennedy—nevertheless did quietly remark, during the agitated discussion of the late fifties, that nobody interrogated Hubert Humphrey about his Congregationalism or Richard Nixon about his Quakerism the way Kennedy's Catholicism was being explored.

Kennedy had to face a certain myopia on this point. As Al Smith was forced to learn what an "en-kick-lical" was, so John Kennedy was forced to learn more about churchly problems than would be expected of a Congregationalist or Episcopalian, more, probably, than he wanted to. John Cogley, who was later to be the religion editor of the New York *Times*, tells of a note candidate Kennedy passed to him on the campaign airplane on the way to the famous encounter with the ministers in Houston: "It is hard for a Harvard man to answer questions in theology. I imagine my answers will cause heartburn at Fordham and B.C." (*i.e.*, Boston College, in Catholic academic and theological circles).

I experienced some of the heartburn effect, too, in an interview with Kennedy in the spring of 1959, when talk about a "Catholic candidate" was becoming a major national topic.

There were all these questions about Catholicism and American democracy in the air; why not (I asked myself) talk to the man whose candidacy chiefly brought them to the fore? He was obviously an intelligent man. Why not discuss the relation of Catholicism—not as an institution or power bloc, but as a substantial body of thought and values—to American politics? Surely as a sophisticated Catholic he deplored the treatment of Catholicism simply as *power* and never as *substance*. Why not ask about the relation of Catholic social thought to American liberal thought? Why not ask about the social principles of the papal encyclicals? About Maritain and Gilson and Father Murray and Joseph Pieper and Don Luigi Sturzo? About the relevance of Catholic teaching on natural law? About the guidance of the church's moral philosophers on political questions? Why not, indeed?

A meeting with Kennedy quickly dispelled these academic fantasies. He was just back from a successful trip to Wisconsin and

Indiana, and he and his staff were busy, bouncing, and optimistic, full of beans and bills and polls. Religion? Yes, well, that's the most overrated of all issues. There's nothing much in it. The thing to do is to subordinate that issue. A Catholic can be elected—look at the governors in California, Colorado, Oregon, the senators in Minnesota, Michigan, Maine. Polls that Lou Harris took show it can be done. Look at the towns in Massachusetts—overwhelmingly Protestant—that he had carried by a large majority. He cited a town in Massachusetts that Adlai Stevenson had carried by 16% and he carried (in the senate race) by 80%. He had these facts all ready to go, and ticked them off fast; it was my first experience with the rapid-fire fact-citing aspect of John Kennedy that became familiar during the campaign debates and the press conferences of his presidency.

Of course, he said, *some* Catholics can't be elected—you can't elect a crook. But *some* Catholics can be elected. The whole import of his remarks, as I might have expected, was to show that a Catholic could win—or, rather, to destroy the notion that a specific Catholic could not win. ("I do well with Protestants.") Anything beyond that obviously was in somebody else's field.

He gave the swarm of questions buzzing around a Catholic candidate the same direct, objective, pragmatic treatment that he gave everything else. He moved directly to the political point, with no philosophical embarrassment: what is it that bothers people? What is it I can say to win them over? "I've satisfied both Paul Blanshard and Cardinal Cushing; what more can they want?" "They're crazy to think I wouldn't lean over backwards."

As to his relationship either to church agencies or to church thought, he could not have been more detached. Asked about a priest who is a Catholic social thinker, he said he only saw him and others when they spoke for "the church's interests" at hearings; why, he asked, should he talk to him when he could talk to Ken Galbraith? I had an answer to that, but I didn't give it.

The subject about which to talk with the Massachusetts senator obviously was not religious social thought, but politics.

I told Ted Sorensen it had been a revealing conversation, and went back to the university. But in my heart I thought something was a little wrong. For Kennedy to subordinate the "religious issue" (or even to turn it into a mixed blessing, as he did with reference to the Democratic nomination) is quite understandable, *politically*. But politics in that broad and simple sense is not the whole of life for a president or a citizen, however it may be for a candidate. One defended Kennedy, of course, against the stupid anti-Catholicism of many "liberals." But putting all that aside, turning instead to one's own thought, one would have hoped that John F. Kennedy had taken into himself more of the best of his own heritage than in fact he had.

If one asked where one could find a view of the "technical" world, of the relation of "ways and means" to guiding moral-political ends, one answer would have been in the oldest continuous intellectual tradition of the West, developed and maintained within the Roman Catholic church. Kennedy could have found in modern Catholic thinkers ("opening the windows" at Vatican II exactly during his presidency) an understanding of "sophisticated" judgment, and the place for "ways and means," far better than in most "American" alternatives. On the one side there was the uncritical endorsement of "scientific"-technical-operational reasoning by much of "progressive" America. On the other side there was the dark "existentialist" European reaction against Technology Land, gathering strength in the United States in the sixties and bursting out in a simplified version in the New Left of 1965–70. The latter tended to be a mirror of the former, with the irrationality of a NOW generation in its beads throwing out much of the best of the historic tradition of the West along with modern technology. Far better than either was, for example, Jacques Maritain, in whose work "technical reason" is neither exalted nor repudiated but, rather, put in its proper place, subordinate to moral reason. There in Kennedy's own heritage was the Person and the Common Good. With all due respect to John Kenneth Galbraith and Arthur Schlesinger, Jr., on these fundamental matters Kennedy would have done better to have drawn upon the best thought of his own church. Robert Frost recommended at the inauguration that he be more Irish than Harvard; one might add, with reference to that speech as a symbol, the wish that he had been more Catholic than Yale.

. . .

That was not to be. Instead we were to have the explicit rejection of "philosophical" and "ideological" answers of the old-fashioned kind, and the specific and invidious endorsement of specialized knowledge. When President Kennedy gave the Yale speech, he ended, as was his wont (or Ted Sorensen's), with a Bartlett quotation. It seems that Thomas Jefferson had once said that our "new circumstances" require "new words, new phrases, and the transfer of old words to new objects." This is not, however, what Kennedy's "technical answers" speech really had been calling for. Rather, he had seemed to say, forget about the mere phrases in favor of "sensible and clear-headed management." He even said that it is upon such "management" that "the very future of freedom" depends. Never mind about the mere *words*—new or old—but attend to those "sophisticated judgments" on "hard and complicated facts" case by case.

But from a different place in the academic procession one could believe that the Jefferson quotation really suggested the better view: that in the end high political leadership should not be an applied science, but a liberal art.

5

On Pursuing Something
More than Happiness,
on Not Waiting for the Facts
to Speak for Themselves,
and on Not Building
Any Great Societies

In the late sixties the students in a college class had some trouble locating modern American "conservatism" (although they knew that its family name is Buckley), and they had a hard (though enjoyable) time distinguishing old lefts from new lefts; and they discovered that the word "radical" can be used in many ways, and rootless words like "moderate" and "militant" in even more ways, but all of these difficulties paled beside those that surrounded the honorable old name "liberalism." Of all the confusing labels in politics that one was the worst. When the professor mentioned John Locke and John Stuart Mill and what liberalism meant a long time ago (some of it—the individualistic and anti-institutional part—sounded like the New Left to those students) and when he explained that America is a liberal nation historically, so that our conservatism conserves classical liberalism, and that often when a European says "liberal" he means, at least with respect to economic matters, almost what the Indianapolis *Star* means by "conservative," and that F. A. Hayek and Arthur Krock did not think recent American liberalism is very liberal, and that there is a great deal to liberalism beyond Hubert Humphrey, beyond even Franklin Roosevelt—when the professor tried thus to explain liberalism, the students were ready to break their pencils and cry.

In addition, although in general they had a rather surprising interest (as compared with previous generations) in that most important and neglected subject applied political philosophy, most of them really did not care much about liberalism (whatever it is or was) except negatively. If I understood their position on liberalism, it was that they did not know what it was, and they were against it. They had not read the books and articles about the "end" and "decline" and "death" and "bankruptcy" and "failure" and "poverty" of liberalism or the things inevitably called "Beyond Liberalism" or "After Liberalism—What?" but they had lived all of their conscious political life in the atmosphere that called forth those books and articles, and they took that atmosphere for granted, as we do when we are young, as given, final, and absolute. Generally speaking, they found the whole subject of liberalism, what it might be and not be and what its condition is or was, as one student wrote, rising to indignant capital letters, his passion stronger than his spelling, BOREING. Let us, they would plead, their eyes beginning to glow again, go back and talk some more about the student left and the Black Panthers, and the greening of America and the wretched of the earth, and women's lib and gay lib, and revolution and repression and the Great Refusal, and Angela Davis and Mao Tse-tung, and the evil deeds of General Motors, and populism old and new, and all politics beginning at the barrel of a gun, and sexual politics or sexual anything else, for that matter, and racism and drugs and technology and the counterculture, and riots and violence and blowing up buildings and all those truly interesting subjects. And forget about liberalism.

College students are not, the implication of many writings of that period to the contrary notwithstanding, the absolute center of the universe, but as children of the *Zeitgeist* they are a handy barometer for the political weather. What they felt, their elders felt, too, although the elders came to the feeling with a different history and expressed it differently. Liberalism had by the late sixties been BOREING for some time.

And then it (whatever it was) had become something worse than boring: morally discredited. "The American dream was killed by the liberals"—Columbia University senior, 1968; "Liberalism is now a dirty word"—W. H. Auden, 1970; "A liberal is a radical with five kids"—Bill Russell, basketball's leading philosopher, 1970.

In those disputatious journals in which the intelligentsia call each other names, the Vietnam war was often said to be a "liberals' war," perhaps for more of a reason than that a liberal intellectual or two advised the presidents who made the decisions about it. White conservatives, and white radicals, along with black militants, were more than eager to see that "white liberals" got at least their full share of the blame for America's racism and racial hypocrisy; they were willing in fact to extend the word "liberal" to cover some quite unlikely suburbs, school districts, states, regions, and individuals in order that the indictment of "white liberals" be the more powerful.

What was called "liberalism" had become vague or multiform in meaning; it was, or seemed to be, pervasive in articulate circles, and therefore prone to predictable expression; and it seemed to be in power—therefore responsible for the ills of society. As the memory of FDR and the Depression faded, and a new middle class arose, and issues changed their shape, serious contending political positions appeared. There had been a time when only a discredited conservatism used the word "liberal" (often thus, in quotation marks) as a term of reproach. Those were the good old days, when just the "primitives" and the Chicago *Tribune* attacked the liberals; then God was in his heaven and all was right and left with the world. About 1965, however, the New Left arose, providing liberalism with an unsettling enemy to the left to match its more familiar enemy to the right, which meanwhile had become intellectually more formidable. The two, with their nominally polar opposition, had a surprisingly large number of ideas in common. They both fed upon the individualistic and anarchistic strains in American culture, the romantic antagonism to government, bureaucracy, and organized life. They both appealed to an outsider's feeling that an "establishment," if not a conspiracy, had led the country astray. They formed a kind of pincers movement at the end of the sixties that decimated liberalism. This left and this right shared a detestation of liberalism, for one ironic reason:

each blamed the liberals for being too soft on the other. Then came Nixon, and a revived conservatism; then Watergate, the impeachment proceedings, and ideological confusion.

/

Liberalism will return, of course, in some form, perhaps in many forms. As the nation recovers from these events, and the fury over Vietnam and "revolution" fade in memory, and the cold-war simplicities are discarded, the issues about the good society must return to the center of the political conversation. And the time will come for American democratic reform, despite all the battering it has recently received, to raise its head once more—the position, that is, that (unlike conservatism) has social justice as its primary purpose, and (unlike the violent left) seeks to realize that purpose through democratic politics. Despite all the obituaries, that tradition will not die. One may say with a confidence founded on a considerable stretch of American history, and on the logic of contemporary society as well, that ("revolutionaries" and conservatives to the contrary notwithstanding) there will once again come on the scene a version of the long, conglomerate American tradition of "reform" politics. The question about this tradition is, not whether it will vanish, but what intellectual and moral form it will take, now that in a chastened condition it must cope not only with more complicated issues but also with more robust rivals, to the right and to the left, than those to which it has been accustomed for three decades at least.

Some brief suggestions about the form in which this tradition might reappear, based on its difficulties in the sixties and before, might now be made. It has acquired over recent decades some associations and philosophical underpinnings that are not essential. For anyone who is sympathetic to the policies but not necessarily to these associations and underpinnings there may be value in sorting them.

There has been a rather inflated liberal view not only of the presidency (as, after Richard Nixon, observers hastily were saying on every hand) and of the federal government, of government itself perhaps (as conservative critics regularly charge, and some of the newer radicals as well), but also of the entire political-governmental arena, in the larger human setting.

This can be explained by an example. There was, as many readers will remember, a famous memorandum written by Arthur Schlesinger, Jr., in 1959 urging the Democratic party to provide the sort of "creative leadership" the times demanded. In this memorandum there was a theme that did not receive as much comment as did the more overtly political part. This was the theme of a "spiritual unemployment," as Schlesinger called it, that was to be overcome, along with, presumably, the more conventional economic unemployment, by an exciting new liberal political leader, fulfilling the cycle of American politics. Schlesinger, it may be remembered, described an "inherent cyclical rhythm" in American politics alternating negative with positive government at intervals that would bring around the positive side at a moment conveniently close to the arrival on the scene of the president to be elected in 1960. In Schlesinger's *A Thousand Days* he tells us that John F. Kennedy appreciated this memo—as well he might.

Schlesinger also referred to the "cultural" signs of an impending "resurgence of the national vitality." These signs at the end of the fifties included "rising spiritual discontent" in a "self-estranged social order," the "beat generation," "the interest in *Dr. Zhivago*," the "religious boom (Billy Graham, etc.)." These were said to show a "widespread yearning for spiritual purpose of some sort in life." All this, the memorandum implied, could result in and be fulfilled by a new *political* movement, with an activist leader like Theodore Roosevelt. This political movement would seek not the "quantitative liberalism" (hours and wages) of the New Deal, but a new, "qualitative liberalism" (schools and parks) "dedicated to bettering the quality of people's lives and opportunities."

Schlesinger wrote that under a Teddy Roosevelt-like leader and a political movement dedicated to qualitative liberalism "we will move on to the more elusive and complicated task of fighting for individual dignity, identity and fulfillment in a mass society."

One felt that this was an appeal of a sort that ought to have been avoided. By making so direct a link between cultural, even "spiritual," conditions and the right sort of political leadership these paragraphs overrated the place of politics in the human situation in a way that American liberals have often done, and ought not to do. This memorandum could almost have been taken to have confirmed the conservatives' complaint that liberal Democrats think they can do everything by political movements and governmental policies: "Hello, Jones. Spiritual yearnings reported in Omaha. What is the Department of Interior doing about it?" There are purposes that cannot be, or should not be, achieved by some organized collective political movement, with or without Teddy Roosevelt (with or without John Kennedy), and they most especially include the old, very complicated, and often rather lonely struggle for "individual dignity, identity, and fulfillment."

That Kennedy's 1,000 days, following upon this memorandum, were to a degree a fulfillment of its expectations does not necessarily justify it. After Kennedy was shot, there was a strain in the popular mourning that went beyond the grief and sorrow one feels for a slain statesman. There were the talismanic purchase of books and coins and symbols and relics, the pathetic poems and songs, the weeping by grown men and women, and an atmosphere for a time that went far beyond affairs of state. It was a phenomenon that is not altogether gone from our politics to this day. One young man at Yale used exactly Schlesinger's word, "spiritual," to describe his own link to John F. Kennedy; this was Gary Hart, later to be the campaign manager for a rather different leader, George McGovern. One should note all this with respect for the depth of feeling it reflected. But perhaps one may be permitted now gently to say this: it went beyond the boundaries to which government and politics should reach. It had been true at the death of Lincoln and of FDR also: the United States has more religious ingredients mixed with its nationalism, and more nationalism mixed with its deepest emotions, than it ought to have. But in the cases of Lincoln and FDR the people had lived with these leaders for a long enough time through great enough events to give a weighty content of shared history to their grief. In Kennedy's case the time was so short, and the accomplishment, for that and other reasons, so much less, that the public attachment had a larger component of sheer celebration: of "spiritual employment." The new instruments of publicity played their larger role, developing Kennedy as a national figure in 1956–60, and as a celebrity when he was president. With all respect to a people's strong feelings (feelings that one shared), a liberal ought to draw back from this mixture: not to encourage it, but to discourage it.

Politics, even in the thermonuclear age, deals (or should deal) only with the surface of life—the very important surface, to be sure. But still, even the nation itself, let alone a particular political movement, should not pretend to provide the sources of value, and the springs of cultural renewal; these should not give men and women the symbols of ultimate meaning and evoke their final loyalty. Such loyalty and meaning should come from the realms of freedom, truth, and mystery that lie beyond the social ordering that is the task of politics. That is the way we have come to understand the place of politics particularly in the *liberal* tradition out of which we have come—the tradition of Western civilization, with liberal democracy as its fullest expression to this date.

The universities, the churches, the arts, the work of science and intellect, the development in a culture's conversation of its moral understandings, and the search by individual human beings for meaning in life should all precede the work of government, and of political movements and leaders however "creative" and "bold" and "new." And they should extend beyond the work of politics and the state. Politics and government are, or should be, limited and responsive; such moral initiatives as are appropriate to them should arise beyond their reach; they then should be moved by values they did not create. They should rest on the consent of governed, and be moved by cultural and religious and moral and intellectual springs they do not and should not control. So we have traditionally believed.

This does not mean that there cannot be a politics that is a meaningful activity in its own place. Perhaps in a more sober and careful mood, a mood that keeps politics away from the realm of final values, we can have a better politics. One felt in 1959, and one feels now, after the brief Kennedy administration and a great deal more has come and gone, that one should work in politics in the narrow sense for the specific persons, parties, and policies that will do the things that need to be done, that will serve justice and the common good—but leave the "quality" of life to another department.

2

Critics of recent American liberalism say that it is hedonistic, materialistic, and shallow; that it seeks by stream of government programs to make all men "happy," and fails. An American neoconservative, lumping liberals and radicals, quoted, as the refutation of both, the title of an article Kenneth Keniston produced at the height of the youth revolt: "You don't know what Hell is like unless you grew up in Scarsdale!" He said contemptuously that "liberalism" had as its purpose turning all the world into a hellish Scarsdale; that is the way welfare-state liberalism ends—in an emptily materialistic suburban life.

Surely that is an unfair charge, if one looks at the whole constituency of American social reform, and at its longer history, before the most recent crop of conventional liberals. "Social justice," rather than "happiness," was the primary value; that means a more worthy and serious picture of man and his purposes. Is it really fair to say that Jacob Riis and Lillian Wald and Jane Addams wanted to alter life in the slums and the tenements solely in order to make the immigrant population "happy"? Or to say that materialistic Scarsdale "happiness" was the objective of the civil-rights movement in Montgomery or of the Poverty Program in Bedford-Stuyvesant?

"Happiness" and "fulfillment" are conditions that remain problematical and finally beyond the reach of social arrangements. Nevertheless, justice requires that the social order eliminate as far as may be the impediments to attaining them, and provide as far as may be the conditions for attaining them. It requires this as what is justly due to men and women, arising from the possibilities of their society. What is due is that they be treated with respect for their humanity. Material conditions, and material comparisons, do enter into that just treatment, but only as one part of it. Shaw writes that one must understand that the poor are not only hungry but also humiliated, and that is an important truth. It is the unhumiliating treatment of men by their social arrangements that a democrat must seek.

At the same time, being hungry is in itself an evil, and the threat of the alleged evils of Scarsdale should not prevent us from caring about the ways the hungry are to be fed.

"Happiness" is not a weighty enough name for the true object of living—which is both more and less than happiness. But surely it is callous to conclude that one should be unconcerned about the gross social unhappiness that spreads as far as the eye can see, block after block, across South Chicago. A little more happiness there would not hurt.

Perhaps in the interests of disentangling the social democracy one wants to support from the hedonism one does not, one should disavow that notion of a "qualitative" liberalism. At least as it modulates into the phrase "quality of life" and brings echoes of the advertising world, it may imply a refined hedonism one repudiates. A "quantitative" liberalism will suffice, for purposes of governmental action.

There is no necessary connection between reform democracy and a hedonistic outlook on the world. In the United States much of what passes for conservatism is hedonistic, too, and without the redeeming intention to spread that pleasure around. It wants itself to remain Scarsdale while the rest of the world is relegated to Bridgeport.

The charges against recent American liberalism do have a foundation. We liberals have been tempted, especially in the recent decades of comparative wealth and comparative complacency, to a certain excess in language and rigidity in method, to grandiloquence and predictability. In the days of the Great Society one could observe some of the features of liberalism that are desirable and also some that are not. The outpouring of significant legislation, bill after bill, came mostly in 1964 and 1965; the Promethean atmosphere seemed to cover most of Lyndon Johnson's years. The pretentious label the "Great Society" reflected some of its less desirable qualities.

A certain recognition of direct hits made by the critics may be implied by reproducing here the following document. It was found (as the humorists say) beside a shattered typewriter in a room much like thousands of other rooms off a corridor much like a hundred other corridors in a mammoth rectangular building, much like other such buildings, at the end of a long, long, long day in the Johnson era.

As will be seen, it deals, as did so many of the efforts of those years, with an aspect of public life that had been around for a long time prior to the Great Society, and that is with us still, but that nevertheless was addressed by Johnson with a peculiarly sweeping grandeur.

EYES ONLY

Augmenting Our Prose Resources for All America:
A Message to the Congress of the United States

Thirty-five years ago our great President Franklin D. Rooosevelt said, "The only thing we have to fear is fear itself." And I say to you today, let us face the messages of the future without fear.

Although commitments in Vietnam make this a time of restraint, it must not be a time of retreat. We can—and we will—meet the crucial challenge of official statements at home, while carrying on the sober responsibility of official statements abroad.

In the last four years a wealthy and abundant America has produced more official prose than ever before in the entire history of this great land.

We have done much.

But we must do *more*.

Our annual rate of message output rose by 16% over the previous year, 150% over 1960—more than three times the rate of growth of the Gross National Product, of which it is itself an increasingly important part.

In producing this prose flow we have employed 16,804 persons with advanced degrees, 64% of whom are members of Phi Beta Kappa, and 34% of whom—more than one in three—were graduated *cum laude* or higher.

We have composed more paragraphs in the past four years than was done by the entire federal government from the presidency of George Washington through that of Harry Truman.

This is a record of which we can be truly proud.

But it is a record which—working together—we must now surpass.

Despite our efforts in these last four years there are still many Americans untouched by this rich outflow.

—Our senior citizens, for too long left in the shadow of neglect, have been isolated in their Golden Years from the vital mainstream of American messages.

—Our children and our youth, our nation's greatest resource, have not received the full Enrichment of our messages.

—Millions of our new babies have yet to hear their first syllable of governmental prose.

—Many Americans who suffer from message-neglect are the victims of poverty and racial discrimination.

34.6 million disadvantaged Americans have incomes below the poverty line; of these, 34.6 million, or one out of every one, are blocked from official proclamatory documents by the cruel blight of poverty.

—Among our Negro males, the average rate of those who show no interest whatever in messages is 100%.

—Among our white males, the average rate is also 100%.

—Among our females—both Negro and white—the rate is the same.

We are not reaching our sturdy farmers on our tranquil farms, our strong workmen in our mighty factories, our great Indians on our great reservations, our lovely streetwalkers on our broad and lovely streets.

Let us recall the words of the poet, "No man is an Island, Entire of Himself."

We must attack this deprivation with every weapon at our command—and we will.

Our goal must be clear: Abundant messages for an Abundant America. A compassionate society will insist that every American, whatever his color, his income, his blood type, or the section of this great land from which he may come, from the giant boiler-room attendant in Peoria, to the little Shoshone grandmother in Thermopolis, to the medium-sized karate instructor in the farthest reaches of the Bronx, shall have all the official prose that he can stand.

On Pursuing More than Happiness

Creative Federalism in
Preserving Our Rhetorical Heritage

Official statements are not the work of the federal government alone. They are produced by every agency at every level throughout this great land.

State and local government, which are closer to the people and their needs, do their part in producing messages, speeches, and prose of every kind.

Private and voluntary agencies have always done much in this critical field. Many of our individual citizens produce prose on their own initiative.

But the federal government must also do its part.

—The message gap, like the pollution of our air and the contamination of our water, recognizes no political boundaries.

—The pressures of a rapidly expanding population will require more prose each year. It is estimated that by 1980 our population will require 3.2 paragraphs of official prose per day, for every man, woman, and child.

—We are increasingly an urban nation, and vital unmet message needs increase by seven to one in our great metropolitan areas as against our rural areas and our small towns.

The Task Force on the Nation's Future Message Needs and Prose Personnel Requirements, in its distinguished report, "A Voice for the Voiceless," estimates that the average sentence in Government Documents for fiscal 1968 will bear the stamp of twenty typists, thirty-three research assistants, and forty-seven editors for every actual writer. In some cases there may be no original writer whatever.

Thus we must take action to:

—upgrade vital stapling skills;

—strengthen programs for comprehensive and co-ordinated cutting and pasting services, especially in areas of severe prose deprivation;

—expand research into innovative techniques of message production, by computer, Xerox machine, and closed-circuit electronic typewriter.

As the prophet has written, "Where there is no vision the people perish."

I recommend the enactment of the Partnership for Prose Manpower and Training Act of 1968.

This will:

—provide for two prose production centers, on a pilot-project basis, scattered throughout this great land;

—foster regional development of arrangements to co-ordinate more efficiently our governmental language production with that of our great foundations, our great business corporations, and other representatives of our private sector;

—initiate a program of grants-in-aid to our states and our cities to fund initial planning for innovative programs in the dispersal of prose facilities and the delivery of prose services to all our people in areas of dire prose needs.

Conclusion

We are a great people. We have done much. We have come a long way. But we must do more.

Just over a century ago Abraham Lincoln said, "The world will little note nor long remember what we say here."

Marching forward together on this solid foundation, we must do our part to make Lincoln's promise come true.

4

There were more serious shortcomings in the Great Society than flatulence of prose style. The shortcomings satirized above go beyond the use of words, to ways of thinking not uncommon among liberals: the lumping-together, with its corny and patronizing terminology, partly euphemism and partly insult ("senior citizens," for example, in their "golden years," or "older Americans," with its rather irrelevant nationalism). One is uneasy, too, with sentences on the same subject like those Sorensen-Kennedy reverse-parallels: "it is not enough for a great nation merely to have added new years to our life; our objective must be to add new life to those years." Who is doing this "adding" of what "new life," and for whom?

One could compose a seriocomic examination of the culture's moral troubles using the shifting standard terms for the "poor," and "needy," the "minorities," the "disadvantaged," the "culturally deprived"; James Baldwin has written about the curious term the "underprivileged."

The humane sensibility may send a warning: watch out when

you are classified, and especially when you are classified as a "disadvantaged" group; as blacks, the poor, and persons who find themselves in other "underprivileged" classifications know, a generalized and patronizing good will can sometimes be as offensive to human dignity as a generalized hostility. It may be a little demeaning, and even dangerous, to be lumped together and set apart under a label and a sentimental group picture, with the implication that one is fundamentally different (although like all the others under the label) and burdensome. The categories social reformers use are much like the categories of bigots, and have the same tendency to harden into stereotype. And accompanying the reformer's stereotype, at least in the Great Society period, there was that proprietory "our"; and the inevitable overstated "great," and that insistent nationalism: our great program for our senior citizens in our great country.

The criticisms of the Great Society are familiar by now, and to some degree accepted. It would be hard to deny that the inflated language about a "war" on poverty, to "abolish" it, promised too much, aroused expectations that could not be fulfilled. It was true that many of the legislative reformers of that period, like American activists of past periods, too easily assumed that problems could be "solved," and perhaps that "social science" could do the solving: one defect in American liberalism is its link to the simple optimism of the Enlightenment and of more recent American "progressive" and "pragmatic" thought. The temper and caution and judgment and language of the Great Society certainly could have been better—wiser, more sober, more careful, more candid. In making such alterations in the social-reform tradition, though, one would not want to discard the underlying purpose. It is by no means clear that the critics share that purpose.

The editors of a sober and discriminate series of assessments of Great Society legislation, published in a special issue of a journal (*The Public Interest*) that has carried some of the higher order of postliberal criticism, wrote in their conclusion, in quite a different tone from presidential messages:

Often, though not always, the intended beneficiaries of social legislation do benefit. There are sometimes unintended and unwanted side effects; and some public programs simply don't work or prove too costly.

But there is nothing in the history of the 1960s to suggest that it is a law of nature that social legislation cannot deal effectively with social problems, or that state and local governments or private enterprise will always do better than the "Feds."

The record of the Great Society is one of successes mixed with failures, of experiments that proved themselves at least partly successful and experiments whose returns do not appear to have justified the effort. In other words, it turned out about as any sensible person would have expected.

5

Now a word or two about the relationship of liberalism to pragmatism and to empiricism: to getting the facts and looking for what works. These attitudes are all very well as far as they go, which now is not far enough. One should be empirical, but only about empirical matters; one should be pragmatic, but only about pragmatic matters. And it is particularly important when one is insistently pragmatic and empirical (a good thing to be) at the level at which this insistence belongs—get the facts, find out what works, learn the particular circumstance—that one then not impart these sound attitudes unsoundly to that other level on which they do not belong: what is good, what is just, in what direction we should go.

Before John Kennedy and Lyndon Johnson became president of the United States, American liberalism had had a long association with "pragmatism," both as a formal philosophical position and as an informal attitude. In the United States for three or four decades at least we had had an explicit recommendation of pragmatism, and of compromise and realism, and also a fierce condemnation of "doctrinaire" and "ideological" politics, coming from an unusual source—from reformers and progressives.

In the historic panorama of politics one would expect the counsels of adjustment, workability, and realistic accommodation to the limits of the possible, and the condemnation of abstract ideologies and useless visions, to come from conservatives: from people, that is, accustomed to identifying with the powers that be.

One would expect to find more of the practical and realistic note in John Adams and Alexander Hamilton than in Tom Paine and Thomas Jefferson, more in Calhoun than in Thoreau, more in Edmund Burke than in the philosophers who prepared the way for the French Revolution. Usually it is the conservative who is the realist and (as we have come to say) "pragmatist," the opponent of visionary, abstract pictures of the ideal society. It is the man who does not want society to be changed—who is often also the man who wants to hold on to power, position, and advantage—who tells us how limited social action really is, and how much it is circumscribed by necessity and bound by intractable facts.

But as the history of this somewhat unusual country has unfolded, the "progressives"—the democratic improvers of society—have come into an unusual ideological and political situation. In this new world, with its democratic "American Creed," the egalitarian advocate of change for the benefit of the common man has been able to appeal to the founding documents, the national ethos, and a considerable tradition. He had not been necessarily as much of an outsider as such people have been elsewhere; he could plausibly claim to stand within a received tradition and given set of values. It was then relatively easy, and politically useful, for him to take his social ideals for granted, as those shared by the society as a whole, and to argue only about their practical application. It was tempting to do so, too, because like all Americans he felt more at home with practical applications than with general ideas, and got the better hearing when he dealt with the former. "What can we *do* about it?" is always the American's question, whether he is conservative or progressive or nothing.

American "progressives" have had an association with pragmatic and empirical attitudes going back at least to the turn of the century. The association was mightily reinforced by the great triumph and lesson of FDR and the coming of the New Deal, against the background of a Great Depression in which 13 million people—one out of four of the work force—were thrown out of work. The New Deal's succor to the unemployed, the downtrodden, and the whole economy was interpreted as a victory for

pragmatic, experimental, untheoretical, conglomerate, undoc-
trinaire, realistic, coalition-building liberal politics. It was done
by a series of "experiments," some of the early ones discarded,
some of them better than others, practical, *ad hoc*, social reform.
While visionary intellectuals called for socialism, the New Deal
created, instead, the Federal Deposit Insurance Corporation. "I'm
not faced with a theory," FDR would say (or supporters would
quote him as having said), "I'm faced with a problem." He also
compared himself once to a quarterback (presidential references to
football antedate Nixon), whose complex practical situation on the
actual field of play was very different from that of the cheerlead-
er, who had only to proclaim the ideal ("We want a touch-
down").

And the triumph of the quarterback of the New Deal, facing
"problems" and not theories, took place in an intellectual setting
that was already strongly committed to "pragmatism," to "instrumentalism," to what was called in a book that dealt with a relevant piece of American intellectual history "the revolt against
formalism." Look at the *facts*, and at what *works*, not at some a
priori abstract "formal" doctrine. If you ask who was the chief intellectual precursor of the New Deal, and, to an extent, of American liberalism ever since, you have to go back to the philosopher
of "instrumentalism," John Dewey. There are not many other
candidates. He and Keynes were the intellectual pillars of a New
Deal that did not cast up much fundamental social thinking.
The chapter on the intellectual atmosphere of the twenties that
prepared the way for the New Deal, in the first book of the
Roosevelt series by Arthur Schlesinger, Jr., features John Dewey
first of all, and then Thorstein Veblen, Charles Beard, and Herbert Croly. The primary stream of thought that flows into New
Deal liberalism is empirical and practical, finding its impulse "in
life rather than logic," in Brandeis briefs loaded with facts, rather
than in abstract ideas. John Dewey's volumes assail one capitalized word after another from the storehouse of the "formal" thinking of the past: Certainty, Goodness, Truth, Justice. None of
these should be treated as absolutes carved somewhere in stone
forever; each should be reduced to lower case, and subjected to
endlessly self-correcting examination by the instrumental method

that is science and democracy (science and democracy thus linked in Dewey's view).

But in John Dewey there was still a solid remainder of the longer intellectual heritage out of which he had come, and a real enemy to fight. The pragmatic progressive's "revolt against formalism" took on power while "formalism" was still alive, and unmistakably conservative in its political implication. As the years passed and what was once a "revolt" became itself an established political attitude, the situation changed. American liberals have in their more subtle way the problem of revolutionaries presented fictionally by Arthur Koestler in *Darkness at Noon:* how does the younger generation that fought no battles, but received the result as a birthright, keep the faith?

The workings of history left New Deal liberalism for a long time rather complacently in possession of the American ideological field. Liberalism came to have too easy a time of it, intellectually speaking, and after the New Deal, against the background of the gargantuan object lesson of the Great Depression, won its vindication. By 1949 Lionel Trilling could write, in the introduction to *The Liberal Imagination*, "In the United States at this time liberalism is not only the dominant but even the sole intellectual tradition." We can see now, in retrospect, that the dominant intellectual position of "liberalism" in the late forties and after, to which Trilling referred, was temporary and accidental, unlikely to recur, and rather unhealthy.

The "pragmatic liberalism" of Roosevelt's New Deal had been vindicated not only by its own partial success, assisted by the war, but also by the way the alternative positions to the right and left had been discredited by the events of the thirties and forties. When Trilling wrote that sentence he could not find in America any conservative or reactionary *ideas* (as distinct from conservative or reactionary impulses) that were worth mentioning, and he did not even discuss the possibility in America of serious Marxist, revolutionary, or radical ideas, as these might be distinguished from liberalism. Marxism and the left had by then been undercut by so many traumas and disillusionments that the Henry Wallace movement of 1948 did not have moral and intellectual prestige remotely resembling that of the left of the early and middle thirties. The right wing came out of its performance in the face of the Depression, its furious opposition to Roosevelt, its generally isolationist position in 1936–41, with seriously impaired dignity and respectability.

The New Deal received a kind of retroactive endorsement from many intellectuals who had not necessarily been enthusiastic about it while it was happening. And the patriotic unity and reaffirmation of American democracy that accompanied the fight against Hitler had occurred under the leadership of the liberal Roosevelt, Dr. Win-the-War's prestige helping to vindicate Dr. New Deal. The liberalism of the New Deal had won a belated intellectual triumph, assisted by the rediscovery of cohesion and patriotism elicited by the fight against Hitler and then by the flood of disillusioning information about Russia and communism in the formative years of the cold war. So "liberalism" prevailed.

But in the longer run this easy predominance of a vaguely "liberal" outlook in the articulate circles of the nation has not been healthy. When it was joined with an anti-intellectual practical man's outlook—on goals we all agree, let's take each item case by case, with no theories, please, only facts and ways and means— the distinct emphases of the American tradition of social justice have been somewhat muted, especially as time has passed and the memory of the Depression and the New Deal have faded.

This tradition—if one may call it that, despite its variety and incoherence—has had in it a much clearer perception that man is a social animal than Americans, with their individualism, generally have had. It has been at least implicitly aware that men are dependent and interdependent to a degree that the American myths of self-made man and self-reliance and Horatio Alger heroes thoroughly obscure. It has been aware that this interdependence is much increased by the modern industrial world: the current versions of American democratic politics arose in the late nineteenth century in response to the evils of industrialism. The social-reform tradition has had as its norms social justice and the public interest (the "common good," as it might be called in another setting), which stand in some contrast to the celebration of self-interest and individualism of much of the American ethos.

And the social-justice tradition would have had—should have developed by now—its criticism of the collective egotism of the American nation, in the international field, too. But the sound of all this was muted by the comparatively unchallenged place of diluted liberalism in articulate circles, and by the deliberate abandonment of general ideas in favor of "facts," "science," and what works.

Originally the practical and factual political method American liberals developed was a secondary message, a borrowing from historic political wisdom (not necessarily liberal—more often from conservative sources) and also a recognition of the unusual possibilities of American constitutional democracy, for the noncatastrophic accomplishment of democratic ends. These themes were *secondary;* the social democratic ends, the humane rearrangements of society, were primary. But then when that primacy faded, and these subordinate themes became the first message of liberalism, it began to fade away—to fit in altogether too well with the inclinations of the society as a whole. And, fading, it became boring and then discredited.

6

"Social justice" is a phrase that has, like all the high abstractions that on the right occasion bring some tingling of the blood, often and grossly been misused. But we cannot for that reason discard it, any more than we can discard the word "liberty" because of all the crimes that have been committed in its name.

The formal meaning of the word "justice" is, of course, to "give every man his due"; to each what is his, what he deserves. There is a balance of the one side with the other, as in the scales held by the blindfolded figure in front of the courthouse. In its pure abstraction the concept allows, to be sure, for endless varieties of interpretation. It is perversely amusing to read, for example, the old new conservative Russell Kirk, indignantly rejecting the concept of *social* justice, reading into the definition of justice "to each *his own*," a foundation in the very nature of the universe for private property

(*His Own;* what is *his*). Kirk's view reminded me of the satirist's imaginary name for the only course at Yale the young William Buckley approved of, "The Divine Origins of General Motors." Those of us who do not believe in the divine origins of General Motors—who believe that motorcar company is just a human construct and not a direct product of the Creator's will—may also believe that the same is true of the institution of private property itself: that it is not written into the very foundation of the moral order everywhere, anywhere, and always, but, rather, is another human construct, to be tested and judged and hedged and discriminated about by antecedent moral principles. And we surely understand by the phrase "his own" something other than his own plot of land, his own garden, his own stocks and bonds, his own yacht and country home, as in the unintentionally comic conception of Kirk. The phrase "his own" may better be rendered, "what he deserves"; it would not be altogether wrong to use the vernacular phrase "what he has coming to him." Whether what a man justly has coming to him includes the farther reaches of the holdings of ITT is the proper subject of moral and political argument.

To many a modern mind the pure abstraction of the formula quoted seems not only empty—in a sense it is empty—but also meaningless, worthless. As an economics professor would say: Okay, so who's against it? A political scientist, later to be the president of the American Political Science Association, pouring daiquiris on his porch on Prospect Street in New Haven, typically complained about a book by one of the scattered few of his more philosophically minded colleagues: "But he doesn't say what justice *is!*" What it *is*, in application, we debate. The abstract idea of justice itself serves as a point of beginning: it gives the debate meaning and makes the occasion for serious moral contemplation and instruction and self-correction. It is one of those central formative patterns for the mind and conscience, developed out of centuries of conversation about the right way for men to live together, that ought to have been built into the John Mitchells of our society—to choose only him from all the tempting examples—into all of us, for that matter, more soundly than they have been.

Social justice, then, is to some extent a distinct and a modern idea, as already suggested in the remarks about Juvenel. It has, of course, as he said, achieved a wide currency in the modern world, and like all great ideas may be put to a pernicious use. It almost means what he says it means: that the arrangements of society, independent of the moral quality of the individual, shall be such as to "give each man his due." It means that—except that those of us who hold to it as a central idea do not believe in the implied "supreme legislator" who does the arranging in a manner untouched by the human citizen's hands. In the still developing tradition of American reform democracy, as also among social democrats everywhere, the citizenry, through the institutions of a free people, work out the concrete content of justice in society—work it out; today, and again tomorrow, and continually. There is no finality, no utopian point of arrival. No day ever comes when justice in society is *achieved*. It is a continuing purpose of the democratic deliberation, of the conversation in the culture of a free people. And it should come to be as much a part of the moral equipment of the individual as the virtues that have a longer tradition: social justice as a personal virtue. We have this modern phrase "social conscience," which has some reason and some use. One wants "social conscience," which, for example, most Americans developed after 1954 on race, to bear on other issues as well.

Social justice means that ordering of society whereby each man is given his due. What is his due? That he be treated according to the full stature of his humanity.

It is, of course, a condition that, like justice between individuals, is never perfectly achieved. Nevertheless, it is continually to be sought.

A socialist like Shaw can flatly slap down on the table, like a dealer playing his trump card, the names of his purposes: socialism, which means equality of income. Bang. An American liberal cannot be unequivocal at that level. He does not necessarily hold to the socialism his conservative friends accuse him of. He is, at the most, a creeping socialist; moreover, he may well be content to be forever creeping—content that his creeping never arrives at "socialism" (whatever that term may now mean). He is not committed to "Public Ownership of the Means of Production," although he is not in all cases against it either. He is not, with Shaw, committed to Equality of Income as a simple ideal, although he would now favor a redistribution of income in the United States to diminish the inequalities and guarantee a livable minimum. It is no longer illuminating to say "mixed economy," as we used to in my youth; we already have a mixed economy; one wants a better mixture.

If his disagreement with the left is his acceptance of capitalism where it serves as humanely as is now possible, his disagreement with the right is his unwillingness to defend it where it does not. As Public Ownership is no final principle, neither is the "Free Market" or "Private Property." Principles come at a higher level than any of these. These constructs of the capitalists and socialists are to be tested against antecedent standards of the stature of humanity. The free market may do the wonders of impersonal, noncoercive allocation its defenders claim, but that is exactly the place for some pragmatism and empiricism: in fact, does it do so, in the particular case? Does it work in reality as the economists and the ideologues say it works in their books? One finds most of the real problems (that consumers' incomes are not equal, and that many producers have immense power over prices, over the market; and so on) are assumed away in capitalist theories.

How about government regulation? Quasi-public corporations? TVA? Amtrak? Public television? We have been inventive in this country in making up all sorts of mixtures that do not fit the purity of the old socialist-capitalist debate, and that is good. The pragmatic reform tradition has played a major role in that, and that is good. The "market" and the "corporation" and even the "state" are all instruments of the community to serve its good . . . to serve the common good, social justice, and the liberty of the human being. They are all, in other words, to be tested by antecedent moral principles that the older socialist debate by-passed.

Of the role of the state, with its unique ability to coerce, the same is true. Liberals need not hold to the automatic preference for action by the federal government that conservatives, and now sometimes radicals as well, try to attribute to them partly for debating purposes in the antistatist American atmosphere. We need in this country a healthier view of the role of government in society, but that role nevertheless must be put in its place, subordinate to objectives that may have other means of realization. The liberal should refer to the "Jeffersonian ends" and insist that they are controlling; the "Hamiltonian means" are subordinate, to be tested by whether they are truly serving the Jeffersonian (that is, democratic, egalitarian, humane) ends.

This means that the American democratic reformer may say, in the argument with right and left about the "state," that he does not necessarily prefer action by the central government to action by the lower-level governments. That depends. Neither does he prefer action by government to action by nongovernmental agencies. Certainly he does not, or should not, support all the actions of governments, whether they move in the direction of social justice or not—a ridiculous position once you state it that way, but one implied in some attacks on alleged liberal support for big government. He believes as much as the next American (perhaps more) in the limits of the state, the stature of the human being that goes beyond the reach of the state, the dangers of the omnicompetent and omnipresent totalitarian state. Really it is the limits on *society*, and on the *nation*, that can never claim the whole of a person or be his final fulfillment.

All this is not to imply a rejection of the "welfare state," either of its accomplishments in the United States so far, or—as it is important to say—of the objective of completing what has not yet been done. We ought to have done that long since, without all the hullabaloo. Men may tire of particular lines of political talk well before they have accomplished their purpose, or independently of any such accomplishment; people of the World War II generation were already saying they were "tired" of hearing about what was then often called the "Negro problem" before the civil-rights movement had even begun. The notion that the "social gains" of the New Deal's welfare state are completed and passé, though widespread, is mistaken.

Let me quote, about the welfare state in the United States, a "radical" who in other places in his writing has many barbs for liberals, Irving Howe:

. . . the welfare state has meant that large numbers of working-class people are no longer ill fed, ill clothed, and insecure, certainly not to the extent they once were. That automobile workers in Detroit can today earn a modest, if insufficient, income; that through union intervention they have some, if not enough, control over their work conditions; they can expect pensions which are inadequate but far better than anything they could have expected twenty years ago—all this is *good:* politically, socially, in the simplest human terms. To dismiss or minimize this enormous achievement on the lordly grounds that such workers remain "alienated" and show little awareness of their plight, is to allow ideology to destroy human sympathy.

One expression of American democratic reform, but only one, is state action to share the risks and succor the victims of the movement of history: the welfare state. But the heart of reform goes beyond that to the never-ending quest for social justice and the common good.

6

On Not Overthrowing
the System

Politics moves by repulsion, flight, and bad memory, as the obvious sequence in recent American history indicates. The Nixon scandals had many roots, but an important one was the shocked reaction by ordinary folk against the outrageous doings of the young left, and the turmoil of militant protests and polarizing events of the late sixties. That New Left and that turmoil, in turn, grew in some part from the deficiency in American liberalism just described.

Watergate represented (along with everything else it represented) a gross overreaction, by a man and a group with a well-developed siege mentality, against the "revolutionary" left of 1965–70. This overreaction was mingled with "backlash" against left-liberalism and even against Great Society–New Frontier liberalism; the aforesaid siege mentality was not inclined to make nice distinctions among what it called, in one of its own unappetizing epithets, "radiclibs." Although the attack on the left, and the blurring of the line between the left and the liberals, was of course filled with strategic political considerations, at the same time one assumes an admixture of genuine conviction. One can find both the strategy and the conviction in those strange documents the transcripts of the taped White House conversations.

Among some of the allegedly "silent" and "forgotten" and "middle" constituency, the fear was authentic, and extended not only to bombers and busers and leakers of Pentagon papers and hordes of demonstrators claiming they would "stop the government," but even to George McGovern, the Methodist from South Dakota. For a few moments in 1968–70 there had seemed to be a faint scent of anarchy in the air; at least, many citizens thought so, and reacted.

At another level, the neoconservative or "revisionist" intellectual movement that came into prominence during Nixon's first term was also in large part a reaction against the sixties, and especially against the left—against radical politics, radical "counterculture," radical chic. One might almost say it was nothing else.

And that New Left, that youth revolt, had among its several causes the vacuum in liberalism. The brief radical outburst of 1965–70 was the result, to be sure, of a complicated configuration of historical events—above all, the Vietnam war—and of social conditions (even of demography: the multitudes of American young from the postwar baby boom). Part of it was world-wide. Nevertheless, it was also the outcome of an intellectual and moral situation in the United States, a condition of Belief, of Value, and of thought, or of their opposites.

As a nonradical American democrat, I feel the justice of the wounded retort made by an alumnus of the youth revolt to criticisms of the sort made in these pages. What you have written is unfair and too negative, the younger man said plaintively, looking back on his own mild fever of radicalism: "What other viewpoint was available to us?"

Intellectual movements do matter, and our heritage of New Deal liberalism did not, by the late sixties, have much to offer. There was the Vietnam war, to which we had at best an ambiguous relation. We did not have thinkers of stature. Alliances forged in the thirties and forties were clung to still, beyond the point of their true application. The old liberalism's late forties' alliance with cold-war nationalism and with pragmatic politics and philosophy and with "consensus" social theories gave it a complacent aspect repellent to many who were newly discovering America's defects.

And this liberalism had strong ties to the scientism of the universities. I believe that the positivistic atmosphere of college classrooms in the fifties and early sixties prepared the way for the irrational outburst of the late sixties. That scientism fit rather neatly, at least in its disdainful rejection of moral language and of general ideas, with the no-nonsense, "hard-nosed," "tough-minded" syndrome of the practical men in Washington. And the resulting moral and interpretative vacuum was one source of the bizarre developments among the young and some of the intelligentsia in the late sixties. Humane young persons, provoked by the Vietnam war and Southern "cops" and the comedy of a consumer economy, searching, as the young are always searching, for a large, constructive grip on the world, tried to fill the empty place their elders had left them with some makeshift thing made up of pieces of Malcolm X, Herbert Marcuse, Herman Hesse, Norman Mailer, Bob Dylan, Timothy Leary, Frantz Fanon, Zen Buddhism, Che Guevara, and the kitchen sink. That jungle suddenly grew because there had been only a desert before.

1

The youth of the fifties, it need hardly be said, were not like the youth of the sixties. The first time I saw a large gathering of young men from the private preparatory schools of the Eastern seaboard, at a conference of some kind early in that decade, I noted how proper and homogeneous they appeared to be: well-scrubbed, well-combed, little three-quarter-sized embryonic organization men, in their three-quarter-sized Brooks Brothers' suits, with their three-quarter-sized shirts with button-down collars, with their three-quarter-sized copies of the New York *Herald Tribune* under their arms and their three-quarter-sized versions of Henry Luce's opinions, preparing to go off to Yale and Harvard and Princeton to become the stuffed shirts of tomorrow. I looked at them critically then; many of us did. They were said to be a "Generation of Bureaucrats," young fogies, passively willing to accept what they were told, uncritical, unrebellious, desirous only of a secure place in an organization society.

But fifteen years later I winced when I scraped up from memory what I said and thought in those very different years. I even remembered with a certain nostalgia those days when we were all deploring the passivity of students.

We said they were too easily adjusted to the social order, too complacent, too unrebellious. We tried to say that America as it stood was not quite as complete a victory over mankind's problems as these young people seemed to think. But the young people did not believe it. They would often maintain that the only remaining political problems were in the international field, that America's domestic problems had been essentially solved.

Some professors tried to tell these students that racial discrimination was no mere surface matter of individual attitudes but a persisting "structure of injustice," and that despite the wonders of American capitalism, there were poor people left clean out of the picture. The eyes of the young people would glaze over at the mention of these poor, whoever they were, if there were any, and they would soon change the subject. At the height of the complacency of the middle fifties, such words went whistling out the window to the place dead lectures go.

In the fifties a college teacher regularly argued that student opinion to his right. By the late sixties he regularly argued with student opinion to his left.

With much of what young activists said, he probably agreed, and muttered to himself, Where *were* you fifteen years ago? (After enough years of teaching one may stupidly blur together all those classes and all those students, quite unfairly lumping together all their faults. They have sat in the same chairs in the same rooms, after all, and, except for hair style, they look alike.)

When in the late sixties we thought back to the fifties' efforts to rouse the students from their apathy, one of the old jokes would come floating into memory: the one about the preacher whose supplication for rain was followed by a cloudburst and a flood; "I know, Lord, that we prayed for rain, but this is ridiculous."

One Sunday in the spring of 1968 I gave my oldest daughter, a girl then sixteen years old, a ride home from church. She had with her a boy friend, one of her fellow workers at the headquarters in New Haven, Connecticut, for the Eugene McCarthy presidential campaign of that year. The church at the door of which I picked up these two young politicians was no ordinary house of worship, no little brown church in the wildwood, but Battell Chapel, the Church of Christ at Yale University, at which the preacher was William Sloane Coffin, Jr.—Jeb Stuart Magruder's ethics teacher, among his other distinctions. The congregation was predominantly young, and vibrated with moral outrage every Sunday at the evils of American society.

At some of the evils, at any rate.

That there was a certain selectivity in choosing the evils to be vibrated against was one of the points I would meditate about, as on intermittent Sundays I myself dozed along pleasantly, as one does in church, in that particular congregation.

On this Sunday, however, it was my daughter and her friend who had done the meditating, with somewhat different results from mine. They were unequivocal in their enthusiasm for what they had heard. As they got into the car, these two members of the Now generation (the *then* Now generation) said that the preacher was—oh, wow!—Terrific, Fan*tas*tic.

As a member of a non-now generation, I asked for specifics.

It seemed that if Jesus were alive today he would be put in jail for draft resistance. It seemed that if Jesus were alive today he would be criticized by university professors for not being "objective." It seemed that allowing alcohol while prohibiting marijuana showed the hypocrisy of society. It seemed that Yale alumni were making *some* progress in their social views, mostly because of the influence of their children: "If there is one thing Yale alumni are more afraid to lose than their property, it's their children." It seemed that even if you won the rat race, you were still a rat. It seemed that—the preacher borrowed a philosopher's phrase—the world was hanging not by a thread but by a wet Kleenex. It seemed that—here there was a borrowing from Norman Mailer—all the obscene words in all the obscene books ever written and banned from libraries were not half as obscene as one minute in the mind of General Westmoreland.

I thought about what to say in response to all this as I drove down Whitney Avenue. The ethos of Battell Chapel was a subject that had to be approached with circumspection. Coffin, who was then under indictment for his leading part the previous fall in a draft-card turn-in at the Department of Justice, was a considerable hero to many in New Haven, including my daughter. A year later she was to be one of those in her high-school graduating class who would successfully recommend inviting him to be their commencement speaker; when he would arise to speak, she and all her classmates in their white dresses would also rise, to give him a rather touching gesture of honor. And on balance I did not mind that this was true.

Therefore any qualifications I wanted to make at this late date would have to be stated with discretion.

"You know," I said, "when I was young, I heard preachers in Kansas who would take a swipe at Franklin Roosevelt. I would look around at the congregation sitting there pleased as punch in the pews. They were all what I suppose we would call middle class. Undeniably they were Middle Western, and residents of a small town. Almost to a man, or, I should say, to a lady, they were Republicans. I used to feel that digs at President Roosevelt were not really what these Kansas Republican ladies needed to hear, in order to enlarge their spiritual horizons."

(Perhaps large concessions were now in order.)

"I realize, of course, that there are vast differences between that Kansas situation and the one in Battell Chapel today, if you go out into streets and compare church opinion with local public opinion. In the Kansas case they coincided, and in the present case they certainly do not. Moreover, there is the most important point of all, whether the opinion expressed—no matter who agrees with it, or disagrees—is right or wrong, is or is not on the side of justice and truth as you understand it. Maybe you say that that consideration overrides all others. Maybe you say that being Against the War, loudly and firmly, is all that really counts.

"Still, I have to say for myself that when I sit in a pew and hear about the draft and marijuana and the police and the young and that really rather crude item about General Westmoreland, and then look around at the congregation, I have something of that feeling I had back in Kansas. They are hearing what they already believe anyway."

My daughter and her friend did not appear to agree with these remarks, coming as they did from a member of the middle class, from a person over thirty, from a *parent*. I suppose what I seemed to be saying to them was something like Walt Whitman's amusing admonition to his young disciple Horace Traubel: "Be radical, be radical, be not too damned radical!"

That Sunday night another older fellow gave a speech, the president of the United States, Lyndon B. Johnson. As it drew toward its end, I called my daughter to come see it on the television set, because something about the president's phrases and manner was causing an expectant tingling in the spine.

The satisfaction created by the president's withdrawal from the election race did not last long. On Thursday night of that week in 1968, I was in Washington, sitting with friends in a Hungarian restaurant. An older man, an employee in a red-jacketed Hungarian outfit—a rather incongruous messenger—came soberly to the table with the news.

"Dr. King has been shot," he said. "In Memphis."

After a preoccupied evening, I watched a late symposium, in my hotel room, in which Whitney Young and Roy Wilkins and another black American were asked implicitly insulting questions by a white reporter. I was ready to kick in the tube that night to silence that white newsman. Martin Luther King was only a few hours dead: it was a time to honor him, to remember him, to grieve for him. But this agitated white newsman kept asking, "Who will succeed Dr. King as a Negro leader?" and "Will there be a new spokesman for nonviolence?" and "What will the reaction of Negroes be?" This white man asked such questions not just once, but repeatedly, and virtually to the exclusion of questions about Dr. King's life and work. Wilkins and Young, with a patience almost incredible under the circumstances, kept quietly turning his questions aside. (When I asked him about that program later, Young said, with quiet understatement: "That was a difficult evening.") They kept refusing to name some black who was suddenly supposed to take Dr. King's place as "Negro leader"; they kept declining to suggest (as the white interviewer almost in so many words asked them to do) that black viewers should refrain from a violent reaction to Dr. King's death. At one point, this television newsman felt called upon to volunteer the statement that he and all his white friends didn't hate Negroes.

This newsman is one of those whose Establishment liberalism was later to be deplored by the Nixon White House. Whatever he represents, it did not serve well on that evening. Nor were others much better. A major-network anchor man commented gratuitously, and actually a little inaccurately, on the "dignity" of the King funeral. Many other whites said foolish things in the days that followed. The obvious, immediate, explicit white feeling was *fear*, not grief; and that was all too plain.

Shortly after noon the next day, I checked out of my hotel and got into a taxi. When I told the white taxi driver my destination—Union Station—the driver put his head down on the steering wheel in dismay. I was accustomed to the disappointment of Washington taxi drivers on learning their fare would be only the sixty cents for Zone One, but I had never seen anything quite like this. Finally the driver lifted his head and resignedly drove through midday Washington. He did not, however, take any of the usual routes passing through the Seventh Street ghetto area. Instead, he went all the way around by Pennsylvania Avenue. Reading the papers on the train, I learned why: bands of angry young blacks were burning and looting and rioting up Seventh Street.

Government people and black leaders had been meeting all that day at the White House, but little came of that. When I called Washington friends over the weekend, they told me about flying into a smoking capital city that looked as though it had been bombed.

On the following Sunday I went to Battell Chapel; I went from time to time, perhaps as an application to myself of the positive principle implied by the negative comment on Kansas. Over the years I had worked out about the right annual dosage of Coffin I required to keep my organs working properly. But on this Sunday—Palm Sunday, as it happened—I went not as a part of my annual dosage, but because, whatever the mixture of my feelings in general, I did want to be there on this particular Sunday.

The church was crowded. It was quite an extraordinary congregation, diverse in age, race, dress, and no doubt in many other ways as well. Although Coffin explained in the announcements that black leaders wanted to have "a sort of a boycott on whites for a while," still there were quite a number of black persons in the congregation.

In the middle of his sermon, Coffin spoke with some passion against those who were presenting King simply as a "spokesman for nonviolence."

"He was the spokesman for *direct action* that was nonviolent. To leave that out, to present him any other way, is to dishonor Martin's life and work."

It was obvious enough, but I had not heard any other white person speaking in public say it so clearly.

Despite all that was predictable, tasteless, foolish, and dangerous in the late sixties' conglomerate of protests, militancies, liberations, and revolutions, there was also mixed with it an occasional penetration to the moral heart of the matter. And the New Left after 1965 (mostly inadvertently) made it possible seriously and explicitly to examine American institutions and American values more fundamentally than had been possible for a quarter of a century. One hopes that effect will not be lost.

Most of us have to live through a number of years and several historical turning points in order to get a feel for the pitch and roll of history. In these matters, much goes by reaction, counteraction, alternation; sons repudiate their fathers; students see where (they think) their professors were wrong; most of all, middle-aged men perceive their own youthful mistakes. The great changes of history change one's mind in ways that as a youth one does not anticipate. Where a man first begins to formulate his adult ideas, in that important part of life from about age sixteen until about age twenty-five, he ordinarily has not yet had time to have felt any of the large sea changes of history. Though his elders often tell him that his mind will change because his historical experience will change, he does not believe it. He does not believe it because this alleged wisdom of the elders is a cliché, and because these elders are discredited by the evils they seem to have tolerated. They have coexisted with those evils.

The social ideas of a young person, reinforced by his peers, are felt by him to be exempt from the flux that made the ideas of his elders now so laughably outdated. The world is new to him, and his ideas about it seem to be unique in their finality.

But they are not final. They change. The expatriates and hip-flask people of the twenties sobered up remarkably after the Crash; in the thirties, the Adonais of the flappers, F. Scott Fitzgerald, wrote to his daughter that she should be reading Marx's savage description of The Working Day. Thousands of the college students in the early twenties who signed the Oxford Pledge never to fight in another war fought bravely all over the world in World War II. Many properly conventional young of the fifties discovered in pot parties of the late sixties unconventionalities they had shunned in their youth. The younger brothers of the wild ones of the late sixties began to be more thoughtfully sedate, and the much advertised generation gap suddenly vanished.

Orwell wrote some sentences about childhood, in his essay about his schooldays, that may be applied to the political ideas that develop in the later period of our youth.

The child and the adult live in different worlds. . . . It will have been seen that my own main trouble was an utter lack of any sense of proportion or probability. This led me to accept outrages and believe absurdities, and to suffer torments over things which were in fact of no importance. It is not enough to say that I was "silly" and "ought to have known better." Look back into your own childhood and think of the nonsense you used to believe and the trivialities that could make you suffer. . . . The weakness of the child is that it starts with a blank sheet. It neither understands nor questions the society in which it lives and because of its credulity other people can work upon it, infecting it with a sense of inferiority and the dread of offending against mysterious, terrible laws.

Our budding social and political ideas, when we are growing out of childhood's ignorance, are often marked by the freshness and sweep of a new discovery, with the first stark perception of all that is wrong with those once-mysterious, terrible laws. But at the same time, this sweeping discovery is made with what is still almost a blank sheet, upon which the personally felt record of historical change will one day be written. What one hopes for—not something easy to achieve—is the deepening and sophisticating of those youthful perceptions, and a correcting of them also, to be sure, without losing touch with their moral directness. This will not happen without a more serious political education than has ordinarily been our practice.

4

Those who were, like my daughter, young in the late sixties felt the sudden simultaneous impact of many forms of American protest, dissent, and radicalism. Many protesting movements re-enforced each other, and created a new spirit of native anti-Americanism—a heresy against the American creed in culture, politics, and economics—that seemed to me to go beyond anything in our past.

I said the "American creed." Perhaps I should use, instead, the vague and rather fatuous phrase that was widely heard in the very different decade preceding, and say that in the sixties there was a new level of both serious criticism of and nose-thumbing directed against the American Way of Life. A predominant mood of the sixties kicked the national pieties of the fifties in the seat of the pants. A significant part of the protest movement of the sixties also took up serious social reform and national self-criticism, again in contrast to the comparative complacency of the years that had gone before. And then toward the end of the decade there developed, on the left, something else: a movement that went beyond irreverence, reform, and national self-criticism in the direction of what is called "revolution." At its extreme it stood in opposition not only to the national failings but also to the national ideals and established procedures. It was in protest not just against the fifties but against the whole sweep of the American experience, at least according to its most ferocious spokesmen. It stood in opposition not to particular injustices, not to the excesses of capitalism, not even precisely to American capitalism as a whole, but to the entire system, the entire, vaguely defined and virtually all-inclusive "Establishment"; in other words, not only to the specific faults of America, but to America itself, including its moral core, constitutional procedures, and liberal democracy. And of course a reaction on the part of ordinary citizens against all this anti-Americanism began to gather strength.

Several kinds of protest and revolt, out of the past, came back into American public life simultaneously and in force. These older rivers of protest, dammed or diverted, now burst over the dams, returned to their channels, and flowed together into the flood tide of radicalism in the delta of the late sixties. Some of the feeder streams may be identified, at least symbolically, with decades of the past. We may say that the sixties saw the simultaneous return of the cultural protest of the twenties and the political-economic protest of the thirties.

The stream that came from the twenties had mainly to do with culture, higher and lower: with items of behavior and attitude, of manners and morals, of values and leisure activities.

The affinities of the twenties with the sixties were noticed fairly often: one sexy, prosperous era of short skirts and youthful revolt calling out to another. If you reread *Only Yesterday*, you will find much that reminds you of the sixties: endless discussions about the Younger Generation, with middle-class young people in rebellion against the middle-class standards of their middle-class parents; endless discussions of sex, with a rapid change in the role of women and in mating mores and morals; endless fascination with popular culture—the Jazz Age, radio, Paul Whiteman's orchestra playing "It's Three O'Clock in the Morning." The standard word for the twenties, of course, is "disillusionment"; there is an important aspect of the later sixties to which that word applies, too. In both periods there were widespread and visible evidences of escapism, hedonism, frivolity, dropping out: the hip flask and the speak-easy in one period, the drug culture, the hippies, the pot party in the other. In both periods it is not only the young who reject the authority figures and mock the representative national characters; celebrated intellectual leaders do the same. It marks quite a shift in national mood when H. L.

Mencken supplants William Dean Howells as the literary arbiter. In the late sixties there emerged a whole new set of "countercultural" spokesmen and publications. In both decades the most talked about of the intelligensia mock, criticize, deplore, and satirize national institutions and prevailing national standards.

The twenties saw a rebellion against the middle-class family; a "revolt against the village"; a rejection of what was rather mistakenly called "puritanism." These dissenting movements opened fissures in the national culture that were then more or less papered over during each of the three decades that followed, for reasons each of the decades provided. Then in the sixties the cultural divisions burst open again.

Both these decades saw the city asserting its values against those of the small town and countryside; each saw the old stock and conventional cast of American characters lose visibility and prestige.

The Harvard-Catholic-Boston-sophisticated figure of John F. Kennedy, who of course was immensely important for the spirit of the sixties, was not only the first president born in this century but also perhaps the most remote in all recent American history from the ethos of Main Street. He calmly explained to a farm audience on his Western tour in the fall before his death that he was a city boy who had never milked a cow or plowed a furrow, straight or crooked.

In these two decades the urban variety of the real United States made itself felt against the uniformities of the mythical United States of Main Street, the New England Yankee, and suburbia. In these two decades American culture seemed livelier, richer, more heterogeneous than in the rather stuffy periods that preceded them. At the same time, there came—especially in the late sixties—a sweeping repudiation of authority and of standards that was not as welcome a development as the other one.

There was also a connection between the sixties and the thirties, when the Depression brought quite another kind of criticism of the nation's institutions.

The characteristic protesters of the twenties had not been much concerned with politics and economics. They went to Paris. They read H. L. Mencken and laughed at the American boob. They satirized *Main Street*. They may have laughed at Harding, Coolidge, and Hoover, but not out of any clear-cut contrary political judgment. They were contemptuous of the nation's Babbitts, but not only of any clear-cut contrasting economic ethic. If you reread *The Great Gatsby*, you will find a good deal in it that reminds you of the sixties, but except for some incidental disapproval of the reactionary opinions of Tom Buchanan you will not be able to make out Fitzgerald's political and economic views. Some of the figures of the twenties turned out to be unalloyed political conservatives: Willa Cather and, in his own way, of course, Mencken. The itch for political and economic reform was, in fact, an expression of the "bilge of idealism" of people like the "Archangel Woodrow," and then in the thirties of a certain presidential "radio crooner" that Mencken and the supermen of *The American Mercury* looked down upon.

The Crash, the coming of the Depression, the "American earthquake," as Edmund Wilson was to call it, changed all that. In the spring of 1932 Wilson looked back at the attitudes of the twenties, which he said already "seemed a long way off"; from the thirties, he said, "we can see how superficial they were." The first of these attitudes was that of the "Menckenian gentleman, ironic, beer-loving, and 'civilized,' living principally on the satisfaction of feeling superior to the broker and enjoying the debauchment of American life as a burlesque show or a three-ring circus. . . ." Farther along in his article Wilson said that it could now be seen that all the suddenly outdated attitudes from the twenties "represented attempts on the part of the more thoughtful Americans to reconcile themselves to a world dominated by 'salesmen and brokers' . . . that they all involved compromises with the salesman and the broker. Mencken and Nathan laughed at the broker, but they justified the system which produced him and they got along with him very well, provided he enjoyed George Moore and had pretensions to a taste in liquor. . . ."

In the thirties these "more thoughtful Americans" no longer made compromises with "the salesman and the broker."

C. Vann Woodward wrote about this period:

On Not Overthrowing the System

In the thirties and well into the following decade there occurred the most thoroughgoing inquest of self-criticism that our national economy has ever undergone—not even excepting that of the muckraking and Progressive Era. No corner nor aspect nor relationship of American capitalism was overlooked, and no sibboleth of free enterprise went unchallenged. The prying and probing went on at every level from the sharecroppers to holding companies and international cartels. Subpoenas brought mighty bankers and public-utility empire-builders to the witness stand. Nor was this activity merely the work of the wild-eyed and woolly-haired, nor the exclusive concern of one of the major parties. It was a popular theme of the radio, the press, the theater, and even the pulpit. . . . Universities hummed and throbbed with it. . . . Then in the mid-forties something happened. It happened rather suddenly. The floodstream of criticism dwindled to a trickle and very nearly ceased altogether. It was as if some giant sluice-gate had been firmly shut.

The shutting of that sluice gate by the celebrational atmosphere during and after World War II perhaps helped to make the backed-up flood stream more of a torrent when the sluice gate opened and that criticism flowed out again in the sixties, as it certainly did.

That the American economy became again the object not only of criticism but also of attack in the sixties was evident in every one of the institutions Woodward mentions, and in television and especially in books and magazines. He referred to muckraking and the Progressive Era, which might stand as the next previous historical antecedent to the thoroughgoing criticism of capitalism in the thirties. The muckraking magazine article reappeared everywhere in the sixties, including appearances in publications in which it was quite incongruous: in *The New Yorker*, that prestigious survivor of the spirit of the twenties ("not for the Old Lady from Dubuque"), which ran long columns of social criticism side by side with advertisements for two-thousand-dollar diamond clips from Van Cleef & Arpels; in such an all-American entry as that hinterland Bible *The Saturday Evening Post*, in its last days; and even in the flagship of the American century, Henry Luce's *Life*. Crusaders and crusading books and articles tumbled over each other. Church and university had a new leftward flavor. As to the theater, the cinema, and books, I have already suggested that one reason for the severity of the rebellion of the late sixties may be the coinciding of different kinds of protest, antipuritan and anticapitalist; in the theater and the movies and on the newsstands, one heard them all at once, at full whistle.

5

This radicalism was especially difficult to deal with because the cultural revolt was joined with the political one. A nonradical might object not only—as was commonly said—to the tactics sometimes employed (violent, illegal, coercive, defamatory), but also to the underlying cultural revolt. America, despite all its particular ills, is not as the radicals pictured it. Moreover, one did not want this nation to be made over according to the values implicit in the methods they employed and the attitudes they exhibited.

One had to admit that the inadequacy of the heritage of liberal reform was one cause of the protests. And one did accept as accurate many of the particular criticisms of American society. But one certainly did not believe the evils in it would be corrected by a holistic rejection of that society, by an unbuttoned hedonism, or by tactics of violence and abuse.

Meanwhile, there came to be decals of the American flag on the windshields of every other car that went by. They represented the repressive reaction that was gathering force against the outbursts of those years, one course, in turn, of the misdeeds of Watergate and Richard Nixon.

In a way, what happened in the late sixties was that a worldwide anti-Americanism developed a powerful native branch. The Vietnam war was of course the most important single cause, among white citizens at least, of the radical protest. In line with my remarks about the decades, and with all those fluvial metaphors, we may observe that there was another stream of dissent that was dammed in 1939 or 1941: the protest against war and the military. The revulsion against "merchants of death" in the aftermath of World War I and the strong pacifist and isolationist movements of the thirties were thoroughly discredited by Munich, Pearl Harbor, the unity of the nation fighting Hitler, the revelations about the concentration camps, and then, after the war, by Stalin's activities in the developing cold war. The debacle of Vietnam made a kind of antiwar view intellectually and morally respectable again, and made it politically possible seriously to challenge the military.

Antimilitarism, antipuritanism, anticapitalism—and antiracism. When one speaks of America's treatment of the black man, one has to deal, alas, not in decades but in centuries. I think this stream of reform was dammed in 1876. That does not mean one should ignore or deprecate—as some of the fierce new fellows did—the long steady battle by, for example, the NAACP, through almost all of this century, for Negro rights; but it is true that the battle has not been in the center of the nation's politics. In the nineteenth century, of course, it was—from the abolitionism of the eighteen-thirties to the end of Reconstruction. But then it was dropped, even by reform movements. After a brief interracial beginning, Populism did not help the Negroes' cause, and some of the worst racist demagogues came from a Populist background. The Progressive movement does not seem to have had much to say for the Negro beyond Theodore Roosevelt's entertaining of Booker T. Washington in the White House; during Woodrow Wilson's presidency, social segregation was instituted in federal government buildings in Washington, and the early years of the century—the Progressive Era—are sometimes called the nadir of the struggle for Negro rights since Emancipation. Certainly the cultural critics of America during the twenties did not make any serious campaign for racial equality; Mencken, who regretted that he missed a chance to report the lynching of a "blackamoor," surely would not have regarded such a campaign as a suitable occupation for gentlemen. The New Deal does not have as impressive a record on racial equality as one might expect; FDR won over the votes of the traditionally Republican black electorate primarily on economic issues. He gave in on the wartime FEPC in 1941, in response to pressure and without conspicuous enthusiasm. I think it can be said that racial equality was not a chief feature of any progressive movement that played a large role in American politics from 1876 until 1948 or 1954. (I say 1948 because of the Truman civil-rights program, the desegregation of the armed services, and the fight over the civil-rights plank in the 1948 Democratic convention.)

It is as though the nineteenth-century trauma over this moral paradox at the heart of American democracy exhausted the nation, exhausted even the reformers, some of whom quite explicitly checked slavery off their list of "social questions," and turned to other matters, like the labor question. It is as though Americans, during this "lost century of civil rights," looked back upon the Emancipation Proclamation in something of the way they look at the Declaration of Independence, as a complete declaratory accomplishment that made real its objectives at a stroke. For whatever the reasons may be, the broad white American public, from the end of Reconstruction until these past few years, has suppressed the truth about the treatment of the black man. As the civil-rights movement and the Black Power movement forced this historic injustice upon the attention of the white Americans, they raised also in the minds of the young and the critical other questions about a nation that could so long have tolerated so manifest an evil. The Vietnam war and the black movements had the side effect of making more plausible the criticisms of the nation in other fields. In the eyes of some, America was morally discredited, and the national evils are not particular, separable items, but a general condition.

The women's movement was dammed after World War I, with the gaining of the vote. For four and a half decades, especially during the Depression, war, and Eisenhower, there was little change. But now the broadest stream of social change has flooded the highlands as well as the lowlands. Other groups took the cue, and sought their "liberation" and their "power."

Among many other criticisms of the nation, those directed against "conformity" and "mass society" and big bureaucratic organization, which became common in the fifties, were given a sharper anti-American edge than they had had: the ills of technological society, too, are the faults somehow of "America" and of the Establishment.

6

All of these quasi-cultural movements, unlike those of the twenties, had a political edge. The Berkeley outburst and Harlem disorders of 1964 had been the first big signs of something new. The escalation of the Vietnam war and the Watts riot of 1965 brought it fully into American politics, and it reached what is so far its worst expression in the terrible period of 1967–68, from the Newark and Detroit riots, through the march on the Pentagon in the fall, the assassinations of Martin Luther King and Robert Kennedy and the Columbia University riots of the spring, to the Chicago confrontation in August. This phenomenon—not new, of course, but expressed at a new level of intensity—was the politics of violence, provocation, confrontation, the polarizing and potential unraveling of the nation. The ideological accompaniment of this phenomenon on the far left was a hard-line and explicit anti-Americanism that rolled all the objections to different parts and aspects of American society into one big ball and saw in it one evil plan of an "Establishment." That was a primary fault: it is always bad political thinking to consolidate into one single unit the evil of the world. It is too convenient; it invites fanaticism and self-righteousness.

Many interpreters in those years stressed the continuity of the youthful idealism with the American past; somebody in writing the Scranton Commission's report, after the Kent State–Jackson State killings, composed a sentence saying that these young people want "to remake America in her own image." Although that is a rather generous way to put it, it was true indeed that this youthful protest had much in it that was continuous with the tradition of American social idealism, trying to make America be the ideal America, the America, as in Langston Hughes's poem, that has never been yet.

But one may also say that the New Left was continuous with American themes in a negative way. Ironically, this new anti-Americanism was very "American" in its style: moralistic, antipolitical, anti-intellectual, contemptuous of the past, a simplistic crusade against a conspiracy.

To be against tradition and authority and established institutions is as American as apple pie and H. Rap Brown. To be eager to respond to the whims of the young is as much in the spirit of the larger culture as the next cigarette advertisement. This country has been having *now* generations since at least the eighteen-nineties. That is one of its faults. A self-indulgent hedonism is the essence of suburbia even if it is lived in the Haight-Ashbury. To be cynical about "politicians," city hall, political parties, and the doings of diplomats is entirely in the spirit of the cracker-barrel philosopher in the general store. To hate central planning, and to romanticize local autonomy is as fresh as John C. Calhoun and Robert A. Taft. The notion that from "Participation," much talk, and still more participation some social benefit necessarily arises is not unlike the outlook of the middle-class social worker's buzz group. "Do Your Own Thing" is as American as Ralph Waldo Emerson, from whom it came.

To be an anti-intellectual "activist" (act now, think later) is as conventional in this country as being a two-fisted businessman Getting Things Done; and not altogether unlike the attitude of the vigilante who grabbed a gun off the wall, shot first, and asked questions later. The "counterculture" had many of the characteristics—the faults—of the culture it is supposedly countering.

This included a staggering generational self-righteousness. One had to see the immensely popular motion picture "The Graduate" in a theater crammed with college boys and their dates, with lines upon lines of young people waiting to see it twice, three times, and four times, to hear them laugh and cheer with a passion rare in a motion-picture theater, fully to perceive what a strong personal meaning young people found in that systematically antiadult production. The full blame, the empty and materialistic suburban world of "plastics," rested on the parents. The young were innocent, put upon, finally triumphant despite all: the faults of the world are somebody else's, not theirs.

But may one suggest—even in the simple-minded terms of that movie's own plot—that after all the young hero, so put upon and misled by his elders, was a college graduate, a man old enough to bear some of the responsibility for the shape of his own world.

We could not condemn the simple-minded and stereotyped view of the young and the left taken by all too many of the silent majority and leave uncriticized the simple-minded and stereotyped view many of them took of everybody else. For a time it seemed to be too closed systems colliding, condemning each other but at a deeper level alike.

In the late fifties and early sixties, in the sit-ins of 1960, the Freedom Rides of 1961, the Mississippi Summer Project of 1964, the early community-action antipoverty projects, and in other activities not so well publicized, individual young persons were an important part of significant social achievements. This was before the interest in social causes became a conventional part of the young people's world, when there was no automatically supportive peer-group attitude. Young activists had to take initiative and risk and make sacrifices. But in the later period social idealism often hardened into a moral cynicism, became superficially so widely shared as to be something like a fad. And then it abruptly faded.

There was a period in the late sixties when one perhaps more often admired the careful independent student who dissented from the dissent than the many marchers in the troops of "protest." One might become exasperated with the naïveté and self-righteousness of some student militants; be inclined to despair at the lack of persistence and perspective in the general run of the off-and-on students; be shocked by the unintelligent and inhumane way many made huge jumps in argument ("We've tried electoral politics and it didn't work, so there's nothing left but violence"). Then when one went to a student meeting all cranked up to argue with these common failings, one would find one student, and another, and another, in whom the prevailing characteristic was not any of these failings but a simple uninformed innocent earnest social idealism. (That was true more at Indiana University than at Yale.) One would be forced to put away one's fierce arguments against the student extremists and to deal with naïve virtue.

7

But that did not vitiate the arguments in their proper place of application, as, for example, against this radical's statement of the meaning of "the movement," sharply distinguishing it from liberal reform:

Efforts to resolve problems, correct injustices, or protest outrages are not enough. The insistence now is that all these problems are symptomatic of a more fundamental corruption—call it capitalism, call it imperialism, call it racism, call it liberal democracy, call it consumer enslavement, call it the arrogance of power, or call it everything at once. The point is that the evil is inherent in, and not accidental to, the American Way. The offense against humanity is by habit and not by exception. Not this or that malfunction (which, in radical analysis, is not a *mal*function but a too perfect functioning) must be remedied, but The System Itself must be changed. This is the distinctive dogma of the Movement.

Those who object to this distinctive dogma—that America is inherently and habitually "evil"—do so not only because we make a different appraisal of the United States but also because we object to the political mentality this outlook reflects and encourages. Notice in the quotation that the sweeping condemnation of a *general* and *essential*, not a merely particular and accidental, evil is combined with a tumbling row of ungraded candidates for the specific identity of this evil—call it this, call it that, call it the other thing. Included in this list, not incidentally, is "liberal democracy," about which many of us would made the opposite moral judgment, if indeed the radical writer seriously means what he seems to be saying: the hard-won combination of constitutionally protected civil liberty and popular rule that has been worked out in the liberal democracies, to some degree built into institutions and the habits of the people, is a historical accomplishment of the first rank.

One objects also to the sweep and indefiniteness with which a whole series of items are named, in this "Revolution Without

Ideology." Every specific injustice becomes merely another example of this all-embracing evil, perhaps not very important in itself and no longer a discriminate, specific, and objective phenomenon to be dealt with. Who remembers what happened to that
gym in Morningside Park in New York?

There is an older, more serious and honorable radicalism, a
radicalism of greater intellectual power and lasting moral authority, than that represented by the youth revolt of the sixties: the
radicalism of Irving Howe and I. F. Stone and, more recently,
Robert Paul Woolf and Michael Harrington, to name just a few
persons whom one must respect. And there can be a radical ingredient in the political outlook of persons who are not themselves a
part of the left. That radical ingredient is the examining of institutions to their conceptual roots, as became possible for a moment
in the late sixties. One could be radical in moral and intellectual
inquiry, though conservative in culture and reformist in politics;
reformist, not radical, in actual policies because the real world
changes in ways our imagining cannot foresee, and there are real
people whom those changes affect. Confronted with one of the
many evils discoverable in any society, the mind can jump immediately to its abolition; tasting any of the goods of social life, the
mind can jump to its universal enactment. The imagination can
combine all the evils in a bundle to be extirpated, unite all the
goods in a utopian vision. In real life it is not so easy. The effort
to abolish an evil or enact a good may be quite a different matter,
in the full range of its results.

When you begin assuming perfect conditions, where do you
stop? Henry Sidgwick, the notable nineteenth-century English
moralist, pointed out how different utopias can have quite contradictory assumptions about what the ideal will be. One example he
gives is Plato's *Republic*, a sufficiently utopian conception, which
nevertheless contemplates war as a permanent and unalterable
fact to be provided for in the ideal state; a modern utopia would
include the removal of all war. There are utopias in which some
kind of perfection of marriage is the ideal, and others in which
free love is the ideal. With respect to the distribution of economic
goods, is the perfect ideal to be conceived as perfect charity on

the part of the wealthy or perfect equality? "In short," says Sidg-wick, "it seems that when we abandon the firm ground of actual society, we have an illimitable cloudland surrounding us on all sides in which we may construct any variety of pattern states; but no distinct ideal to which the actual undeniable approximates, as the straight lines and circles of the actual physical world approximate those of scientific geometry." When one makes a radical assumption removing characteristic ills of actual society, one cannot know what new ills one would thereby be introducing. In life we do regularly bear the ills we have rather than fly to others that we know not of; in the political fantasies of our mind's construction, however, we think only of the good and not of the ill that radically altered constructions might bring. To act well in politics, close to the practical decisions of our life, it is well to seek continuing modest reform rather than to try to leap out into that cloudland.

Because in our utopian mood we picture society perfected as it cannot be, we develop a kind of contempt for reality—a reality that never comes up to our standards. That contempt then may sour our relation to the institutions we share with our fellow citizens. I think that happened with many of the sixties' young left.

In the old chestnut of a poem "Maud Muller," Whittier sentimentally lamented the missed moment when the judge riding by had not seen the maid, and added the familiar sentimental ending: "For all sad words of tongue or pen, / The saddest are these: 'It might have been!' " Bret Harte wrote a parody in which he pictured the dreadful result when the judge actually saw and married the girl in a wholly unsuitable marriage. He added to Whittier's lines: "Sadder by far are these we daily see; it *is*—but hadn't ought to be." This is the spirit of the reformer's critical realism as distinguished from sentimental radicalism.

8

In October of 1970 I found myself in New York City having lunch with a friend who worked for *The New Yorker*.

"Did you read that long piece by this fellow Reich?" he asked, after the soup.

"Sort of," I said. "Glanced at it."

"Really very good. Very interesting," he said. "I think he has something."

After lunch, when I went to one of the offices I was to visit, the man there said: "Say, did you read that long article in *The New Yorker* called 'The Greening of America' ?"

"More or less," I said.

"Very interesting. I think he has something. His picture of 'consciousness II' is—well, is just like some of our friends here. You ought to read it. He says the revolution is going to come by the 'seepage' of this new youth consciousness."

Later that afternoon I visited another office in New York City.

"I have reprints here of something you will want to read," said the man there.

" 'The Greening of America'?" I said.

"Why, yes," he said. "How did you know? I have Xerox copies of it, to give out to people. I think he really has something."

On the plane home I read Reich's article, up to the point about the "corporate state" forcing us to choose between peanut butter with chunks and peanut butter without chunks, denying us *real* peanut butter.

The next day, in the Middle West, a professor of economics asked me whether I subscribed to *The New Yorker*, and I said I did.

"I just happened to buy a copy in an airport a couple of weeks ago," he said. "Do you know who this fellow Charles Reich is? I really think he has something."

An assistant professor of American literature asked what I thought of that article in *The New Yorker*.

"Applesauce. Full of prune whip all the way up to the eyebrows. Not rigorous. Not analytical. Irresponsible."

"Of course he's not 'analytical,' or 'rigorous' or 'responsible,' " this man answered. "He's a *poet*. I liked it. I think he has something."

Former Secretary of Interior Stewart Udall visited the university for a speech and included a favorable reference to "The

Greening of America" and Consciousnesses I, II, and III.

"Did you know Charles Reich at Yale?" he asked afterward.

"No. I can remember seeing him at the law school, and loping around campus."

"I think he has something," Udall said.

Shortly thereafter W. Willard Wirtz, the former secretary of labor and speech writer for Adlai Stevenson, also visited the university for a speech, in which he also referred to "The Greening of America" and Consciousnesses I, II, and III.

"I think I am about Consciousness two and a quarter myself," he said. Wirtz also made clear that he thought Reich had something.

Every day for a month in the New York *Times* it was Reich on one page, consciousnesses I, II, III on the next page, Greening of America on the next page.

At a dinner party the wife of the chairman of the political science department, an intelligent woman, asked whether I had read this long *New Yorker* article about the "Greening of America."

"Ummm," I said with a sigh.

"I think he really has something," she said.

Why was this article (and book that followed) so popular? Part of the answer has to do with the unusual combination Reich managed to bring together. The book mixed a ferocious and unsparing indictment of the consumer society with the picture of a most appealing sort of "revolution"—one that would come not by violence or even by organized effort, but by the peaceful spreading of a change of "consciousness." It would "seep." It would bring down the corporate state by nonco-operation; it would bring the green again up through the concrete. The book was thus able to satisfy two quite different impulses at the same time. It had in it something of that gratifying sweeping totalism of the radical, who sees in society one single monolithic evil, with all the particular evils conveniently rolled into one big ball (the corporate state, for Reich). Merely particular ills and merely "piecemeal" remedies may all therefore be loftily disdained.

But there are many books like that—"radical" books. What Reich did was to combine this radical attack on the one side with optimistic evangelism on the other side. Most radical critiques of capitalist America are not optimistic, but grim. They are not individualistic appeals for conversion, but relentlessly collective and realistic. But Reich combined radicalism with piety and optimism. In addition to this unusual combination, there was a little of the Galbraith Effect—the imbalance between an overt verbal criticism of and a covert affection for the ridiculous concrete details of the giant machinery of modern capitalism. And there was something of that middlebrow fascination with an amateur sociology that provides handy classificatory schemes, I, II, and III.

One mentions this now faded flower to disagree with both of its themes. Modern America is not as monolithically evil as Reich said, and such evils as there are, are not so simply identified; nor are they so simply soluble by "seeping" changes of "consciousness" (a notion quite reminiscent of the "change of heart").

Reich blamed the ills of American society on this entity called the "corporate state" (that is, the present polity, economy, and culture of the United States, bound up in a bundle), as though it were an agent with a will. He set it in stark contrast to the green grass and flowers of the new consciousness of youth. But in fact the undesirable features of Americn society arise in part not from the manipulation of some Power Elite, but from the unmanipulated attitudes and authentic values of the people, very much including young ones. They arise, also, from the accidents of history and (Reich and his young people did not like it when one said this) the perennial limitations of the human condition. One cannot blame all that is wrong on the "corporate state," whatever or whoever that is. It is ethically misleading to do so (Reich's book was obviously a kind of a moral treatise, enthusiastically preaching a set of values and of moral interpretations). If one blames everything on a personified, capitalized evil entity apart from oneself and one's companions—the Corporate State, the Power Elite, the Consciousness II people—then one is in danger of exculpating oneself. If correspondingly one exalts uncritically another entity (Consciousness III, the youth culture) as the bearer of all the values the other has violated, then one may simply vindicate oneself, if, as is likely, one secretly pictures this group as an extension of oneself.

And one may also by this melodrama load an unbearable moral burden on the messiah group, in the way the Marxists did with the proletariat. One obscures their humanity—their frailty and deficiency—and lays the foundation for tyrannical action done in the name of this sure agent of a new humanity. And for a crushing and destructive disillusionment. They will not in any event transform humanity or transform this earthly life, and should not be expected to. One felt in 1970 the likelihood that this "greening" would be very temporary, and that the "concrete" would be back soon; and that proved to be correct.

Some of the evils and difficulties of present-day America do have their root in the human condition. They come from the situation of a man trying to live with other men anywhere: his egotism; his mortality; the limitations of his physical and intellectual make-up; his tendency to praise, advance, and serve himself in many ways, blatant and subtle. This green-America group did not escape from that . . . the radical imperfection of mankind.

One reader who liked Reich's book, though, was the decent senator from South Dakota, who not so long afterward was to be the Democratic candidate for president of the United States. Perhaps George McGovern, looking at the book one day in 1971, remarked thoughtfully to an aide: "You know, I believe he has something."

7

On Resisting the Temptation
to Become a Conservative
(or Even a "Centrist")

It was not easy, after 1967, to avoid calling oneself a "conservative," or even to go beyond labels and become one. Or to become a "centrist" or a "neoconservative" (a neoconservative, that is, of the recent variety: politics, an inexact science, produces an endless flow of recycled terminology). I want to explain this temptation and then to suggest why one should not yield to it.

1

The recent history of American conservatism seems to go something like this:

Once upon a time, in nineteen-fifty-one, to be exact, there came upon the scene a "new conservatism"—the *old* new conservatism, if you follow me. It proved to be more lasting and significant than many of us nonconservatives thought it would ever be, when William F. Buckley fresh out of college gave Yale professors fits by producing a book called *God and Man at Yale*. Unless you were attacked by it, it all seemed pretty funny back then. I remember one professor waving the book in front of his students and saying that it did indeed show the failure of education at Yale, but in a different sense from that Buckley intended. Russell Kirk was building what seemed to be ridiculous intellectual castles in Spain with books like *The Conservative Mind*; Clinton Rossiter was harmlessly grouping a considerable section of our intellectual history, back to *The Federalist* and before, under the title *Conservatism in America;* Peter Viereck, whom many suspected of not *really* being a conservative, perversely insisted, for some crotchety reasons of his own, on calling himself by that name. The *real* American conservatism, meanwhile—the practical conservatism that wins votes in precincts and blocks bills in Congress—had plenty of power but no intellectual appeal. It had come out of its nonperformance and callousness in the face of the Depression, its furious opposition to Roosevelt and the New Deal, and its generally isolationist position of 1937–41, with seriously impaired dignity and respectability. It seemed a reflexive, selfish, almost mindless resistance to Roosevelt and the modern world, using ancient American antigovernmental themes to protect the parochial outlook of George Babbitt, and the narrow interests of the business community. It did not have visible connections with serious ideas of any kind, including those of the "new conservative" writers. Once, when the most distinguished leader of this practical conservatism, Senator Robert Taft (a better man than most of his followers), was asked whether he had read Russell Kirk's *The Conservative Mind*, he responded with a reference to a James Thurber title—*Let Your Mind Alone*—and said he did not have much time to read books.

Most liberals in the late forties and the fifties looked with amusement and disdain upon the effort to revive conservatism in America by means of philosophical and literary exercise. The conservatives might control the House Rules Committee, the American Medical Association, and the county organizations of the Republican party, but the land of books and ideas belonged to progressives. This "new conservatism," they thought, was a frothy indulgence in nostalgia that would soon blow away.

But somehow it did not. It gathered to itself a rather quaint but not altogether unimpressive collection of ex-communists, Catholics, Austrians, elegant Southerners, Middle Western classicists, University of Chicago economists, and Ivy League yachtsmen, plus some new critics of literature and some old critics of progressive education, and with many sober references to Edmund Burke was already worth taking seriously—at least a little seriously—even before the ideological fireworks of the sixties.

Then, with the stimuli of that remarkable period, there came a rush of new converts, if not exactly to Barry Goldwater, or even to *The National Review*, then at least to other brands of something like conservatism. These new brands were in general more intellectually complex and more interesting than what had gone before.

That unavoidable barometer Norman Mailer, rather typically I think, wanted in the early Nixon years to outflank liberalism in *both* directions by calling himself a "left conservative." Emanations from the Cambridge area suggested that Harvard and MIT professors were road-testing together a new model of conservatism, a *new* new conservatism, one supposes. Typically, in an academic setting in those days an older professor of mathematics, with a European background, would respond to favorable comments on George F. Kennan's writings with the remark, intended to be praise, "Yes, he is *conservative*." Many ex-liberals, fleeing the apparently sinking ship of the liberal faith, would soberly roll off their tongues the word "conservative," try out the sound, and find that it was not so bad after all. There was a considerable group of writers variously called, sometimes by themselves, by new or substitute labels: "centrists," "radical centrists," "progressive centrists," "conservationists," "neoconservatives."

It often happens that labels that are originally epithets are picked up and worn proudly—defiantly—by those to whom they have been applied. In the late sixties one could feel that defiant impulse rising, in face of the New Left attack. In the memoirs of Dean Acheson, *Present at the Creation*—written during those years—he responded to the charge that he was really a conservative with a casual admission of guilt. He remarked, by way of explanation, "I don't much believe in revolution." So the "revolution" people set the terms of definition.

Back when these new things were just beginning, in 1960–61, out in Santa Barbara I talked to a harbinger of the New Left that was to come, an older philosopher who had been a supporter of Henry Wallace in 1948 and who even back then was always referring portentously to Herbert Marcuse (Marcoo-oo-se). He turned in the middle of a political argument and said, in tones of gravest accusation, "Why, you're a *conservative!*" The implication was clear: his interlocuter was thereupon to roll over dead. One was tempted to say, if from his angle of vision that was the way it appeared, so be it.

A conservative political outlook became, to one's surprise, rather tempting and for the most honorable and straightforward of reasons: there was much solid matter in the writers who called themselves by that name or something like it. One could not help but notice that Buckley, mellowed through the decades since he left Yale, often had a sound point to make, and that the same was true of the columnist James J. Kilpatrick. The newer new conservatives included, certainly, some of the most provocative and perhaps also most valuable social commentators of these years— the ubiquitous Daniel Patrick Moynihan, for one inescapable example, doubly or triply important because of his earlier identification as a liberal Democrat and because his government service seemed to lend authority to his views. He could casually and rather typically remark, "I believe I am the only person to have served in the subcabinets of all three of these presidents, Kennedy, Johnson, and Nixon." There were associates of his, including Nathan Glazer, who are, or were, in Cambridge together. (At this time, Moynihan is in New Delhi charming the Indians; Edward Banfield, the neoconservative political scientist who wrote *The Unheavenly City*, has left Cambridge for the University of Pennsylvania.) Irving Kristol, before Watergate, at least, was said to be the Nixon White House's favorite intellectual; the magazine he edits, called *The Public Interest*, and his columns in the *Wall Street Journal* stated many of the postliberal themes. Kristol went so far as to remark that "my instincts are—I have indeed come to believe that an adult's 'normal' political instincts should be—conservative." Many others uncovered in themselves these allegedly "normal" and "adult" instincts. Norman Podhoretz and some articles in the magazine he edits, *Commentary*, provided further examples from the higher journalism. In the academy, a number of sociologists and sociological writers who think the larger thoughts and comment on public policy began to describe themselves as conservatives: Peter Berger, as well as Glazer. The thoughtful writing of Professor Robert Nisbet, another sociologist, began to coincide with the spirit of the times.

One read that Glazer, who is wiser about society than many of his colleagues in that discipline, described himself as once "a radical, a mild radical . . . who felt closer to radical than to liberal writers in the late 1950s," who then became "a conservative, a mild conservative, but still closer to those who call themselves conservative than to those who call themselves liberal in early 1970." Glazer's article on "The Limits of Social Policy," in *Commentary* for September 1971, was perhaps the most important single article of this new movement. There were in it political scientists (James Q. Wilson, perhaps) and of course many economists (Milton Friedman the best known). There were social commentators who had been commenting for a long time whose work coincided at points with this new movement: Peter Drucker, on occasion. Even our greatest living political columnist, the Lippmann for all seasons, described himself in an interview as a conservative, and halfway praised President Nixon for doing his disagreeable anti-Jacobin job satisfactorily.

All across the nation men said: It didn't work; we tried to do too much; there are limits to what social policy can do; money alone cannot solve society's ills.

I do not mean to identify the views of any one of these quite diverse people with those of others—all thinkers object to being grouped into a "school"—or to lump obviously quite distinguishable people together. They differ widely, and the views of one should not be attributed to the others. But there was a movement, or at least an atmospheric condition, larger than any of them, in which they all more or less participated. In the early seventies they seemed to be just about the most stimulating group of American political commentators one could find.

That, of course, was before Watergate and Nixon's resignation. Afterward, one of them remarked: "Nixon has done for conservatism what Stalin did for socialism."

2

One reason for the blooming of these hundreds of neoconservative flowers, obviously, was a recoil from the New Left, the youth revolt, the fashionable radicalism, the militant counterculture. George Orwell wrote that Jonathan Swift "was one of those people who are driven into a sort of perverse Toryism by the follies of the progressive party of the moment." It is apparent that much American neoconservatism was of that shocked, reacting, and perhaps perverse kind.

The follies of the New Left of the late sixties were multitudinous and spectacular. Persons who were spat upon and vilified by the outbreak of immature left radicalism during that period perhaps understandably recoiled into the shocked sobriety of real conservatism. It would be hard to find a "progressive party of the moment" more loaded with folly that the American New Left of the late sixties, because much of it was sheer brattishness, because it was to a marked degree avowedly anti-intellectual; because it lacked cultural roots and was at least as much cultural rebellion as political movement.

Perhaps "folly" is not a strong enough word for the repellant features that many people saw when they read the manifestos or were shouted down at a meeting. It was by no means unusual for older witnesses with a European past to feel the shock of comparison with Nazi and fascist youth. The young left tended to dismiss the comparison contemptuously as the worst kind of propaganda, but there certainly were people in whom it was not feigned, or propaganda, to make the all too familiar attempt to score a point by linking one's opponent to Hitler, but instead a genuinely felt shock of remembered association. An older professor, once a refugee, looked out the window of a college building and saw a marching and chanting band of youth, fanatical and absolutistic, irrational, glorifying "action" and violence, calling their opponents by the names of contemptible animals: was that foreboding and terrible memory that he felt merely propaganda? Writers with a European background—one a refugee from Mussolini—drew the comparison between the glorification of "under 30" youth in the late sixties' New Left and the anthem of Mussolini's Italy, which began "Youth, youth, springtime of beauty."

In both the New Left and the Nazi and fascist movements there was a deliberate irrationality; a passionate cult of youth and "action"; a rationalization of a necessary, even noble, violence; an absolutistic contempt for "dialogue" and "procedure" and all those "soft" and merely "liberal" values; a thrill in chanted slogans and extremes ("Up against the wall!"); an unrestrained denunciation of their foes.

"The Movement" combined a romantic utopianism, on the one side, with cynicism on the other, these reinforcing each other and filled with passion. That was a bad combination on every count, and, against the impassioned self-righteous irrationality and violent behavior they produced, it seemed that one might counterpose a thoughtful, skeptical, "humane" self-critical conservatism.

These ideological terms, of course, are inexact, shifting with shifting circumstances, and if that new kind of radicalism for that brief period defined the terms of politics, and if there are to be only two choices, if one must be on one or another side of the barricades: all right, then, one might say, I am a conservative.

Here is a quotation (by no means unusual) from one of those "radical" manifestos of the period 1965–70:

The "best" of reformers must be ranked with the regime itself as enemies of the revolution. Second-phase armed revolution in the United States at present requires the effective elimination of persons such as Galbraith, McGovern, McCarthy, Randolph, Harrington, Goodwin, Chavez, and if someone had not already seen to it, Martin Luther King.

Reading that sentence one may understand why many people say: If the alternative to a view like that is conservatism, then I am a conservative.

When the New Left tried deliberately to create extreme situations, in which the bourgeois society would show its ugly, violent face, show itself As It Really Is in its police busts and jails, and thus "radicalize" new recruits for the movement, their actions also had an opposite effect on other people, as they intended. To "polarize" people, and "radicalize" some, is to "conservatize" others; it is to make others choose the other side of the barricades and show themselves to be enemies of the revolution, and so forth. One subordinate reason to resist the temptation of conservatism is this: one should not accept the radical's effort to force an absolute choice and to divide society in that simple two-sided way. The arrogance with which some of the new radicals presumed to do so was one of the many objectionable attributes of their movement. Nevertheless, they are a mixed bag, too, and by no means simply an evil thing. We should keep on refusing—not a Great Refusal; just a small refusal—to respond to moral and historical choices in the way that the revolutionary mentality tried to force us all to do.

I do not mean that there were no deeper reasons for being tempted to conservatism than the recoil against a particularly obstreperous but momentary form of the left. The much more important source of temptation came from the disillusioned aftermath of liberal efforts of the sixties, and even of the liberal efforts of the four decades since FDR took office: the liberalism of government programs, federal action, social programs and bureaucracies. The conservatives both old and new have of course repeated many of the familiar criticisms, sound or unsound, of the welfare state. But their versions of these criticisms sometimes showed yet another, deeper reason why these newer versions of conservatism are tempting. This one is more fundamental than skepticism about the specific legislation of the Great Society and much more fundamental than one's recoil from the New Left and the counterculture.

America's political ethos, for an assortment of historical and cultural reasons, has had since the nineteenth century a thread of simplism and sentimentality, a shallow distortion of the complexity of social life. In recent years, for another assortment of reasons, that thread has been prominently identified with liberalism. Therefore an intelligent conservatism, at least before Watergate, could plausibly present itself as the bearer of a wiser view, a more mature and skeptical view of the "limits of social policy," and the limits of politics—even of the "tragedy of the human condition"— than its progressive rivals.

There are those half-truths or three-quarter truths that are just about the very definition of conservatism: there are values built

into the institutions that exist that have developed over generations of human living. They have proved themselves through
time. Men are, among other things, creatures of habit, of tradition, of memory, and shared uses. They live by regularities and
expectations and memories; they love the old schoolhouse and the
flag and their comrades from the war (especially now that they do
not see them any more); they develop ways of doing things that
come to be part of their very being. When you try deliberately to
change society, you do not have the knowledge to comprehend all
of that: Edmund Burke kept criticizing the French revolutionaries'
notion that out of their own bare reason they could construct a
New, Better, Different, maybe even Perfect, Society: they cannot. The "democratic society" the Students for a Democratic Society thought it could bring into being would quite evidently not
have been better or more democratic than the one it talked about
overturning. Michael Polanyi and F. A. Hayek and Bertrand
Juvenel and Michael Oakeshott and Karl Popper in their different
ways have taught their readers to recognize the limitations on
human reasoning about society, on "total planning," on constructing utopias, on grand designs for the total remaking of society.
Constructing utopias, in which characteristically one assumes
away at the outset the hard part (that men are egotistical and different and even contentious by nature), is not a very useful exercise—often it is a destructive one. Expecting total "planning" of
the social order is foolish. Abstract pictures of a world that never
was, and doctrinaire devotion to such abstract pictures, cause
much harm in the life of man, as the history of the twentieth century in particular ought to teach us. It takes generations of living,
and the reason and experience of many men, to build humane institutions; it cannot be done by one mind, one group, even one
generation at a stroke.

The attempt to build new societies, moreover, has undesired
and unanticipated side effects. Somebody is hurt by the change.
People do not want the change, even though you think they
should. They respond to it in ways you did not expect: society is
not an artifact, to be rebuilt by man, like a house; it is a living
thing, to be tended by men, like a garden.

Max Weber describes that "ethic of responsibility" in which a responsible political man *is not permitted* to pretend that collective man is better than he really is: a responsible leader *must* deal with the "average deficiencies of humankind," and not allow himself, as radicals, visionaries, dreamers, devotees of the "ethic of ultimate ends," allow themselves to do, to imagine them away. And thus from a hundred other "wise" conservative thinkers (mostly European, but some American Founding Fathers, too).

Since the United States got itself into its modern mental state at some point in the nineteenth century, we have not had in our national make-up much of this necessary and attractive social wisdom. So it is tempting to endorse it. Its humane skepticism may chasten our tendency not only toward inflated rhetoric but toward inflated expectations as well.

Nevertheless, I think one should not succumb to this new new conservatism, or to any other. Why not? In part because it is to such an overwhelming degree (as I said) a politics of recoil, of reaction, of antipathy to what went before. And in larger part because that recoil was shared by a large segment of the population.

If there had not been a New Left of 1965–70, and the Great Society outpouring of legislation and promises in 1964–66, this new-conservative intellectual movement could scarcely have uttered its first audible sound. Such a recoil—so easy, after all—is not a sufficient basis on which to shape one's political ideas.

And before Watergate this recoil was timely. It was current, popular, atmospheric . . . as one who believed in it said, a "groundswell." Everywhere prominent intellectuals were saying, with a sigh of worldly wisdom, that there are, after all, "limits to social policy" and "unintended consequences" of social action. They said, quite rightly, that the arousing of expectations that cannot be fulfilled has bad results. They pointed, also to some degree rightly but perhaps too exclusively and too often, to the defects of "liberals" and of "intellectuals." They borrowed, and used in a rather different way, from Lionel Trilling, his phrase about an "adversary culture." Many older social thinkers were still reeling from the repugnant features of the New Left.

And some were unstrung by riots, open admissions, protests, busing, militancy. A friend from graduate-school days of twenty years ago who had been an original sitter-in in the founding days of CORE during World War II, a progressive activist, a boy-cotter, full of Causes, sat now in the Brookings Institution and explained that Spiro Agnew has a point; Edward Banfield has a point; Jensen, and Schockley, who finds differences in the IQ of the races, may even have a point. The black movement was already off the tracks, he said, at Selma. He is not a racist, but . . . one does not need to grant equality to *morons*. He used both the phrases of the real conservatives: GO SLOWER and IT'S THEIR OWN FAULT.

Many a man in the street, with President Nixon's encouragement, had his own curmudgeonly version of the conservative themes. On many particular points these new postliberal antiradicals may be right, but when the points (right and wrong) are added together, and added together several times over and by many people, and oversimplified by the ordinary man, they then create an ungenerous public mood of unbenign neglect, spiced with anger, contempt, resentment, and even what Irving Howe has called "social meanness."

Conservatives, of both the old and the new variety, often refer to the importance of a society's moral foundations, and in this regard, as in so many others, they are right. The basis of the society's health is indeed to be found, just as they say, in the values of the people. But that is what is worrisome about this conservatism at this historical moment . . . its effect on the values of the people. The new conservatives may be right about some specific defects in recent social legislation, and they certainly are right in many of their criticisms of the counterculture, but the cumulative effect of all of the writings is damaging to the fragile social conscience of the nation.

Before Watergate, the president and his people played the current conservative themes with a big brass band for the larger public; conservative writers meanwhile played a more sophisticated chamber-music version for the orchestra seats. Together they embroidered themes of negation, complacency, and callousness, thereby drowning out other themes that ought to be heard—specifically the themes of the common good and of social justice. Those themes have never been as well established for the broad population as they ought to be.

At the risk of sounding like an inverted Spiro Agnew, I suggest that these writers in Cambridge and New York and Washington may not fully realize how their themes reverberate in the genuinely conservative territory where liberals have no limousines, where intellectuals attend no Georgetown cocktail parties, and where there is no radical chic . . . perhaps no chic of any kind. "Remembering the Answers" to one's own youthful radicalism is not enough, especially when those who overhear and use one's remembered answers never had the faintest trace of radicalism in themselves, and not very much compassion . . . who have at bottom a very different set of values from one's own. I write from Indiana, and from the heart.

In the United States it is not easy to disentangle the humane social wisdom of the larger European tradition of conservatism from an inhumane endorsement of competitive individualism and Herbert Spencer and Horatio Alger, which is an "abstract," unreal, and "doctrinaire" as any of the progressive utopias the conservatives attack. And it is incomparably more powerful. In this country it is the practical content of, and the powerful practical supporter for, any real conservative party.

Although it is true that American liberalism has been shot through with superficiality and sentimentality—so, too, has America's practical conservatism. There are some broad cultural characteristics that affect Americans of all stripes, left, right, and center. But the right has better connections than the left.

These political ideas do not exist in a vacuum, a cloister, or a debating society: they have links to power and to group interest. In American society the conservatism of one kind (social wisdom and Edmund Burke) is in constant danger of serving the conservatism of another kind (the Nixon party arriving by private jet to deplore welfare chiselers around the swimming pool of John Connally). It is in danger of shielding the interest of the most powerful plutocracy in the history of the world, and of encouraging the uglier side of popular opinion.

At present American conservatism is an unresolved mixture of the American orthodoxy of capitalistic individualism with the more profound and at many points very different themes (*e.g.*, the theme of an organic community) of historic European conservatism. The latter has much to teach American political thinkers of all parties.

But with its vision of the community as real, as a good, linking past, present, and future, in the way described in famous paragraphs of Edmund Burke, and its emphasis on tradition and authority, it goes against the grain of American antiauthoritarian "progressive" individualism of all political positions, not least the position that calls itself conservative in the editorial columns. It is a long way from Edmund Burke to Barry Goldwater, and the distance between Richard Nixon and Benjamin Disraeli was repeatedly and amusingly demonstrated after that brief White House effort to link the two.

In America such social wisdom as conservatism may have supplied has been applied to government and deliberate social action but not to profit-making technology. The "brake upon progress" that conservatism, in all times and places, is supposed to represent, has been quite *unevenly* applied: to undertakings of the central government so severely that, as we nonconservatives often point out, the United States has so lagged behind the civilized world in provision of collective support and service as not yet in some regards to have attained what the German nation attained under Bismarck. On the other hand, that "brake" has rarely been applied to technology in the hands of commerce.

Conservative social wisdom is supposed to be aware of the undesirable side effects of "social change" (as it is now called), especially "rapid" social change. It should have that awareness because of its realism about what human beings are like and its knowledge of the complexity of society—of the accumulated value of existing institutions. But if such an awareness is the test, one would have to say that the so-called conservatism of the capitalist party of McKinley, Coolidge, Goldwater, and Nixon at least—we shall see about Ford—has not been conservative. It has resisted social change from government but promoted the far more important social change that has come through the combination of commerce and modern technology. Our society has changed radically—not as much through the ideas of reformers as through the unregulated, almost unexamined impact of the railroad, the telephone, the automobile, the life insurance company, the television industry, the airplane, the "agri-business," the aerospace complex, the strip miners, the bulldozers tearing up the hillside for the real-estate developers: more than a century now of mammoth rapid alteration of life through the ramifying impact of the industrial-technological machine.

A thorough conservatism would be wary about the impact of this modern technology on man as a creature of habit, of tradition, of order, of a desire for continuity and regularity, of preservation and slowly accumulated ways and values. One has the spectacle of the conservative president, resisting even mild social programs, vigorously defending a much more disruptive new phenomenon like the SST.

Senator Barry Goldwater, the politician most unequivocally identified with conservatism in recent American political history, the author of a best-selling book called *The Conscience of a Conservative*, the maker of speeches about nobility and excellence and heroism in aristocratic ages, and about the central virtue of patriotism, has, or did have, at his Arizona home an *electronic* flagpole that puts the American flag up and down at sunrise and sunset automatically, without human effort. Millions of American "conservatives," one may safely guess, would see nothing amusing or contradictory in that. It would not seem to them that old-fashioned patriotism had been compromised by this association with effort-saving decision-removing technological automaticity.

Conservatives in the United States in the late twentieth century are not well equipped to understand the compromise this symbol represents, or its contrast with an older conservatism. The machinery of modern "progress" is fully endorsed and exploited, but its meaning for political philosophy and policy is left unexamined.

6

In these efforts at social criticism it does matter who you are, and when you speak, and what effect you are having. In the larger issues of society one cannot refer only to the abstract "truth" of one's statement, without reference to its context and effect. I am emboldened to say this by the neoconservatives themselves: they attack liberals and radicals for various awakenings of the sixties that they claim to have been undesirable in their effects. Fairlie's suave and often telling criticism of the Kennedys calls what they did a "politics of expectation" that had a damaging effect upon the American public. Banfield criticizes the promulgation of the idea that the poor and the blacks have been badly treated, not exactly because the facts are wrong but, rather, because interpreting the facts in this way has a bad effect, morally and practically, upon the poor and the blacks themselves. I want to turn this around on Banfield.

The spread of the idea that the poor and the blacks have been mistreated, he said, encourages crime and rioting. In chapters on those subjects, he wrote (or at the least strongly implied) something like this: *Don't* encourage Negroes and the poor to believe they have been unjustly treated, because to do so is to appear to give them "a quasi-right to commit crimes." Do-goodish environmentalistic talk breeds the "feeling that the victims of oppression have a license to break laws." These ideas, in other words, have an unfortunate practical effect upon particular hearers. Very well then, I suggest that we make the same sort of test of practical function and moral effect for Banfield's own themes, and those of his fellow revisionist conservatives. They will have a bad effect upon those who may be expected to read their material, which we may assume will not be circulating vigorously in the ghetto.

There is necessarily a certain *ad hominem* in these matters—or, rather, not an argument to the man so much as an argument to his audience and his relation to his audience. If this man (Banfield, as a symbol now of this whole movement) were himself poor and black, writing or speaking out of and to the under class, then a brave defense of personal responsibility and of restraint and of law observance even in the face of social injustice would have a very different moral quality (much higher, I mean) than it has in his book, with its authorship and readership. Or if, being who he is and writing for those who will read his book, he had tried to work his way around the full circle, and had included, along with his indictment of the sentimentality of do-gooders and the self-indulgence of some black militants, an even-handed indictment of the escapism and callousness of white suburbia and the petulant self-sympathy of the blue-collar whites, and so on, then perhaps one could respect that, too—if it were effectively done all the way around. But Banfield did none of these things, except for attacking the sentimentalists and the poor. The Americans who read this book learned nothing for their moral improvement. Instead, they found what they already believed vindicated by a Harvard professor's references to social-science studies.

So long as the city contains a sizable lower class, nothing basic can be done about its most serious problems. . . .

. . . the serious problems of the city all exist in two forms—a normal-class and a lower-class form—which are fundamentally different from each other. . . .

The lower-class forms of all problems are at bottom a single problem: the existence of an outlook and style of life which is radically present-oriented and which, therefore, attaches no value to work, sacrifice, self-improvement, or service to family, friends, or community.

Banfield's definitions of the "classes" are so sharp and so invidious as almost to amount to this: the problems of the city are caused by BAD PEOPLE, different from you and me. It is so sharp an either/or definition, without degrees and changes, as to be untrue to the complexity of human beings.

Large segments of the population are already concentrated exclusively upon this one sharply defined and isolated feature of the social landscape, and to believe that the problem of the city is the problem of misbehaving, undisciplined "lower-class" people, quite different from themselves (implicitly: racially). To believe that is morally and politically (and financially) convenient, relaxing any moral tension and placing the entire fault and responsibility on someone else.

This does not seem a cultural situation in which the readers of important books on the "urban crisis" need to be told that the city's troubles are really the fault of the "lower class"; that efforts to help will do more harm than good; and that given time everything will improve anyway.

One of the criticisms that new conservatives have made, accurately, in my opinion, of reformers of the sixties, is that they overstated the possibilities, raised hopes, promised too much. But that is not the world's only error. The first item in a list Banfield gave of recommendations that are "feasible" but not "acceptable" is this one:

Avoid rhetoric tending to raise expectations to unreasonable and unrealizable levels, to encourage the individual to think that "society" (e.g., "white racism") not he, is responsible for his ills, and to exaggerate both the seriousness of social problems and the possibility of finding solutions.

If one agrees with that recommendation, one may match it with another, of which the new-conservative's constituency stands in greater need:

Avoid rhetoric tending to increase complacency and callousness, and to encourage the comfortable individual's feeling that somebody else, not he, is responsible for the problems of urban life, and to minimize both the seriousness of social problems and the possibility of finding humane ways to ameliorate them.

Banfield held that the nation is oversupplied with activism and do-goodism; DON'T JUST SIT THERE, DO SOMETHING! and DO GOOD are, he says (rising to sarcastic capital letters), the mischievous mottos of too much of America's upper middle class, and it is they who stir excessive talk about urban ills and racial injustice.

To me it seems that though there is, indeed, much mindless activism in America, that activism is not confined to, or expressed at its worst in, the humanitarian social-reform tradition. Something like it appears in a more dubious form in the go-getters of

American commerce. Similarly with American do-goodism. It is true that there is much naïveté and nonsense in that direction. Can you really say, though, that this foolish upper-middle-class sentimentalism is America's major failing? Hardly. It is one difficulty. The much deeper one is the callousness and prejudice of the large and comfortable American mass.

In the United States today there are simultaneously three kinds of insensitivity that must rarely, if ever, have come together before.

One is the perennial selfishness of the privileged, wary about the ragged folk outside the gates.

The second is the pseudo-democratic and populistic appeal to numbers and to the "common" man, against the different, the minority, the makers of unpopular noises.

The third is the individualist and competitive ethos, the victors in life's race satisfied that they have deserved their victory, being hard-boiled about those who lost: It's tough, but that's the way life is.

There is nothing new, of course, about those who are "well off" being callous and complacent, or contemptuous or antagonistic, about those who are not "well off." The capacity to identify with those whose life situation is different from one's own, not very great at best, tends to diminish with increasing remoteness. And comfortable Americans today (partly because of the do-goodish spirit Banfield deplores) may not be as bad as the robber barons of our past, or as oil-rich Arab sheiks or as the Bourbons or as the Podsnaps. But at the same time, the well-off have increased so greatly in numbers, in modern America, as to give the problem another shape.

We all believe (in our collective role, if not in every case personally) that we fully deserve all the privileges we have, and probably some more in addition; privileged groups believe that, and the United States has more people who are "privileged" one way and another than does any other society. Layer upon layer of this population looks at the much-discussed "poverty" and "poor" and "other America" as from a great distance. Moreover, we are a 90% white country with a 10% black minority—not an easy arrangement, as much sad history has taught us. These conservatives are right in saying that we should not regard "law and order" as a "code word" for "racism"; still, "racism" (not a word one likes much) does exist, and a subtle version is creeping back into respectability.

It cannot have happened often before that populistic racism, plutocracy, and competitive individualism have coincided and reinforced each other as they do now in the United States. It would scarcely seem to be a situation that requires complacent books by Harvard professors, or repetitive reminders about the limits of social policy, or torrents of abuse for efforts at social reform.

7

Even if there should come into being in the United States a conservative position of a profounder sort, it does not appear to be our primary philosophical need. I think we should not endorse any kind of American conservatism, however one may stretch, repair, renew, improve, redefine, patch, cut, or rearrange it. Why not? Because that social wisdom, even at its best, comes second, not first, in the ordering of one's mind and purpose in society. In the first place there is the claim of justice to the human person, a norm that places all the existing institutions under continual review. One wants an increase in the social wisdom conservatives often exhibit—in order more soundly to achieve objectives conservatives rarely seek and usually oppose.

The guideline is social justice and the common good. The conservative wisdom about how complicated society is, and how difficult and problematical it is to try to change it, is, though important, secondary; it is not the source of direction. One wants Americans to know all of that better than they have—not that they may yield to passivity, prescription, the acceptance of the way things are, but in order that their effort to achieve the common good will be more effective, sensitive, and persistent.

While reading these centrists and conservatives and neoconservatives, I kept saying to myself—but Reinhold Niebuhr already long ago said all that, and said it better. (Or if not "better"—no claims should be made on literary grounds—more profoundly.) He certainly wrote enough about "human nature" and egotism and the pervasiveness of power and the realistic need to balance power with power and the "limitation and fragmentation of all human striving" and the "organic" character of society to satisfy any conservative of the philosophical sort; one of them did remark, in fact (a little warily), that Niebuhr's thought did at least offer a stimulating alternative to the eighteenth-century presuppositions in modern thought. When one finds in Nathan Glazer's article "The Limits of Social Policy" a rejection of the notion that for every problem there must be a solution, one remembers a thousand strokes exactly to the same point in Niebuhr. Some of us grew up reading attacks on "liberals," from that other source. But the result was different from this conservative thing. When it was all said, admitted, explored, and confessed—egotistical man, warped and limited human reason, complex human society, insoluble problems, even the tragic element in human existence—when all of that was said, the conclusion for Niebuhr was never in his life "conservative." Social justice—a social justice we have not achieved, but ought to—remained his idea of the purpose of a man's life as a citizen, throughout the fifty years of tumult in which he wrote on politics. The social wisdom he taught never became (in his own hands, at least) the servant of inhumanity, complacency, or despair.

8

Watergate
and the Dignity of
Democratic Government

The extraordinary events that became a national preoccupation after March of 1973 were, along with everything else they were, a continuously unfolding national morality play. They had elements of melodrama, tragedy, and farce. They were certainly an Epic, with the New York *Times* printing long and changing lists of the cast of characters, like the useful old yellow insert with which one could distinguish Rostovs from Bolkonskis in Simon & Schuster's wartime edition of *War and Peace*. They sometimes managed to combine the tragic, the comic, and the pathetic all at once, as in this exchange:

Senator Talmadge: Who did you think your backers were?

Bernard Barker: Sir, I was not there to think. I was there to follow orders, not to think.

Talmadge: Didn't you wonder who was giving you the orders?

Barker: No. I had absolute confidence in, as I do now, the people I was dealing with, sir.

Talmadge: Who do you think you were working for?

Barker: I was working for Mr. Hunt, and those things Mr. Hunt represents.

Talmadge: What does he represent?

Barker: Eduardo represents the liberation of Cuba. . . .

Talmadge: How do you think you could liberate Cuba by participating in a burglary in Washington, D.C.?

These events offered so rich a vein of comic material that comedians and humorists could not keep up with the possibilities. Even the mighty Art Buchwald, indefatigably writing columns with both hands while holding his cigar in a third and signaling Henri at Sans Souci with a fourth (as it would seem), had to allow many savory items to fall through the cracks. It was a fine thing indeed that Buchwald did in the early days, about God's efforts to warn "Richard" about the men around him. His phone calls intercepted by Haldeman, His telegram lost in the pile supporting the Bombing of North Vietnam, God showed up one Sunday morning at the White House prayer service. "And do you know what you did, Richard? You introduced Me to Pat and gave Me a ball point pen."

Buchwald was good also on his wife's reassurance when he was crushed to learn he had not been included on the Enemies list ("You're still an enemy to me, dear"). Nevertheless, during those incredible months from March 1973 to August 1974, each news report brought two or three more topics that Buchwald or Russell Baker were not able to cover, from the sheer comic fecundity of the thing.

I believe no one did justice to the touching question asked of E. Howard Hunt by Alfred C. Baldwin III, of Hamden, Connecticut, as the two of them fled before the police from the room filled with electronic gear in the Howard Johnson Motel on the night of June 17, 1972: "Does this mean I am out of a job?" What a tribute to the Nixon Work Ethic!

As there was no keeping up with all the comic possibilities, so also the whole story was an embarrassment of riches for the political moralist. And there was much evidence of the failure of his kind. It will be remembered that Jeb Magruder (the most inappropriately named *Jeb Stuart* Magruder, the distinguished historian of the South C. Vann Woodward remarked, as a Methodist might say the most inappropriately named *John Wesley* Dean) made one of the most explicit of the efforts to displace the blame for Watergate onto the left and the protesters, by referring pointedly to the antiwar speeches and activities of his respected teacher, then at Williams College, William Sloane Coffin, Jr. This called to mind an incident in Santa Barbara over a decade earlier, at the height of another scandal—minuscule by the monumental Watergate-scandal standards—having to do with television quiz shows. We were sitting by the Pacific thinking large thoughts about the nation's moral condition. One man slowly lowered his head and confessed: "I was Charles Van Doren's ethics teacher."

But if Watergate was jammed to the point of public indigestion with evidence of the shortcomings of American political culture, the whole story of the revealing of the Watergate misdeeds and the change of presidents contains also much evidence of the other sort. It has become fairly common to list individuals and institutions who rose to the historical task: the night guard at the Watergate, Fred Wills; the Washington *Post*, its publisher Mrs. Graham, its editors and reporters; Judge John Sirica, who became *Time*'s Man of the Year; Senator Sam Ervin, the folk hero of the summer of 1973; Elliot Richardson and William Ruckelshaus, who refused to carry out the presidential order to fire Archibald Cox; Peter Rodino, rising soberly to the unique demands of his chairmanship; Chief Justice Warren Burger and the Supreme Court, with their unanimous decision on the yielding of the tapes in July of 1974. But one should not make a list of heroes—feet of clay are easily found, and a search for heroes makes the wrong emphasis. The point is, rather, that the ethos, in its openness and diversity and moral substance, did have in it much that we can respect and build upon. That remains true though the primary emphasis in the pages to follow is on the shortcomings.

1

One wants to connect these events to the underpinnings of American politics. But before doing that one must be careful to set aside the repeated efforts to displace or distribute the blame—the effort to say not only that Watergate never happened but also that it was somebody else's fault: the left and the protesters caused it, the press invented it, national security required it, the prankster Dick Tuck started it, the Democrats also do such things, all politicians do such things, in fact everybody does such things.

The persistent inability of some of the central figures seriously to admit they had done anything wrong showed forth at its baldest in Ehrlichman and Haldeman. Their position was not only a total denial of any wrongdoing but also an obliviousness to the moral implications of their own words and deeds.

As it was not irrelevant to the understanding of John Foster Dulles that he was a Presbyterian elder with a Calvinist upbringing, and of Dwight Eisenhower that he came out of a Middle Western evangelical sect, and of Woodrow Wilson that he was a Southern Presbyterian minister's son, and of Dean Rusk that he also came out of Southern Presbyterian heritage, and of George McGovern that he was a fundamentalist minister's son converted after the war to Methodist social-gospel idealism, so we may observe that Ehrichman and Haldeman are both Christian Scientist. So is Egil Krogh, the onetime head of the plumbers whose straight-arrow moral journey had an ending that included admitting error, thus demonstrating that this, like other sorts of religious (and nonreligious) training, can have its positive as well as its negative effects.

With reference to the other two one may repeat the following joke.

Three men in Hell are sweltering, boiling, miserable from the heat.

The first man (let us take stock figures for stories of this type), perspiring profusely, said, "I was a Catholic priest, but I loved meat and ate it on Friday."

The second man mopped his brow and explained, "I was an Orthodox rabbi, and I kept a kosher home, but I loved ham sandwiches."

The third man—the one in whom we are interested—said, "I am Christian Scientist, and it is not hot, and I am not here."

"Watergate" is a symbol for a set of political evils that were real. They were not to be wished away, or excused by reference either to past misdeeds of Democrats or to violent demonstrations in the late sixties or a general moral condition of the nation. The central point was established early. It was, in the language of the second article of impeachment, the "abuse of power." There had been a gross violation of democratic procedures and of the public trust.

Men used their lawful power for unlawful and immoral purposes—first of all, "by whatever means necessary," as the extreme left used to say, to get their leader re-elected. They evidently intended to tighten their grip on the national government for the long future. They virtually extorted funds from corporations; they systematically disrupted and manipulated their opponents' campaign; they tried to turn the instruments of government illegally to their own purpose—to intimidate the press, damage their "enemies," cover their own misdeeds.

This betrayal of public trust was the heart of the matter, and it was sufficiently clear long before the impeachment proceedings in the House Judiciary Committee.

For that betrayal no one else could be blamed. As the minority that had defended Nixon on that committee finally had to say, in their rather poignant minority section of the committee's report to the House:

We know that it has been said, and perhaps some will continue to say, that Richard Nixon was "hounded from office" by his political opponents and media critics. We feel constrained to point out, however, that it was Richard Nixon who impeded the F.B.I.'s investigation of the Watergate affair by wrongfully attempting to implicate the Central Intelligence Agency; it was Richard Nixon who created and preserved the evidence of that transgression and who, knowing that it had been subpoenaed by this Committee and the Special Prosecutor, concealed its terrible import, even from his own counsel, until he could do so no longer. And it was a unaminous Supreme Court of the United States which, in an opinion authored by the Chief Justice whom he appointed, ordered Richard Nixon to surrender that evidence to the Special Prosecutor, to further the ends of justice. The tragedy that finally engulfed Richard Nixon had many facets. One was the very self-inflicted nature of the harm.

On the point about the assignment of political responsibility, let us for diversity turn briefly away from Watergate to one of the many moments when we American liberals did not perform well.

In 1948 the victory that pleased many of us, in some cases more even than the stunning re-election of Harry Truman, was the election to the Senate of the young mayor of Minneapolis, who had led the civil-rights forces in that year's Democratic convention.

Six years later, Hubert Humphrey was to run for re-election, and his victory was by no means assured: Minnesota, until that time, had not had the habit of electing Democrats, and in 1954 there was a cloud of McCarthyism covering the nation's politics.

And so it came to pass that on the floor of the United States Senate on August 12, 1954 (with the election coming in November) there was a debate about a bill to outlaw the Communist party. The bill had been introduced by a number of liberals, among whom Humphrey was the most prominent.

The bill was presented suddenly, without hearings, at the end of the session, in an election year, in a form that had been drawn up, it was said, between midnight and one o'clock the night before. "I am tired of reading headlines about being 'soft' toward Communism," said Senator Humphrey. "I am tired of reading headlines about being leftist, and about others being leftist." "I will not be lukewarm," he said. "I do not intend to be a half patriot."

If we meet the arguments of our opponents, not on grounds of our own responsible conviction, but on grounds they have selected to suit the mood of the times, then whose is the victory?

Just as McCarthyism was chiefly the responsibility of Joseph McCarthy and his defenders, and Stalin's purges and mass murders were to be blamed not on the czars or fascists or capitalism, but on the Stalinists, and Republican policy is to be blamed on Republicans, so liberals and Democrats had to bear the responsibility for their own acts, in 1954, and before then and after.

Back to Watergate, nearly twenty years later—nobody else can be blamed for the corrupt atmosphere in the Nixon White House. As young revolutionaries should bear responsibility for their own bombings, and not blame them on the police or capitalist society; as evil deeds by black militants cannot be excused by reference to white racism, or those of hard-hats by reference to student "provocation"; as liberals should bear the responsibility for the hollowness and misdeeds of recent liberalism and not blame it on conservatives or radicals; so the Nixon group could not properly excuse themselves by reference to the uproar of the young left, the actions of Daniel Ellsberg, or the doings of LBJ. They had to bear the blame and responsibility for their own misdeeds.

Having said that, one may then observe that at quite another level there *is* an important link between Watergate and the nation's moral and cultural condition.

It is something like the relationship of society to miscreants of other sorts—a relationship that the Nixonians themselves particularly object to mentioning.

If you can with an effort think back to the time before Watergate burst open, there was a presidential message on crime: criminals, it said, in a phrase that turned to irony in the Watergate cases in court, criminals should be treated "without pity." The message rejected environmentalistic explanations of crime. In the Great Society days, the then minority leader, Gerald Ford, speaking at the Illinois State Fair, condemned what he called "the soft social theory that the man who heaves a brick through your window or tosses a fire bomb into your car is simply the misunderstood and underprivileged product of a broken home." During the urban riots of 1965–69 there was an intense moral dialogue all across the country on just this ancient point, the apportioning of blame to the individual and to social conditions for evil deeds. In the ghetto riots some blacks heroically protected whites against rioters; others looted and burned. They may have had the same background. Obviously there are moral differences among them, and each is responsible for his own actions. But that does not excuse a society that creates Harlem and Watts. Though the young man who threw the rock or robbed that bank or liquor store must bear responsibility for his own deeds, that does not obliterate the simultaneous responsibility of a society that creates conditions that provide the setting for acts like these.

And now we may with poetic justice apply that same soft social theory to Richard Nixon and Company. They did the deeds, and they created the White House atmosphere out of which the whole reprehensible Watergate program came into being. That is their doing, their responsibility. Nevertheless, it *is* true that they came out of the environment of American society and reflect some of its cultural themes. We are all implicated in making, or tolerating, that environment. So it is with the black teen-ager from the ghetto; so it is with Richard Nixon, Jeb Stuart Magruder, John Ehrlichman, and Charles Colson.

$\mathscr{3}$

We do have a problem about civic virtue in this country, symbolized by Watergate. A democracy requires democrats—citizens who understand and fulfill its rather difficult moral requirements and restraints. Where is the education for such democrats, such citizens?

The comic circular effort to avoid responsibility on display in the early Ervin committee hearings in 1973—every man pointing to somebody else, each man saying "I didn't do it; somebody else did," the decisions apparently made by nobody—may be taken as a symbol of the problem of moral leadership in the nation. Each Watergate person said: It wasn't I, I just did my part, I was a conduit, I was a messenger; I took the money but I didn't know why; I raised the money but didn't ask how it was spent; I made the call but I didn't know what it meant; I typed a memo but I didn't read it; I was just obeying orders as I had been taught to do in the Navy; I assumed that because the president's counsel endorsed it, it must be legal; I talked to my subordinates and they kept telling me everything was all right. It was a comic circle of self-exculpation and irresponsibility.

We may take that as a metaphor for the United States at present. Where is the moral clarity that democracy requires? Where are the leaders who help shape the values of the citizenry?

When a lawyer made unkind remarks about the role of advertisers and public-relations men in the Watergate story, a PR man pointedly and correctly replied that they were outnumbered by lawyers. That many lawyers are not well trained in the moral foundations of the law was rather too plainly illustrated.

In 1973, while the Watergate hearings were grinding out their many lessons, Robert M. Smith, a former New York *Times* correspondent studying at the Yale Law School, published on the page opposite the editorials in his old newspaper an article called "The Slippery Slope." The article put the blame for Watergate rather more exclusively on lawyers, and for the moral relativism that gave rise to Watergate more exclusively on law schools, than is altogether just. One may wish to give what Smith wrote about law schools a much wider application:

Law school students are introduced to the Slippery Slope fairly quickly. The first slide usually takes this format:

Professor: (Bored condescension.) Mr. Smith, do you believe that the police should torture people?

Smith: (What is he getting at?) No, sir.

Professor: Do you believe that the police should ever torture suspects?

Smith: (Pause.) No, sir.

Professor: (Volume goes up half a notch.) You're sure of that, are you?

Smith: (Longer pause.) Yes, sir. I don't think it would be right.

Professor: (*Sotto voce*) Not right, huh? (Back to courtroom tone.) Picture this situation, Mr. Smith. A suspect is known to have an atomic weapon. He is also known to have planted this weapon somewhere in the labyrinthine tunnels below Manhattan. It is known that the device will detonate in one hour. The police have tried unsuccessfully, after reading the suspect his Miranda warning, to learn from him where he has planted the weapon. It is known that he is very sensitive to electric shocks. Would you allow the police to give him a few quick jolts to find out where the bomb is, or would you prefer no torture—not even a teensie-weensie electric shock—and the certainty that, say, three million people will perish?

Smith: (How much time is left in this class?) Well . . .

Professor: Now, Mr. Smith. You aren't quite sure that the police should never torture suspects, are you? It's really a question of drawing a line somewhere, isn't it? In short, it's like the rest of life—it's all a question of where you want to draw the line.

It's all a question of where you draw the line—if, indeed, there is one. One of the more instructive moments in the Ervin hearings included this exchange:

Senator Talmadge: Now, if the President could authorize a covert break-in and you do not know exactly how that power would be limited, you do not think it could include murder or other crimes beyond covert break-ins do you?

John Ehrlichman: I do not know where the line is, Senator.

One had to see Ehrlichman's shake of the head and outthrust jaw to get the full effect of this.

To be sure, it is difficult to answer such questions at any time, and especially when they arise suddenly in such august and widely publicized surroundings; nevertheless, Ehrlichman's peculiarly bad answer was consistent with his other words, and with his deeds.

Smith went on with a second point, also of much wider application, having to do with the ubiquitous "cost-benefit" analysis—the modern social scientist's and policy maker's variant of utilitarianism—that spreads across the worlds of "technical and sophisticated judgment":

From the Slippery Slope the student is led to Cost Ben analysis. Cost Ben helps the student to decide where the line should be drawn. The instruction takes this form:

Professor: What's the benefit involved in torturing the suspect, getting the information and deactivating the bomb?

Smith: Three million lives.

Professor: Good. What's the cost?

Smith: (The values I came in here with.) The pain inflicted on the suspect. Possible encouragement to the police to torture in the future. A weakening in the public ethic against torture. A dehumanization of the policemen who did the torturing . . .

Professor: Now, Mr. Smith. Don't you think the public would want the police to torture in such a situation? . . . Isn't it fairly clear that they ought to torture in that, and perhaps other, situations?

If you start at the top of the hill marked Presidency, take the first road that says Slippery Slope, climb into the long black Cost Ben limousine and take your foot off the brake, you will soon reach: Watergate.

Professors in general, as I have by now sufficiently said, are not in a good position to condemn others; the behavioral and positivistic revolution universities have undergone in the last twenty years is perhaps the most important moral abdication of them all.

When one attends conferences on "The Media" an outsider is startled to discover how reluctant these TV and newspaper people are to admit their own power to shape values, and therefore to take responsibility for it. Many believe their medium to be only a "mirror" of society.

Alas, perhaps in an ironic way they are right. The black comedy of Watergate presents intriguing examples, perhaps even an intriguing new type of example, of the manipulative rearrangement of the truth in communication to masses that is always associated now with the forebodings of George Orwell. Lionel Trilling's essay about Orwell had the title "The Politics of Truth": scarcely the term for the activities of the United States government in the sixties and early seventies.

Ziegler's memorable phrase, "render inoperative," will live as a symbol of the effort to disavow the past and make a new one. Something of the same quality touched John Dean's remark about the money he took for his honeymoon—that he would replace it in order to "make it whole"—so that what happened would not have happened. Haldeman's testimony seemed to say, about the Huston Plan for illegal mail cover, burglary, and surveillance, that, since it was rescinded after five days in the face of J. Edgar Hoover's opposition, it was as though it had never been approved. Nixon explained at a San Clemente press conference that the burglary of Ellsberg's psychiatrist's office was a "dry hole," seeming to imply that since nothing was discovered the event itself more or less did not happen.

Richard Nixon came out of the Southern California suburban world, and the Chotiner Machiavellianism. His "team" included, however much outnumbered by lawyers, many people shaped in the world of advertising and public relations. His career was that of a debater, a campaigner, a salesman making irrational links to Enemies and evil symbols—in his demonology Daniel Ellsberg replaced Ramsey Clark, who took the place of Alger Hiss. Sophistry and demagoguery come to be more serious problems in the age of mass communication—when the instruments of deception, manipulation, and irrational appeal are more powerful.

Democratic politics requires some trust in the reason and conscience of the citizenry. It requires an honest conversation about what the people shall do. The devices that go around and beneath the reason to obtain a response are at odds with the true foundations of democratic politics in the consent of the governed: there is or should be a sharp difference between selling a product in a market and choosing public leaders in a democracy. The second implies some measure of reason, conscience, and human discourse, if the people are authentically to rule.

Watergate is a symbol at least and also to some extent a product of a condition much larger than the Nixon administration, a slippery sophistry in modern American political culture that is by no means confined to one Southern California fraternity, to Murray Chotiner and his disciples, or to one organization in 1971–72 at 1701 Pennsylvania Avenue.

4

The United States celebrates its political system—democracy—in an ideal form, beyond what other societies have done. But while celebrating democracy we paradoxically disdain the "politics" essential to it. Cynicism about politics and politicians then shapes the Charles Colsons and Tom Charles Hustons of tomorrow, whose activities, in turn, add to the cynicism. Blaming Watergate on "politics as usual" ironically helps to create the atmosphere out of which events like Watergate emerge. Watergate may make the familiar negative-attitude politics worse. I believe Fred Dutton first said that "Watergate has done for politicians what the Boston Strangler did for door-to-door salesman."

Politicians rightly complained that, Nixon aside, the chief perpetrators of Watergate had never run for office—not even county sheriff. Politicians in a democratic polity ordinarily develop at least a minimal political morality: they learn to pay attention to the people whose votes they seek; their much criticized flexibility and compromising has its positive side, in responsiveness and openness; they learn that their opposition to opponents is limited and specific, not general and absolute. They fight with an opponent on an issue today, and join with him on another issue tomorrow. And across both issues they can maintain a framework of shared agreement on the rules of the system—as the nonpoliticians in the Nixon White House failed to understand. John Ehrlichman did not understand *political* morality, however much he would endorse peering over transoms to investigate private

morals. Charles Colson's celebrated willingness to run over his
grandmother to elect Richard Nixon seemed less and less like hyperbole as the revelations continued. John Mitchell's admitted
willingness to do anything to re-elect Richard Nixon, and to defeat George McGovern, exhibited rather a clear-cut failure to understand the moral requirements and limitations of a democratic
political system.

The monarchical atmosphere of recent presidencies, and especially that of Richard Nixon, is inappropriate: Congress, the
press, and the defeated party, among other entities, all play continuing roles in the workings of the government of a free people.

We do not elect absolute sovereigns, even when a politician
wins by a healthy margin. And healthy margins do not appear to
be particularly healthy for the polity—Franklin Roosevelt in '36;
Lyndon Johnson in '64; Richard Nixon in '72; possibly Dwight
Eisenhower in '56.

As the former attorney general seemed complacently to assume
that McGovern was so obvious an evil and a threat as to justify all
tactics used against him, so also many in Mitchell's company tried
to excuse the lawlessness of Watergate by reference to a real or
alleged lawlessness of the left that preceded it. There was not
only Jeb Magruder's reference to the actions of Bill Coffin, his
ethics teacher, and Cuban-American Barker's reference to Daniel
Ellsberg, but many paragraphs in the testimony of Haldeman and
Ehrlichman, and in the conservative newspaper columns, explain-
ing Watergate by the threat of the left. Nixon repeatedly referred
to the lawless actions of the left in the late sixties.

It is true that other movements before Watergate were often
morally absolutist and occasionally lawless. But surely the place
to begin to restore trust was with self-criticism not with self-exculpation.

Moreover, the parallel breaks down. Obviously the serious tradition of civil disobedience is quite different from the Watergate
abuse of power; the former was done in public by citizens willing
to take the punishment, not in secret by trusted officials abusing
the trust they have been given.

Insofar as one may draw parallels—that the United States had
moral absolutism on the left in the sixties, which encouraged the

fanaticism of the Nixon people in the seventies—it is still important to say with Senator Howard Baker that two wrongs do not
make a right. Indeed, two wrongs accentuate each other and tear
at the fabric of law and of trust that holds the nation together—a
fabric more fragile than most citizens realize.

It is true that many dubious things were done and said in the
sixties. It is true that the nation had a series of rending experiences before Watergate. It is true that the New Left in its rhetoric
about the nation often went beyond the bonds of civility and of
discriminate judgment. But none of that excuses Watergate.

America's moral absolutism appears in many guises: no one of
them may excuse itself by pointing to another.

The self-criticism required by democratic morality includes the
principle of generalization: would I want those who hold an opposite position to mine to use the tactics I employ? Or one may
use this test: do not use means that one would not use in the ideal
society. The actual ends we accomplish are more often those implicit in the means we employ than those explicit in the ideals we
affirm.

5

Witness after witness in the Watergate hearings needed to have a
structure of moral principles that transcended, and put under criticism, the pattern of loyalties within their political and governmental life. One central White House horror was to infiltrate the
United States government with men who had no loyalty other
than to President Nixon. Loyalty of higher ideals was reduced to
nationalism, and nationalism to an absolute support for Nixon.

John Caulfield: I felt very strongly about the President, extremely
strongly about the President. I was very loyal to his people that I worked
for. I place a high value upon loyalty.

Herbert Porter: My loyalty to this man, Richard Nixon, goes back
longer than any person that you will see sitting at this table throughout
any of these hearings.

H. R. Haldeman: Those who served with me at the White House had complete dedication to the service of this country. They had great pride in the President they served and great pride in the accomplishments of the Nixon Administration in its first four years.

John Ehrlichman: I do not apologize for my loyalty to the President any more than I apologize for my love of this country. I only hope that my testimony here has somehow served them both.

John Mitchell: And I was not about to countenance anything that would stand in the way of that re-election.

The Watergate evils were exposed because men had other loyalties—to the good name of the CIA, to the Department of Justice, to the United States government, which is more than any individuals who fill its posts at any moment, to a higher moral principle even than these.

Assistant Attorney General Henry Peterson included a discussion of "loyalty" in the last days of the Ervin hearings on TV. Loyalty to whom? To what? In one examination of these matters at about the same time, a constitutional lawyer quoted E. M. Forster's famous remark that if he was forced to choose between loyalty to a friend and loyalty to his nation he hoped he would have the courage to betray his nation. Have you no other choices? Neither one's friend nor one's nation is an absolute. Either one's friend or one's nation may do evil things, and the same is true of the leaders of one's cause, as perhaps the pathetic and exploited Barker has learned by now.

The central place in the twisted system of misplaced loyalties that fills the moral vacuum is held by nationalism—a nationalism reinforced by the national experience in assorted recent wars. One root of Watergate was the wartime mentality, simplifying purposes with a single overriding goal, a single enemy, a single loyalty—by an absolutist and simplistic morality, which is then a justification for all sorts of dubious activities. If you have no other ethical standard for political life, then the tribal wartime sort of nationalism (our kind against their kind) is the final appeal.

The United States rather suddenly became a world power in the nineteen-forties, without much experience of diplomacy and international politics. It became a world power just as the world was learning what modern totalitarianism is like. As a nation we were unprepared for both.

This inexperienced world power made use of the dirty tricks of warfare thought to be required against the totalitarian enemy: the wartime OSS led to clandestine operations in the cold war; they led to the falsified records and the governmental lies about the U-2, the Bay of Pigs, and the secret bombing in Cambodia. The saturation bombings of World War II were one of the precursors of the morally indiscriminate activities by American forces in Vietnam soberly indicted by Telford Taylor in *Vietnam and Nuremberg*.

This grew from the combination of an exaggerated international enmity with the political limitations of American culture, a culture that had not learned (not that it is easy to learn) how to apply its own best ideals to world politics as it is.

The dirty tricks seemed to appeal to a spirit of derring-do, machismo, and bravado in the American make-up—from the frontier perhaps and the masculine image—and were encouraged by the romantic throbbings of international battle and intrigue of the sort that vibrated in the lives of Gordon Liddy and E. Howard Hunt. In Watergate this thought-world was transferred to domestic politics, partly under the cloak of "national security," partly by replacing international Enemies with domestic ones.

The boundless notion of "national security" (as explicitly expressed by John Ehrlichman and his lawyer, John Wilson, as employed by Nixon, and as repudiated in the end by Egil Krogh) is pernicious, not only in that it contained within it this unrestrained nationalism, but also in that legitimate national security is perverted to be protection of the president's own political security. For the Watergate people, these seemed to come to the same thing.

The merit of the United States is its relationship to a social ideal beyond the morals of a tribe. At its best, as Gunnar Myrdal said, the American creed has roots in universal ideals, including the ideal of a limited society (too often just presented as a limited government)—a society under law, which law reflects both a universal moral claim and the claims of the human person, which transcend any social order. At its worst, Americanism is a tribal morality, like any other tribal morality.

The replacement of Richard Nixon with Gerald Ford provides a moment to reconsider what a democracy can do in world affairs without losing its identity—what American democracy can do, and a civilized people can do, and still be what they claim to be. It is not an accident that columnists in this period recalled nostalgically Henry Stimson having said, "Gentlemen do not open other people's mail."

If Watergate is to have the beneficent side effects we want it to have, it would puncture the inflated and rather unchecked nationalism of American society since World War II—indeed one may say almost since our beginning, because we have so often thought we were a people set apart and better than the other peoples of the world.

6

The Nixon scandals were so numerous and so loaded with endlessly unraveling detail as to make it easy to lose the central point in the tangle of tapes, documents, and hearings.

The central evil did not have to do with tapes or with money; one might almost say the everlasting detail on those matters was a distraction. The central evil was the abuse of power, the violation of democratic rules, the betrayal of a public trust.

Nixon's personal self-enrichment represented one facet of the collection of evils under that heading, reprehensible, to be sure, and more appropriable by the public than the other facets—but it was not the central point. The Watergate scandals would have been a moral outrage, a violation of social principles, even if the man at the center had been an ascetic, a scrupulously honest man in his personal finances. The violation that is of much deeper significance than his estates, his heated swimming pools, and his income-tax deductions is the violation of the rules of proper governmental authority and for democratic politics.

The moral vacuum in which these Nixon scandals arose resulted in a paradox: the modern administration elected most distinctly out of a craving for the majestic authority of law became the administration that most flagrantly violated the law, abused its authority, and undermined the majesty of government.

It is evident that Nixon's outlook on the world has been to some degree discredited. What he has done may help to set that sort of outlook back many decades, and it would be a good thing if it did.

It is to be hoped that the sobering experience of his forced resignation has had this desirable result, to deepen the understanding of public institutions and their proper work.

In a very different setting, a sober Austrian Catholic thinker, Joseph Pieper, wrote the following paragraph:

> One thing, of course, is indispensable: that a sense of the greatness and dignity of governing and ruling be revived in the mind of the public. This is all the more necessary since the "intellectuals" of the past hundred years have been virtually defined by their ironical treatment of the terms "authority" and "subject," with the result that nowadays these words can hardly be spoken or understood without bias. Individualistic liberalism is in fundamental agreement with orthodox Marxism on this point, namely that there is no "governmental authority" properly so called. For individualism, authority is vested in agreements between individuals which, as a matter of principle, can be canceled at any time; for Marxism, it is the hallmark of those preliminary stages of society which will one day dissolve altogether within a Communist society.

One must agree, in part—setting aside the remark (too familiar, in our setting too handy a weapon) about "intellectuals." One must agree that the dignity of governing must be restored—of *democratic* governing.

"Politics" is no mean thing, but a serious moral undertaking linking the consent of the governed to the governmental authority and its just powers, its dignity. Politics links democracy to government; the demos must affirm the principle of government for that to work. And government is grounded in law, indeed in that fundamental law that is a constitution superior to and restraining the individuals who serve under it, as the Judiciary Committee's work made visible. And the law and the constitution are grounded in a moral order, a universal moral frame protecting and affirming the human person, or else it is nothing but coercion and tribalism.

We do learn something from the continuing conversation of the political culture, in the bar and the living room and the shop and the television studio. One wishes that the necessary shaping conversation of a democratic culture were more effectively carried on in the formal setting of the classroom, especially the college classroom. We also learn a great deal from examples, including positive examples. By the end of the bicentennial the American people may wish there had never been a George Washington, but it is nevertheless true that models of the citizen's virtue are essential. The events of 1973–74, as I have said, provided some examples of this kind, along with a swarm of the other kind.

But the great moody, trendy demos learns in its own hard way, failing the better, by experiencing terrible historical object lessons. Perhaps Watergate and the replacement of a president will serve to teach something by negation about the moral dignity of democratic government.

As Watergate is appropriated as a symbol by the political culture, it might even be to the polity as the Depression to the economy, and perhaps Vietnam to foreign policy: an object lesson that teaches a valuable public understanding by what it discredits.

9

"There Are People Out There Who Want to Believe": An American Failure Story

In a magazine article published in 1956, under the title "The Debating Career of Richard Nixon," I remarked that the very debating talents that had brought him rapidly to the eminence he had then achieved ("the Vice Presidency," as, in the Nixon style, we could say) might also someday undo him. One could not have guessed back then the altogether unlikely sequence of events that would follow in the next eighteen years before that prediction would finally come true.

And yet it was always true. Nixon's career had been an American failure story from its beginning and throughout—in his meeting with triumph as well as with disaster, those two imposters that he definitely did not treat just the same. That was one flaw in him. He cared too much about "winning" and "losing," and thereby was doomed to "lose" already however his many game plans for life turned out. The Quitter, the Loser, the Failure: he was all of those in the end, because it meant too much to him not to be. He quit, much later than he should have quit; he failed, as he need not have failed, in the very teeth of a mammoth "success"; he lost the highest of positions, by a forced resignation, in a "historic first," because in his anxiety he sanctioned a program he did not need at all to "win."

He failed his way steadily upward, in a grotesque parody of the Horatio Alger story he himself altogether too much believed in. He failed in the unfairness of his first victory over Jerry Voorhis in 1946; he failed more severely in the gross and more visible unfairness of his victory over Helen Gahagan Douglas in 1950; he failed in the insistent borrowing from his role in the Alger Hiss case, as though forever after a grateful nation ought to do whatever he recommended, as though anyone who opposed him on anything thereafter must be in league with communists and with Hiss. He failed in the opportunism that brought him the vice presidential nomination, exploiting the sterile anticommunism of that period and abruptly abandoning Earl Warren's candidacy at the 1952 convention to go with the winner. In the "crisis" of the Nixon Fund of 1952 he failed most spectacularly, creating in his Checkers speech the very model of what not to do in the dangerous age of mass communication. He failed in the campaign of 1952, attacking the Democrats as though Hiss were their candidate. He failed again in the nasty campaign of 1954, touring the Western states linking honorable men like Senator John Carroll, of Colorado, to communism.

When he finally achieved "the presidency" he proved that there is room to fail at the top. His failure endangered even his successes, as he borrowed insistently from his foreign-policy achievements to argue for his retention in office after the Watergate disclosures.

/

Did he fail also in defeat? One wanted to believe he would not. In the 1960 campaign, he was still a fairly young man, and he was emerging at last from the shadow of Eisenhower—no doubt a difficult shadow to deal with. He was a candidate in his own right for the nation's highest office, with the scars of all those Herblock cartoons and all those critical articles stored up inside him. He tried, I think, for the moment to rise to something higher than the stereotype of himself that had developed, and to match the dignity of the office to which he aspired. His speech accepting the nomination was arguably better than John Kennedy's, with nothing like the nasty thrust at Ramsey Clark and the other delinquencies that would mar his acceptance speech eight years later. On the whole, his campaign against Kennedy in 1960 was much less bad than his other campaigns had been. The one dubious thrust was minor, grossly ineffectual, and multiply ironic now: he praised Ike's clean language in the White House as against Truman's swearing.

Nevertheless, the 1960 campaign was otherwise not so bad; it can be argued that the objectionable items—the missile gap, the communists ninety miles off our shores—were on Kennedy's side. Did Nixon do well when he declined, despite the urgings of advisers, to make backhanded use of "the religious issue" by a plea for fairness to *non-Catholics*, too? Possibly. Sorensen gives him some credit for that. But that was political dynamite. Perhaps he was more of a success in his behavior after he lost the election. Kennedy's aristocratic sensibilities were offended by Nixon's bringing his tearful wife before the television cameras on election night, but—oh! the Kennedys! With all of their advantages! What did they know of the struggles of the son of a grocery-store owner and former streetcar conductor from Whittier, California, who had to work and work and work, without charm, without money, without connections to the Eastern elite! The intensity of Nixon's fear-hate-envy-resentment of the Kennedys seems to have been so great as almost to make one sympathize with it for its sheer force.

After the election of 1960, despite its closeness, Nixon did not contest the result, although many Republicans believed the election to have been stolen in Illinois. He took the result, close though it was, and the disappointment of not achieving that high office, with good grace. One relented a little. Perhaps he was at last something of a success after all.

But then came the 1962 election for governor of California, and not only another shoddy campaign (the death penalty for dope peddlers—a thrust at Pat Brown's opposition to capital punishment), but also that unbelievable press conference after he lost.

One kept wanting to say that Richard Nixon was not really quite as bad as it seemed to those of us who had always opposed him ("hated" him, he would say, revealingly, even on his last morning in the White House. Why raise that subject just then? The overt message was: don't hate them back; they can only hurt you if you hate them back. The more powerful covert message was already delivered by his even raising, on such an occasion, this inappropriate subject: there are people out there who "hate" you). Those of us who had long opposed Nixon kept looking for the qualifications and exceptions, for no man altogether fits the stereotypes that develop around him. Theodore Sorensen, the young assistant to the young senator from Massachusetts, one day in the middle fifties nodded at the door of the vice president's Senate Office Building office, just across the hall from Kennedy's, and said: You know, Nixon isn't as bad as people think he is.

I never got in to see Vice President Richard Nixon, back in 1956 when I was working on that article; Rose Mary Woods, wisely, kept putting me off. She discerned, quite accurately, that I was no friend, and she certainly knew the magazine I was working for was no friend, of Richard Nixon. But I was told several times by knowledgeable Washington people, including Democrats and liberals, that Nixon in private was not only more intelligent but also a more decent person than his public reputation in some circles. In his first administration as president, the late Stewart Alsop wrote a column on the "Demonsterization of Richard Nixon"; how people like me who had long opposed him were discovering now that he was not the monster they had thought him to be.

Appointing Henry Kissinger first as the national security adviser in the White House, and then also as secretary of state, and supporting him in what would be called, in the Nixonian hyperbole, "Great Initiatives for Peace": that was something we did not expect from Richard Nixon. His appointing and supporting Kissinger does not fit. At first glance his open doors to China and détente with Russia did not fit, with the irony often noted that this man who came onstage as the rigid anticommunist did what no Hubert Humphrey could have got by with. He proposed a "*full employment* balanced budget," a budget that *would be* balanced, if the economy were at full employment: not so very different from what we liberals would propose. He joined in saying "we are Keynesians now." He appointed Pat Moynihan to the White House staff, and proposed that first possibility of a guaranteed income—the Family Assistance Plan—that Moynihan insists the liberals killed. (Others disagree: Nixon did not fight for it, they say.) He reversed himself completely and instituted wage and price controls in August of 1971. But if one's point is not that he was a consistent conservative—far from it—but that he was an adventurer and opportunist and sophist who calculatingly seized upon popular moods to use them for his "winning," then all of this does not refute the point so much as confirm it.

In 1962, as one of the commentators said, he showed that he was a sore loser; in 1972, he showed that he was a sore winner. He had already showed it in public words and actions from November 1972 to March 1973, even before the transcripts revealed the ugly private side.

Still, when the end came, one hoped for some grace, dignity, honor, success. One sat down before one's TV set on the night of August 8, 1974 wondering how it would be. Those of us who had already found the smoking gun in that same TV set on September 23, 1952 at the latest had been a little impatient with those who required twenty-two years more of proof. Yet, here it was. And after he had spoken, one said it wasn't as bad as it might have been: no rancor, no bitterness, no attacks on enemies, a certain dignity. But not enough. He said that his support in Congress had "eroded," without a suggestion of why: as though they had abandoned him, as though there had been a disagreement on policy. He came perilously close to yet another variant of that Nixonian displacing and diffusing of the blame, now here, now there, now everywhere, now another place, never on himself, that marked the whole Watergate episode, indeed his whole career. There was one brief reference to errors of judgment— nothing more. And the next morning in his maudlin farewell in the White House, and his campaign speech in Orange County, he marred the dignity of departure. What was needed was a strong man's honest and public admission of guilt. The reason that was needed is like the reason Nixon and Kissinger said we needed a slow, masked, "honorable" withdrawal from Vietnam: in order that there not be a festering wound in the psyche of the silent majority. The events of August 5–9, 1974, happened so fast that their full meaning did not have a chance to penetrate the farther reaches of Rabbi Baruch Korff's constituency. There is the danger that the myth will grow and be a part of tomorrow's politics, that Nixon was hounded out of office by that standard list of his enemies.

4

Richard Nixon has been analyzed enough, attacked enough, and exposed enough not to need much more in that line here, but, for a reason that has nothing to do with Nixon, I do want to extract from the torrent of misdeeds one instructive, polluted rivulet that may be lost in the flood.

He was, as it turned out, an unworthy man in several ordinary respects we had not known him for—his avarice, for example, cutting every corner on his income tax and lying to the public and deceiving his own lawyer and supporters. These familiar blatant sins may serve to dilute the lesson of his more distinctive delinquencies. The sample of the latter that I want to sort out of the debris goes back long before Watergate, providing one of its roots; it is his sophistical and manipulative style of argument and of public persuasion, the fault of the old Nixon never abandoned by the assortment of new Nixons. I suggest that this defect in its subtler way can go as deep into the foundations of the Republic as the impeachable Nixonian offenses.

It should be said right away that he was far from being alone in this offense. On the contrary: it is the unhappy underside of all democratic politics, linked in the classic political philosophers to the debased form of democracy, and anatomized in the eighty-seven hundred books of modern political thought dealing with "mass society" and the like. Its ancient form takes a qualitative jump with the coming of the machinery of modern society, and especially the machinery for communicating all at once to enormous numbers of people.

We do not succumb to the temptation of an artificially balanced both-sidedness when we mention just one notorious example from quite another political direction, because that one example had such distinct echoes of Nixon's own performances. I am referring to the way Senator Edward Kennedy presented the dreadful episode of Chappaquiddick to the public in July of 1969. There was a gathering of high-powered advisers and speech writers in sad parody of his brother's management of the Cuba missile crisis; there was a delay, with its transparent message that public relations was the topic of discussion; there was a television speech, with its only partial confession and pseudo candor, and its appeal for vindication to numbers, and numbers most conveniently chosen for a Kennedy—to the voters of Massachusetts; there was the clamp-down of silence after the desired popular response had been achieved. It was an exercise in "opinion management" that might have been coached by Murray Chotiner, Richard Nixon's early mentor. A Democrat watching Kennedy's television speech could not avoid chilling reminders of Nixon's 1952 speech about the Nixon Fund, his wife's Republican cloth coat, and his dog, Checkers.

With that one reference let us pass over all the other parallels, among liberals, radicals, moderates, and conservatives, among Republicans, Democrats, and splinter-party people. Richard Nixon's platform method represented in persistent quintessence one variant of a ubiquitous failing; usually it is found in a more mitigated form.

I suggest that Nixon's embodiment of this particular fault is a chief explanation of the intensity of the pre-Watergate dislike that he detected, rightly, in certain parts of the population. The explanation for that intensity was not that the anti-Nixonians were by and large liberal and Nixon was not, or Democratic when he was Republican. Still less was the explanation geographical—that they were afflicted with undue Easternness. There was something more to it. One may point to a number of un-Eastern conservatives and Republicans—Robert Taft, William Knowland, Barry Goldwater, and, most especially now, Gerald Ford—who have been by no means as disliked in their public personality as Nixon was.

I suggest another explanation. Nixon represented an unalloyed example of a characteristic by which all are tempted, particularly in a large modern democracy. It is a trait that is at once tempting and offensive to *reason*, which helps to explain the composition of the body of Nixon's pre-Watergate detractors. It also offends our sense of human community anywhere, but particularly in the free institutions that rest upon deliberations among reasonable men. An ancient name for this characteristic is sophistry. Another ancient name, more appropriate to our polity, is demagoguery. The use of words, symbols, and arguments as mere counters in a power struggle is of course not confined to Nixon and his Watergate group; it appears, as I have said, continually and on all sides of politics, right, left, and center. But it does not often appear in as pure and obviously calculated a form as it did in Nixon. When the White House transcripts were released in April 1974, the whole world could read a record of Nixon and cohorts doing the calculating. Telling the truth was called the "hang out route" (as in "let it all hang out"), considered briefly for its public-relations value, and dismissed as unproductive.

In that article about Nixon in 1956 I tied his platform method, perhaps a little unfairly, to the worst features of high-school and college debate.

If Adlai Stevenson is the high-minded commencement speaker in politics and Dwight Eisenhower the morale-building football coach, then Mr. Nixon is the bright young debater. Almost his whole life has been spent in the arguing business, and his success has been, in the language of his native Southern California, supercolossal.

He engaged in his first debate, on the subject, "Resolved: that insects are more beneficial than harmful," in the seventh grade. He won. In his California high schools he entered something called the Constitutional Oratorical Contest three times; three times he won. He led winning debating teams both in high school and in Whittier College, and when he entered the Southern California Intercollegiate Extemporaneous Speaking Contest, he won that.

In 1946, the Congressman in California's twelfth district, a well-liked Democrat named Jerry Voorhis, agreed one day to meet his young, unknown Republican opponent, Richard Nixon, in a series of five debates. The first one was held in a high school in South Pasadena, and after it was over Voorhis asked a friend how the debate had gone. "Jerry," said the friend, "he murdered you."

Four years later, in 1950, Congressman Nixon was running for the Senate against Helen Gahagan Douglas, and a leading California Democrat spoke for Mrs. Douglas in a debate with Nixon. "He knew every detail," says this Democrat. "The audience was with him, and he made a monkey out of me."

Two years later, in 1952, Senator Nixon was running for the Vice-Presidency. "I come before you," he said earnestly one memorable night in late September, ". . . as a man whose honesty and integrity have been questioned. . . ." After the telecast, telegrams, letters, postcards, and even gifts of money came in by the thousands.

Two years after that, in 1954, Vice-President Nixon traveled across the country in a campaign expedition that, in sheer expenditure of lung power, is probably unmatched by any in the history of American off-year elections. The President praised him; everybody credited him with Democratic scalps; midwestern party chairmen publicly thanked him for what he had done "for the American people and his party;" and a Republican columnist voiced the conclusion of many when he said, "Virtually singlehanded, he averted a G.O.P. debacle."

Now, in 1956, just ten years from the time he entered politics, Mr. Nixon has talked and argued and campaigned his way to the threshold of the most powerful office in the world. As one of the so-called "committee of 100" that first picked Nixon to run in 1946, has said, "I guess we didn't know what we had hold of. We knew Dick was smart and we knew he could talk, but we didn't know that he was that smart or could talk that fast."

It was not that he hadn't taken positions; it was just that his deliberately designed platform performances were much more central to his public personality than any clear political commitment; his calculated appeal to a crowd was far more noticeable than any restraining set of values. The worthy things he might do or say appeared to be, as in one of the devices that he used in his campaigning, just the preliminary concession to truth or to the other side that one makes in order to win the audience, so that the final, calculated argument will be the more damning. It may just be a part of what you have to do to win.

"Why is there such a widespread distaste for Mr. Nixon?" I asked, back in 1956.

To understand the feeling against Mr. Nixon one must turn not to the substance of his politics but to the character of his polemic.

Though the early ones are now many years gone, none of Mr. Nixon's campaigns has been forgotten; each has left a memorable stain.

For all their victories and acclaim, the champions in the art of persuasion, from the days of the sophists to our own, have been under a bit of a shadow. After the applause has died down and a more reflective mood has set in, one is never sure just where conviction ended and sheer artistry began. In our time these ancient doubts have taken on a new dimension, as the persuasion of men in the mass has become not just an art but a science. Mr. Nixon, in the practice of that science, has gathered not only laurels but also the antagonism that men feel toward its more unrestrained practitioners.

Almost everybody has been made to look the fool by a glib debater, or been sold something he didn't want by a fast-talking salesman, or been put in the wrong before a crowd by the "sincere" and emotional appeal of an opponent. Such experiences are remembered when one listens to Richard Nixon.

It is this trait, both offensive and tempting to *reason*, that explains the intensity of the pre-Watergate antagonism to Nixon. Sophistry is pseudo reason, seeming reason, the false façade of reason. It is therefore both a temptation and an offense in particular to men who are craftsmen of expression and communication and thinking, who deal in language and ideas and arguments and reporting. It is a sin they often commit, and that their professional conscience urges them to avoid. The mutual antagonism between Nixon and the press more recently, and between him and academics and writers throughout his career, has that principal source. They contend the same turf. The press—to take his greatest "Enemy" in his last days—strives to avoid what Nixon represented, and is tempted to the same faults as he.

If one seeks the attention and understanding of a giant audience, one simplifies: "the larger the audience the simpler the communication must be." If one seeks to grasp and hold a giant audience, one dramatizes and appeals to emotions: one deals in symbols already loaded with feeling. One uses persons as symbols: celebrities, heroes, villains. Nixon specialized, as we all know, in villains, but I believe one chapter in the treatise on his rhetorical method could deal with his pious and celebrational public references to Ike, from his first appearance on the center stage in the summer of 1952, throughout his vice presidency and his candidacy in 1960 to his echo of the Notre Dame cry, when Eisenhower was ill, to "win this one for Ike."

Nixon was a master of calculated innuendo, in which one said something without precisely saying it, by word patterns and linkages: Adlai Stevenson as a Ph.D. from Dean Acheson's college of cowardly communist containment. There was also in him an eliding of truth and of candor by a sort of pseudo reasonableness, mock reason: now, they came to me and said I should do so and so, but that would be the *easy* way.

All of these dangerous features of popular communication are found in the press, with its headlines, its celebrities, its spot news, its human-interest stories, its sensations, its eagerness to be attended to by large numbers; the press, too, can falsify while seeming to be truthful, by its selectivity and arrangement. These temptations are increased by the availability of the camera. The serious reporter and responsible editor tries to avoid all of this, and to train the novice in a professional duty to avoid it. In the book by the Washington *Post* reporters Bernstein and Woodward, *All the President's Men* (a book about newspapermen as well as about Watergate), one can read the tug of war among the competing claims, including a hot story on one side and journalistic integrity on another.

The press was not Nixon's only "Enemy." I said also that Nixon's characteristic faults offend the delicate sense of human community: that we can deal in honest deliberation with each other. That Speaker Sam Rayburn and President Harry Truman were deeply antagonistic to Nixon may have sprung from this source: although men in politics are accustomed to disagreement, conflict, attack, and counterattack, there are boundaries. Nixon did not observe the boundaries. Truman persisted in believing that Nixon had called him a traitor and a crook, even though Nixon's spokesmen would explain that the sentences in question had qualifying commas or something.

One of the debater's devices that the young Nixon obviously learned, from Chotiner or earlier, was this one: it is better to deal with an irrelevant point on which one can make an effective appeal to the audience than with a relevant point on which one cannot. And as the cheering audience doesn't notice, the listener who does notice grinds his teeth in frustration. These plus the rhetorical posing of false and unreal alternatives plus the linkages to evil figures, Alger Hiss, Vito Marcantonio, Ramsey Clark, Daniel Ellsberg, plus the carefully worked out alliterative slogans ("Korea, Communism, and Corruption") make a package of dishonesty that is deeply offensive.

It was calculated. Nixon, coached from the start by Murray Chotiner, rose to power in the time of the growing importance of professional public-relations firms in political affairs. He came from the state in which they had their earliest and largest role, with Whitaker and Baxter engaging in the "engineering of consent" and already "merchandising" candidates in his early political years. The result was exhibited at one stage in Joe McGinniss' *The Selling of the President* in 1968; it was to appear in much more devastating form in the revelations of 1974. In the taped conversations there is no rooted conviction in truth or honor or the decent obligation to one's opponents or the legal limits and proper role of governmental authorities; there are "Enemies"; there are "scenarios"; there is the president of the United States serving, according to his own defense, as "devil's advocate" for positions no devil should be advocating in the office of the chief executive of a free people's government. It was always everlasting "PR."

I am not making this harsh argument about Nixon in any effort to persuade any remaining supporter who might happen across these words: every living soul on this planet will have had more than a full opportunity to make up his mind about this individual by the time these words are read. I aim instead at those who agree with what is written here—who agree that Nixon exemplified, in the traits mentioned, egregious faults. If that be so, then there must be a *standard* that he violated—a standard of conscientious deliberation based upon truth, and the moral order, and one's own authentic conviction. Who disagrees? Well, much of the twentieth century has been more relativist and reductionist than those words I have used would imply: has been reluctant to use those words. There has been a merely strategic outlook, a merely operational outlook in many other circles beyond the Nixon White House. If you condemn Nixon's lifelong platform style, then you imply a moral standard he violated. If you reject his mode of public suasion, you imply an obligation to do otherwise: not to look on human beings as a manipulable mass to be managed; as a collection merely of prejudices and "preferences," determined entirely by the psychological and sociological forces that mold them. The institutions and habits of mass manipulation, and the ethos that justifies it, did not start with Nixon. There are members of the urban intelligentsia, very much against Nixon—too much against him, in a sense—who are not without their operational resemblance to him. We may all make a bit of a scapegoat out of Nixon, and further scapegoats out of the Watergate people. Their doings were not unique. The outlook on the world in that fraternity at the University of Southern California, or that Nixon White House, was not unique. The treatment of the public as a mass to be managed is a feature of the world view of many of those most vociferous in their antagonism to Richard Nixon. It will take something other than "hating" Nixon to root it out.

Gerald Ford, a commentator noted, *made* the football team at Michigan, and has not needed thereafter continually to prove himself a man by "winning." Perhaps it would have been better had Richard Nixon made the first team at Whittier. That might have meant he would not have had the drive to "fight," "hang tough," and "stonewall" through his career. He might just have been the football coach, and debate coach, at Whittier College, teaching some American history on the side. He might never have become president. But then, we might all thereby have been better off, including Richard Nixon. And he might have been a success.

10

On the Changing of
Presidents and the
Surprising Value of Politics

Politics, with its conflicts of interests and purposes, its interweaving of individual and collective destinies, its compound of the heroic, the mundane, the despicable, and the fairly good, its full supply of the variety of humanity and its common border with the tragic aspect of life, would appear to be a rich field for the literary artist. In other countries it has been. It says something both about this country's artists and about our national understanding of politics that even in these years of our stupendous power we have not had much serious politics in our serious literature. That is a pity. Perhaps it will change.

I am thinking, of course, not of the many popular and middle-brow writers who have often recently used Washington gossip and nuclear crises and presidential elections and other sensational political events as a background for entertainment. I am thinking, rather, of the artists who, like Henry James, have no ambition except the highest; James himself, living in England, wrote a novel of politics in two volumes. Yet I do not believe that the scholars of American literature would deny that politics, in both the broader and the narrower sense, has not played a large part in our most serious literary art. That art has floated on a raft down the Mississippi, set out from Nantucket on a whaling ship, explored the inner recesses of the New England heart, followed the bulls at Pamplona, returned to the regiment with a tattered flag, ached for Daisy across the lagoon, followed the small-town girl with her suitcase as she got off the train in the big city, chronicled the Southern temper in a Mississippi county. We do not have much of a literature that accepts and plumbs to its depths the dense adult world of institutions. And our literature in this regard is not unlike the rest of our culture.

In the turmoil of the late sixties the trendy and exhibitionistic novelist Norman Mailer did expand his own kind of political writing, to the good book on the Pentagon march of 1967 called *Armies of the Night*, and to the highly personal report called *Miami and the Siege of Chicago*. He explained, however, that his working principle for this enterprise was the deflationary slogan "Politics is property," and much of what he wrote about the mainstream politicians, as distinguished from his fellow revolutionaries for the weekend and his few heroes, did indeed reflect that view. I suggest that the adoption of such an inadequate principle by this ambitious writer confirms the point. That principle does not represent a wise or complex understanding of the political world. It seems to be approximately that Iron Law of Selfishness that has long served in place of a political philosophy for many cracker-barrel commentators, for many comedians and popular humorists, and even for many political reporters. The older type of newspaperman at city hall used to regard a kind of Menckenesque contempt for political man as a badge of the honor of his kind. "Politics is property" seems scarcely distinguishable from the common man's familiar cynicism about dirty politics and the unworthiness of politicians. It is not unlike the viewpoint of those academics who "scientifically" study politics by reducing all of the purposes in it, high ones and low ones, to self-interest. "Politics" in all these views is nothing but a struggle over who gets what—over the advantages of one kind or another that men want for themselves against others: status, financial reward, leverage on other people, even good seats in the convention hall.

Obviously men in politics as elsewhere do care about these things. The question is whether they care about anything else. One would have thought that the nation was already plentifully supplied with the sour negative to that question, and did not need another dose of it from an intelligent novelist.

Let me for purposes of the argument turn that slogan back onto Mailer himself. A writer's "property" is his hold on the attention of a public; without that he is nothing—especially if his name is

Norman Mailer. He has a large need for sheer publicity, a large stake in being colorful, different, interesting. Suppose he came onstage, in his role as political writer, as another liberal intellectual. Zero. Suppose then he were a fiery radical. Quite a number of those now; the Angry Young Man has been done. How about "left conservative"? Ah. That's better. There is a winning move to make to enhance a writer's property. What should he write about Richard Nixon? About the Yippies? About Mayor Daley? Among the unsurprising surprises in Mailer's books were the more favorable treatment of the Yippies, and a longer delay before he discovers that he likes McGovern, than the unimaginative public might have anticipated (but really what else could he have done? There was, for example, certainly no mileage left in yet another intellectual's denunciation of Nixon). So a calculating writer almost unconsciously adjusts, plans his work, protects and enlarges his holdings. Journalism is self-promotion, writing is publicity-seeking, the literary life is property.

Do I really believe all I have said about Mailer? Or the literary life? No, I don't. In fact, what I have set forth, even about so blatant and self-confessedly egotistical and publicity-seeking a writer as Mailer, is really only part of the truth. One can look at writing from the angle of publicity and of reputation, of reviews and cliques and fashions and notices and sales, of fame and notoriety. But in the middle of all the extraneous elements the pure and genuine article may stay in there, too, lodged in the make-up of the human beings who are trying to do their work and want things to be as they should be. Certainly in writing almost anything above the level of labels on cans, the thing gets its hooks in you and you want to get it right for a reason that would be hard to state but that certainly is not, any more, just publicity or vanity or self-promotion.

As with writers, so in their very different way with political men. No doubt political life attracts men who want power, as literature attracts men who want to make their individuality visible. In neither case does that selectivity obliterate all the other purposes and attachments that men can have. A writer has convictions on many subjects, and intellectual and esthetic standards, and an artistic conscience, all built into his being, which qualify and impede and deflect his calculations of pure self-aggrandizement. And something like that happens also with political men. For all his ego and his desire to see his name in print and to receive large royalty checks and have his book sold and read and talked about, a writer—some writers, some of the time—may get hooked a little on esthetic considerations, on "beauty," on wanting to get it right not for any extraneous reason but intrinsically. So political man, for all his love of power, may actually find himself caring about Justice and Liberty and the Common Good, even when he would be reluctant to use those words.

One should not ask that such a motive be exhibited in its pure form, or consistently. Politicians, like writers, differ widely, of course, and even the noblest politician's motives are mixed. So are those of an artist of the highest type. Moreover, the collaborative activity of the political man has different hazards from the lonely activity of the artist. There is a famous paragraph in the letters between Maxwell Perkins and Ernest Hemingway in which Perkins, who must have had a bad day at the publishing house, generalizes Tolstoy's presentation of young Pierre's astonishment at how different the actual battlefield is from his romantic imagining of it. So it is, said Perkins, with a young man's aspirations generally. There are always so many extraneous elements and limiting requirements! In any line of work

> nothing is ever in a condition of purity. . . . It is all bitched up with other things that do not belong in it. . . . A campaign is not conducted on pure military principles, but is all messed up with political, financial, and otherwise foreign elements. Everything is that way. Though, in art, everything can be excluded. But not easily . . . it is really the most shocking discovery a boy makes when he gets into anything.

If the boy goes into politics he should not be shocked: mixture and impurity (in Perkins' sense), with the continual shifting of strange bedfellows, are of the essence of the activity itself. Nevertheless, it has its ethical foundation, its own good, appropriate to the nature of the activity.

The uncovering of the Watergate evils, the removal of President Nixon, and his replacement by President Ford in August of

1974 displayed that political good in a way that stood in contrast to the sordid activities to which these events were a cathartic conclusion.

It is perhaps not necessary once more to call the roll of Watergate and impeachment heroes; perhaps it is better indeed not to use the word "hero." One does not want to defend the meritorious ingredient in American democratic politics quite in the way that young Senator John Kennedy did, lying in a hospital in Massachusetts with his bad back in 1954, working out with Ted Sorensen a list of Profiles in Courage. That conception—courageous self-sacrifice in politics—did not fit well with Kennedy's own career up to that moment, as was noted by the critics who wished he himself would show more courage and less profile. It did not adequately describe, either, the many merits of the rest of his career, which, although it certainly included varieties of individual "courage," had many other more complex virtues as well.

Nevertheless—to return to the events of 1972–74—the publisher and the editors of the Washington *Post* kept supporting the two young reporters on their metropolitan staff who had been assigned to the Watergate break-in in June of 1972 even when the rest of the press did not join in the coverage, and the public did not seem to be responding, and the immensely powerful Nixon White House was contemptuous, dismissive, and threatening. The stock of the Washington *Post* declined. A serious false step would have been a disaster for the newspaper. Katharine Graham and Benjamin Bradlee and Barry Sussman could not know that, in the end, they and Bob Woodward and Carl Bernstein would be covered with glory; they took a chance. Judge John Sirica might not be admired for all his methods by many who praised him in 1973 and 1974 in the Watergate case, but at critical points he did represent the claims of the law in the service of justice. So did the United States Supreme Court, with three justices appointed by Nixon joining in the unanimous 8–0 decision about the tapes in July 1974, a decision that was an essential part of the series of events that forced the delinquent president to resign. The role of Chief Justice Warren Burger is particularly to be noted: although appointed by Nixon, he wrote the opinion himself, and presumably figured in an important way in the internal court negotiations that made the decision unanimous.

It is to our point to extend the term "politics" to include all the participants in public affairs, but these examples—judges, newspapermen—are not drawn from politics in the sense that the man in the street uses the word. Nearer to politics in that narrower sense were the resignations of Elliot Richardson and William Ruckelshaus on the Saturday in October 1973 when they declined to obey the president's order to fire Archibald Cox. And perhaps after all the celebration of the role of the free press, the role of the bureaucrats who fed the press deserves notice: the civil servants who were the anonymous sources often risked a good deal personally to 'serve the integrity of the FBI, the IRS, the Department of Justice, the U.S. government, the public good. In the real world, the human beings who serve in "bureaucracies" do not become the "bureaucrats" of the usual negative stereotype; they retain the moral complexity of human beings everywhere, including the attachment to human good beyond the mere bureaucratic machinery. If "politics" deserves literary understanding, so does "bureaucracy": not Kafkaesque attack or satire or Dickensian caricature, but imaginative understanding.

There were many other honorable examples of resistance to the Nixonian effort to make federal agencies subservient to the partisan projects of the White House: Johnny Walters, one of the two IRS commissioners who resisted the White House people, was specifically praised in the public sessions of the House Judiciary Committee on the bill of impeachment.

Finally, there are the quintessential politicians, the men from Capitol Hill. In the televised Ervin committee hearings of the summer of 1973, and even more in the work of the House Judiciary Committee in 1974, members of Congress participated not only honorably, but also visibly, in the central constitutional process serving the interests of the nation. It should not have been necessary for the public to have television and drama in order to come to appreciate the serious purpose that Congress can sometimes fulfill, but it *was* necessary. It may be that these two examples of Congress making its virtues visible will mark another benefit of the Watergate scandals, and will help to rectify the imbalance created by the president's ready access to television.

Congress potentially embodies an ethic appropriate to a free society more clearly than the modern presidency has done: all sorts of societies, including very unfree ones, have leaders, treated with awe and ringed with majesty, their picture ubiquitous, their presence overwhelming, claiming to embody the will of the whole people. Only democracies, however, give real power to a deliberative body of peers, who must confront each other's egos, ideas, interests, and values, and arrive at a collaborative decision, and who must continually answer to the people for what they have done in this collaborative and deliberative way.

One value, of course, in the legislative ethic, and hence in democratic politics, is that it requires an acknowledgment by each of the existence and interest and differing opinion of another; and that out of that acknowledgment there comes adjustment, compromise, flexibility, and the limitation of opposition. Men are opponents today but not enemies forever: part of the superiority of Gerald Ford to Richard Nixon was said by many to rest here. That *is* a value, or a set of values, but in our "realistic," "political" reaction against the unpolitical naïvité of the surrounding environment, we stopped there, as we should not have done. Adjustment and the limitations of conflict carry you only so far. A political body may adjust downward or upward; it may at its best deliberate its way to a conclusion serving the community's good, as the House Judiciary Committee did in five memorable days before the television cameras.

Public reaction to that televised conclusion to the committee's work was revealing: how well, the people said, those congressmen comported themselves! Was there the trace of an insult in the element of public surprise at the dignity and serious intelligence of the committee's debate? Never mind. Congress has long suffered in public esteem from its complexity and from the mass public's impatience with the slowness and the long patches of dullness and the compromises of a parliamentary body. In other countries that impatience has provided dictators with their opportunity; the striking lone individual in his uniform, with his drama and mass appeal, with apparent efficiency and identification with emotion-laden national symbols, sneering at legislatures, causing people to stand around, and making or promising to make the trains run on time. We are a long way from that in this country, but the exaltation of the president and his family as celebrities, and his access to television, and the growth in numbers and in arrogance of the White House staff have partaken of this other principle: the one man to whom the masses feel (despite the antique Electoral College) they have given their direct grant of power, who encourages that feeling; who appears on their television screens repeatedly with the flag in his lapel, an impressive seal behind him, perhaps even a bust of Lincoln beside him. The televised Ervin committee hearings were one desirable democratic contrast to that theme; the House Judiciary Committee's were an even better one, because in that case the public could see congressmen soberly working their way to a decision of the utmost gravity: high politics at work. People saw young Representative William S. Cohen, Republican of Maine, ask in dismay: "How in the world did we ever get from the *Federalist Papers* to the edited transcripts?" They heard Representative James C. Mann, of South Carolina, soberly respond to a rhetorical question that under his oath every man would receive equal justice under the law, "be he president or be he pauper." They saw Republicans and Southern Democrats for whom the torment of decision was real, and not because they were worried merely about their constituencies. They heard a dignified debate, with the president's side well defended. They saw and heard part of a long deliberative process that came to a difficult result.

After the Judiciary Committee's vote and the Supreme Court's decision, the Nixon drama moved rapidly to its conclusion, with Alexander Haig and other staff members playing a subtle backstage role in the public interest.

When the new president struck the right notes, they represented the congressional ethic, the democratic "political" ethic in a high sense: not only adjustment, flexibility, and compromise, but also all these within the frame of an effort to make decisions for the public good.

Looking back over the whole sequence, one may ask: Can it be adequately described, by the prevailing reductionist views of politics, as merely a struggle of group interests for power? I suggest the answer is no.

In the early days of my own political life I sat in earnest conversation with a much older man, a celebrated Trumpet of Social Reform, beside a Wisconsin lake, not long after World War II.

"I have never in my life voted for a presidential candidate who won," he said, in amusement and some pride.

"And I would never have voted for a candidate who lost," I replied, with at least equal pride.

He had voted always for Norman Thomas or Eugene Debs. What I meant, of course, was that had I been old enough to vote, I would have voted for Franklin Roosevelt four times.

It still does not seem that losing, as such, is evidence of political virtue. But now, after watching one's friends seek power, and some of them achieve it, and after living in and around the politics of the last quarter century, one would be a good deal less cocky about the desire to "win."

We had to argue back then against perfectionist politics—like that of the Norman Thomas voter—who seemed to treat politics as merely a test of ideological purity or personal character, without reference to the realistic work of putting together a coalition, winning elections, and governing. We would say in arguments with men like him that it is not true that the sole important thing in politics is for me and my candidate to be Right and Pure; the question is not the purity and ideological perfection of my position, but its role in the process of shaping the society. Politics is the uniting of purpose with power—that is the sort of thing we used to say. We would quote that sentence from Shaw, against the idea that the world is just a moral gymnasium in which to exercise one's principles. We would say that these pure idealists—the man with whom I was arguing—undefiled by the stain of actual victory, power, or responsibility would be at best a zero in politics and more often a minus quantity, used by the children of darkness for perverse ends. I said to that Norman Thomas Trumpet in 1946 that economic royalists who grew apoplectic at the mention of Roosevelt could be mild or even admiring about Thomas because he was no threat; he might even draw votes away from Roosevelt, and in any case would never be so vulgar as actually to obtain power and to begin doing things.

So the argument went back then. So one would argue again more recently, when a perfectionist politics showed up once more, after we thought it had almost vanished. I did not expect that I would ever have the opportunity to vote for a candidate who had read the complete works of Walter Rauschenbusch; having had that opportunity in 1972, I hope never to have it again.

Those of us who knew that world, and learned to argue against its faults, would resist what we saw to be its separation of ideals from political and human realities. We said that excessively famous statement of Lord Acton's, that power tends to corrupt, is not the only truth: the *lack* of power also corrupts; having power but not using it for constructive purpose also corrupts. There are sins of avoidance, ommission, and laziness as well as sins of strength and tyranny. That is what we would say back then, and it is true. Nevertheless, after one has seen some of one's friends and some of one's own generation in power, one would be more willing to admit that, when all of these additional points are made, still what Lord Acton said, for all its being excessively familiar, is partly true.

Power tends to corrupt. Sometimes power enobles, but don't count on it every time power is transferred.

Is it that power tends to corrupt? Or that power offers many possibilities, and some men tend to make corrupt use of it? As the arrogant youngsters of recent administrations demonstrated, such men weaken the internal institutional restraints upon power—the legal and moral restraints. In this sense we may say that men corrupt power. To pursue Lord Acton one step further, we may add that some men corrupt power absolutely, as the Nixon administration was to demonstrate.

But that is one part only of the story of democratic politics, as a literary artist would tell it. Those figures in the unraveling of Watergate listed above were not corrupted by power. Many used it responsibly; it is not unknown for a man to use it heroically.

Another slogan of these older arguments with the utopian was, of course, that politics is the art of the possible—a banal half-truth at best. High politics, as said before, is the art not only of the possible, but also of the fulfillment of the largest possibilities, the enlargement of what is possible, the making of what had hitherto been impossible come within the range of what can be considered.

There was a time when we were all saying that it was not really possible, under the American system, to supplant a delinquent president. The nation could not stand the "trauma." And there are many peoples on this earth who would not believe it possible to force the resignation of an immensely powerful chief of state who desperately wanted to remain in office—and to do it altogether peacefully, without any guns or generals or barricades. But gradually, by the acts and beliefs of many men, in the United States it became possible, and we did it.

Part Two

Some American Values

Bittersweet
Land of Liberty

The modern United States is not "rotten," nor is it "sick," but like all cultures it has a warp in it. It has a distinct shape, and that shape has its distinct faults—faults not only "out there" in the overpowering machinery of modern society, but also in the "pictures in our heads." A chief fault, in fact, is to be found in the relation, or nonrelation, between the two: between the too individualistic pictures in many American heads and the ever more tightly interconnected and powerful social machinery that the citizens of this country are collectively trying to manage. A large number of Americans are trying to cope with the interdependence of an advanced technological society with a defectively individualistic culture: with the age of energy crises, Polaris missiles, cable television, and transplants of human organs with an outlook rooted in the small town, the farm, the revival meeting, and the corner grocery store.

Although, if one has a taste for complexity, one may say that the defects are many and subtle, one may also truthfully reduce them to a small number, or even, almost, to one. If forced to do this, to get the point, to summarize America's fundamental troubles while standing on one foot, one might use the very same words that the man in the street, or the president, or the national scriptures would use to say why America is "great": "individualism" and "freedom." That is why the problem is subtle: one must make close discriminations between central virtues and central vices, which stand close enough to each other to be called by the same name.

While writing this, I saw a small item about Horatio Alger, Jr., in the New York *Times*. Yet another novel from his hand had just been discovered. This brought the total of his known productions to 119—most of them the American melodramas about "Ragged Dick" and "Paul the Pedlar" and "Tattered Tom," the poor boy who makes the million that we associate with Alger's name. The *Times* story also reported this staggering, if somewhat loose, statistic: it is estimated that there are between 200 million and 400 million copies of the Alger books in print. These are certainly figures to make a writer's mouth water, a success story indeed. Then at the end of this newspaper account of the discovery of the new book there appeared this paragraph, gratuitously and a little unfairly put there, one assumes, by some envious reporter inclined toward negative thinking:

Horatio Alger's own life did not end as successfully as his stories. He died, alone and unhappy, at 65, after three tragic love affairs and the death of a boy he had adopted.

Life, even in America, is not like the plots of stories by Horatio Alger. Achievement is not automatically crowned with happiness. A man's plans go astray. Men probably are not captains of their souls and certainly are not masters of their fate. The impossible does not take "a little longer": it is impossible. No man is a self-made man. The race is not to the swift, nor the battle to the strong . . . nor yet riches to men of understanding, nor yet favour to men of skill; but time and chance happeneth to them all.

Not only do "time and chance" happen to us all, but the intervention of wills other than our own: other individuals, "pursuing" happiness (in that odd Jeffersonian word) in their own way, and getting in the way of our pursuit, using it for theirs, perhaps. And these many crisscrossing pursuings of happiness intersect to form a giant clover leaf of culture that sharply blocks, guides, restricts the individual pursuits. The idea of the free individual "pursuing" his own happiness, the centerpiece of American civilization, one might almost say, works out this way: when all the "pursuits" by all the free individuals are added, the result is a situation with which not so many are as "happy" as might be expected—as they expected. And not so many feel very "free." And the complex of individualisms is not very individualistic.

The accumulation of unintended side effects from the decisions we each "freely" take is a different world from that any of us individually intended. That is the story of the economy built around the "free" market. The invisible hand comes up with visible results that many do not want. Or *should* not want. And that is the story also of technology and of its cousin, bureaucracy, which are not provided for in America's individualistic theory but are omnipresent in modern American reality.

Two forces intersect to make our characteristic modern American difficulty. One is the excessive individualism of our moral, political, economic, and intellectual heritage, in which there is not enough recognition of the shaping of persons by the community and the need of the self for community. The other is the mammoth centripetal force of modern technology, gathering us ever more tightly together in an interdependence our theory is reluctant to recognize or respond to.

I say the "centripetal" force, but, as many modern social analyses make clear, there is simultaneously something like a centrifugal force: as society is driven toward more centralized power, so at the same time men are spun out into a more fragmented and separated condition. One of the standard statements on these matters, Karl Mannheim's *Man and Society in an Age of Reconstruction*, put it this way:

. . . the interdependence of all its parts makes the modern order much more sensitive than a simpler form of economic organization. Indeed, the more minutely the individual parts of a large mechanism fit into one another, and the more closely the single elements are bound up together, the more serious are the repercussions of even the slightest disturbance. In a well-organized railway, for instance, the effects of an accident are more far-reaching than they were in the stage coach system of transport, where accidents and dislocation were taken for granted from the very beginning.

Mannheim wrote that when the railway was the evident example. In the seventies the daily news and daily life, although still sufficiently supplied with railroad breakdowns (we can get a man to the moon but we cannot get trains regularly from Long Island into New York City), explode with far more pungent examples. A strike by fewer than 2,000 newsdealers in New York

City had drastic repercussions on the American theater and the book trade because the newsdealers shut down the big newspapers, and the Broadway theaters and the bookstores depend decisively upon reviews and advertisements in the newspapers. A handful of Arab oil sheiks in a desert can make a rich nation of 200 million people drive fifty-five miles an hour, line up for gas, shift from Cadillacs to Datsuns. The latest power failure or strike in an essential field, even more, the latest skyjacking, political kidnaping, or terrorist act, shows the vulnerability of centralized and interdependent modern social machinery. Henry Kissinger wrote in his *Nuclear Weapons and Foreign Policy* a remarkable few pages about the impact of a nuclear bombardment on the apparatus of a modern city. Walter Lippmann, back in the twenties, took a modern man's breakfast as a symbol and example of modern interdependence, suggesting to the sociological imagination the multiplicity and range of activities it takes to bring a twentieth-century city dweller his eggs, his bacon, his coffee, and his morning newspaper. Or one may go in imagination down the street and around the square in Winnebago, Nebraska; Lompoc, California; Laramie, Wyoming, to suggest the many links between the modern small town and a thousand remote centers of supply, decision, and control: the Union Pacific; the OEO; the A & P; Piggley-Wigleys; Texaco. In the county seat of Wolfe County, Kentucky, it's the IGA and then a row of federal agencies in dreary storefronts.

It is not hard (it is almost too easy) to bring any American to see what he calls "Bigness" in the dominating giant nationwide organizations, in commerce, manufacturing, transportation, government, and communication. When the young congressman from Maine began discussing in 1956 what speech Adlai Stevenson ought to give, he vibrated with vicarious passion when he thought how the people in his district would respond to a speech attacking "Bigness." Of course they would, then and now. And over in President Eisenhower's speech-writing office someone was no doubt composing (in a less graceful, literate, and allusive version) the same speech.

The bureaucratic commercial and governmental giants are interwoven with all the specialized and interrelated activities that brought Lippmann his breakfast in the twenties and put Neil Armstrong on the moon in the sixties. It is not difficult to make plain a relationship between these giants and the "advances" of technology. Mannheim, in another passage in the same book, uses for illustration and symbol the enlarging numbers of persons who can be threatened—controlled—by "advancing" weaponry: the bow and arrow; the longbow and catapult; gunpowder and early musketry; machine guns and bombs; bombs plus airplanes. He had not yet seen the nuclear and thermonuclear leap in this sequence, which "advanced" and reduced it to the paradoxes and absurdities with which we have been living since 1945. Early in the age of "nuclear plenty" there was a comic movie called "The Mouse That Roared," in which one little Lichtensteinian country with the bomb made all the world submit.

In "communication" the sequence is almost as startling, from the messenger on his horse through the telegraph and telephone, point to point, to satellite relaying pictures simultaneously to hundreds of millions around the world. Bad jokes told in beautiful downtown Burbank are carried instantly to the TV screen of a bar in the hills of West Virginia and to hundreds of thousands of living rooms—to 40 million people or more. Ninety-six per cent of American households, at this time, have those TV sets which show forth their contributions to culture in song and story for six hours and eighteen minutes, on the average, per day. One hundred and ten million people simultaneously watched Richard Nixon's speech of resignation in August 1974; 125 million watched the moon walk in July 1969. TV people used to cite one Shakespearean production in their medium that was seen by more people than had seen all the stage productions of all of Shakespeare's plays in the three and a half centuries since he wrote them.

It is easy enough to see how decisions made in a few central locations affect more people than they once did. The next step is to see the seepage of these decisions, and of nondecisions, and of side effects, into the life of a culture. One asks students to list unintended side effects of the automobile, from the end of Sunday-evening church services and courting in the parlor to the growth of suburbs and Los Angeles smog, and then do the same with TV and nuclear weaponry. All of that is easy enough: centralization, giant organizations, specialized knowledge, the division of labor, dependence and interdependence.

The simultaneous centripetal force, fragmenting and separating persons, is easy enough to perceive, too: the multiple relationships one had to Mrs. Bulwinkle in the idealized small town, not only in the sale at the grocery store but also in the church choir, the junior high school PTA, and down the block at home. It is not so with the salesclerk at Macy's, whom one will never see again; or with the toll collector who takes your quarter on the Connecticut Turnpike. It is not a personal relationship, even though he has his name on a name plate beside his window. "You are welcome, Mr. Barberi!"

The theorists of a "mass society" have dramatized these two simultaneous and only apparently contradictory forces: toward the giant organization, with its enormously powerful center in the situation room, the board room, the network office; toward separation, fragmentation, very specialized work, "loneliness." American young people in a university with 30,000 students, assigned by a computer to a class of 400, have little difficulty perceiving and accepting the "mass society" melodrama. Perhaps they accept it too easily, or in too simple a form: there may be a romanticizing of the small town and the multiple personal relationships with Mrs. Bulwinkle; in Winesburg, Ohio, the result was not ideal. Perhaps, also, many a modern American audience (especially a young one) accepts too readily a caricature of the "mass society," the "technological" society, the bureaucratic and "impersonal" conditions of modernity. "Your name is a number; your number's a case." More careful observers will correct the simple, and usually simply negative, picture of a giant "impersonal" manipulative mass society. It is not that simple, it is not that bad, and the benefits that accompany this modern technology should not be discounted.

Nevertheless, it is a different society from the much simpler one in which an American social picture and American values were shaped.

And that picture was distorted, and those values somewhat

warped, even before social reality took its modern shape. I do not mean in the celebrated Founding Fathers, in whom, if one takes the right passages from the right Fathers, one has something better than what came later. Neither do I mean the colonial Puritans, who with all their defects differed on the major point from the American who was to come. I mean characteristic American social ideas as they grew in the nineteenth century into the individualistic libertarian set of values that still has force today. Already, before the corporations and factories and cities grew and the new inventions spun out their effects upon the social fabric, this American outlook insufficiently recognized community as a fact, a man's dependence upon other men as a fact, our social obligation as a central duty.

This nation has been so thoroughly built on the picture of the separate private individual, fundamentally unrelated to his fellow beings and to society at large, as to impede social understanding even before the swirling complexity of a modern technological society. Put shortly, America, as all the world knows, is too individualistic—individualistic in one sense of the word only: in some other senses, to be sure, it is not individualistic enough. Many writers have observed the peculiar combination of a nation in which there is a conformity of individualism, where men proclaiming the virtues of self-reliance, of individualism, and of each man making his own way, are shocked when a man has a different sort of a haircut or maintains ideas different from the standard individualistic forms.

America is warped in an individualistic, separatist, and voluntary direction because the forces making the culture have tended so consistently in that one direction. In political and social ideas, as an important book by Louis Hartz (*The Liberal Tradition in America*) put it, we are the land of a "colossal liberal absolutism" ("liberal" here in the classical textbook sense). We are a nation whose coming into being coincided with the rise of European liberalism—that is, of the middle-class individualism of the bourgeoisie—and which is therefore "born free" and "does not have to become so." We are a nation with no feudal Catholic corporate past, and no serious revolutionary party: a country lacking those two very different forms of a more collective understanding. We are John Locke writ large, seeing the individual standing separated from and prior to society.

One can extend Hartz's conception from politics to religion: we are the land not only of John Locke but also of John Calvin writ large, or perhaps, as the circuit riders and camp meetings spread westward in the nineteenth century, of John Wesley. This was not only the country with liberalism on the ground floor—and therefore pervasive and unchallenged, in contrast to Europe—but also with Protestantism on the ground floor. And Protestantism of the Puritan and sectarian sort—the more individualistic sort—built around the notion of a "converted" individual. Men are "converted" one by one; the appeal is to the individual will; the revival meeting spread across this country in repeated ways, teaching its lesson of an individual change in a moment in answer to that moment's call. From this country they went out elsewhere with a similar message. This was the land of the missionaries, the revivals, the voluntary associations, the adult baptism, the individual convert who would change society by permeating it with his own individual moral change.

Classical liberalism; free church Protestantism; and, most important of all now, capitalism. Classical capitalist economics has a principle of individualism at its core, and the most effective defenders, early and late, of an individualistic outlook have been the defenders of the free market. The individual consumer freely makes his choice; the market freely indicates to the individual producer what he is to do. This nation, as the leading exemplar of capitalism, has kept reinforcing the competitive individualist picture by the benefits of a productive economy. The most remarkable chapter in Hartz's book is the one on the way the non-business working classes were won over to Horatio Alger Americanism by the discovery of "the capitalist in every man." Instead of looking to one's fellows in solidarity, one looks to one's own individual future, in which one may leave one's fellow behind in an upward rise to fortune. With the giant corporations and the larger body of wealthy citizens, the United States since the Civil War has generated an enormously powerful vested interest in the free-enterprise ideology.

The United States had these great modern forces—liberalism in politics, sectarian Protestantism in religion, and, above all, capitalism in the economy—more fully developed and with fewer rivals than did other, older, nations.

And the individualism they reinforce in each other has been protected and reinforced by the historical good fortune of the nation they have shaped. The United States has had almost 200 years under one written constitution, and extraordinary political success. It has had a continuing economic rise of spectacular proportion, and no defeat in a war. The sometimes maturing lessons of collective defeat, of tragedy, of scarcity have not affected our culture as a whole, through which there runs a vein of sentimentality.

And democracy in our American sense—the equality of condition that Tocqueville examined—has reinforced the competitive individualism by removing other bases of prestige and deference—rank, nobility, family, traditional authority—that might qualify the emphasis on success, the upward rise, the individual in the market.

The result of these influences has been America's quite unusual voluntarism and individualism: the picture of individuals each by his own will achieving what he desires. The historian David Potter wrote, in *People of Plenty:*

Americans have always been especially prone to regard all things as resulting from the free choice of a free will. Probably no people have so little determinism in their philosophy, and as individuals we have regarded our economic status, our matrimonial happiness, and even our eternal salvation as things of our own making.

The well-known fact that our material place in the world, in particular, is seen to be of our own making; and, a very important matter, has well-known and undesirable moral consequences.

It inflates the ego and increases the power of those who are "successful" (successful by a big Cadillac measure) and damages the self-respect of those who are not. It sets before the eyes of its children the goals of big Cadillacs, names on the door with the Bigelow on the floor, names in lights, "I had 700 people working under me." One is told by one's culture that these are worthy goals, that they are indeed the most important goals in life, and even that they define one's manhood. We therefore not only distort the meaning of human life in a tawdry direction but also obscure the element of luck and the assistance of others and the importance of the social fabric in a man's personal fortune. Men have little trouble believing statements, however remote from the truth, that are flattering to themselves: the men sitting around the pool at the Arizona Biltmore give every indication that they believe the American success mythology *in toto*.

Men who have had the foresight—as in the Herblock cartoon of Barry Goldwater—to inherit a department store look down on those who have not been so enterprising.

In the Detroit of the nineteen-twenties, when Henry Ford's conversion from the Model T to the Model A threw streams of workers out on the streets for six months, Reinhold Niebuhr wrote, in bemused exasperation, "What a Civilization this is! Naïve gentlemen with a genius for mechanics suddenly become the arbiters over the lives and fortunes of hundreds of thousands." The naïve gentleman he had chiefly in mind was also taken seriously as a thinker, a leader, a guide and model for the young.

The values were ridiculous, and so was the interpretation of the individual and society. Ford needed the luck to come along at the right moment—not ten years earlier or later—in the development of the internal-combustion engine, and in factory production, and in the economy, and he needed the roads built by government for other sorts of vehicles, in order for his individual effort to be a "success."

Beware the man who has risen to the top from one suspender. And among those not so "successful," by those measures of competition, remember that sad and revealing feature of the Great Depression, when 13 million persons—one-fourth of the work force—were unemployed. That was obviously a collective catastrophe, but millions of the unemployed lost their self-respect and blamed themselves. They took this *social* phenomenon as a *personal* failure, as one can read in Studs Terkel's *Hard Times*. They were humiliated in their own eyes, in the eyes of their children, their wives, and their fellows because they could not find a job.

And on the other side of the tracks there is an unnecessary

callousness toward others differently situated from oneself. The individualistic ethic encourages a lack of imagination about persons whose environment is different from one's own.

This is by no means unique to the United States, to be sure, but it is strong here, and especially notable in a people otherwise marked by charitable and humane activities: we so desperately fear that somebody somewhere is getting something for nothing. Each effort to deal with the plight of the poorest citizen meets an enormous mythology of resentment: the poor man of Five Points will spend the money at the saloon; the WPA worker will spend the day leaning on his shovel; the welfare chiseler drives away in his welfare Cadillac. These recurrent and insistent popular pictures are like that story of the beggar who has half a million dollars in the mattress. They are kept afloat by a popular desire to believe that these others are not genuinely needful.

Finally, the most important for the present argument, the American ethic of competition and success and the voluntary-individualist picture of society encourages neglect of the civic virtues. It makes the public realm far, far less important than the private realm of career, and gives a particular encouragement to the selfishness that (in one form and another) marks human beings in any culture. Other cultures have other forms of selfishness. Another, older, culture, more hardhearted at its core, might be shown in a Henry James novel to be more cynical: men might understand better the social ramifications of their lives, and nevertheless dismiss the moral implications. But our American style is to deny them—to be blinded by the picture in our heads, to tighten up and resist—as American middle-class listeners resist—any criticism of the cluster of values around the idea of competitive self-advancement.

/

A glance at popular culture or a conversation with America in the raw on the highway or in the Middle Western freshman classroom will confirm that this familiar structure of corrupt objectives and distorted understandings still is very much alive. The ethic of competitive individualism is still powerful, given a new boost by some political and social accidents of recent years. The blue-collar worker, and the white ethnic groups, reassert a version of this older ethic in their unhappiness with the radicalism of the late sixties, with black militancy and black pressure, and with the neglect of their own status and problems. We *worked!* Nobody helped us! One might say it is rather curious how we Protestants have corrupted the Catholics and Jews who came to this country! Both Judaism and Roman Catholicism have a more adequate communal understanding than does Protestant Christianity, especially the Protestantism that flourished in the New World. But these older Western religions, coming into this land of liberty with poor immigrant populations, have grasped at least a part of the ethic of upward advance with a particularly intense grip.

The familiar aspects and results of this competitive individualism include the "work ethic" (one should put it in quotation marks); the seeking of *tangible* success (the sort of success that can be seen and recognized immediately by large numbers of ordinary people: visible wealth and fame and power); the focus upon private satisfaction, private career, private material well-being.

On the "work ethic" here is a quotation from an American who, not long ago, had a certain influence:

Recently we have seen that work ethic come under attack. We hear voices saying that it is immoral or materialistic to strive for an ever-higher standard of living. We are told that the desire to get ahead must be curbed because it leaves others behind. . . . We see some members of disadvantaged groups being told to take the welfare road rather than the road of hard work, self-reliance, and self-respect.

Richard Nixon objected to the message these "voices" convey. But as John Stuart Mill observed, men are often right in what they affirm, but wrong in what they deny. So it is with these defenses of an American inclination to put a high value on "work." Work and purposefulness are good, but when they are defended in such a way as to imply a false picture of the world, and to deny other values, they are not so good. Why did Nixon introduce into his homily on work a pointed reference to "disadvantaged groups"?

To do honorable work, for service to other people and one's own fulfillment, for the satisfaction of doing something worth-while and doing it right, and also to pull one's weight in the community, is indeed a value. It is a value that its defenders rightly claim to have been a strength of this particular country. But as with all ethical positions one must ask whether this ethic is applied self-critically. There is the temptation to apply all values in such a way as to vindicate and exalt the self and put down and undercut another. *"I worked—why can't they?"* is the defensive version of the work ethic, a deep and constant American theme, cruel in its social outcome (it vindicates callousness and encourages pride). The dubious feature in Nixon's remark is not his desire to endorse the hard work of the blue-collar and white ethnic Americans, but the clear implication that somebody else (black, poor, "disadvantaged," on welfare) has not worked and has taken a different road from "hard work, self-reliance, and self-respect."

All moral perspectives imply some picture of the world. The success ethic implies that the world is open, in fact, to the success stories pictured in the Horatio Alger books, and that such success is a possibility for everyone, and that it depends entirely upon one's self—one's own self-reliant activity. In fact, it does not. The world is not like that, and our life is not like that. In fact, our lives are full not only of luck, good and bad, but also of a whole set of relations to others: we are dependent and interdependent in the very nature of human life, of man as a social animal. Unless one is Robinson Crusoe, "work" itself is eminently *social*. We are increasingly dependent and interdependent in a world built around modern technology—around the great principle of the division of labor, elaborated more and more thoroughly.

2

Those who take a more favorable view of the American ethos on these matters—for example David Potter, in his *People of Plenty*—argue first that America's wealth (itself a good) is in large part the result of our individualistic work ethic, and, second, that it has made democracy possible.

It is not simply our natural resources, says Potter, that made America a land of abundance. The Indians had those resources. It is not true that "Americans are a people who have wandered unwittingly into a cornucopia whose plenty is accepted with moronic content." On the contrary, the cornucopia is a result largely of the effort and work of the people who came to this continent. Greenland is a different country to the Vikings, to the Eskimo, and to Americans. "The American standard of living is the resultant much less of natural resources than of the increase of capacity to produce and that was the result, directly, of human endeavor. . . ." Some social critics have implied that America's great wealth was simply the gift of the natural wealth of the continent. Not so! It depended upon what was in the mind and the habits of the people who came to the continent. It may not be the most poetic thing in the world to look at a tree and see lumber, and seeing lumber to see dollar signs, and seeing dollar signs to see oneself successful and exalted, but it does have its advantages in material productivity.

And, so the argument goes on, this wealth that came from effort made our American kind of equality possible—was conducive to our political democracy. Our American outlook on equality—equality of opportunity—requires that enough of the promissory notes of democracy actually be fulfilled to keep the myth alive. Abundance allows that to happen. So says David Potter. And, as many scholars say, a certain level of economic development is a condition of an effective function in political democracy. So, the argument goes, not only is the material abundance itself to be counted to our credit, but also its support for a democratic society. Many underdeveloped nations, whose critics may disapprove of American bustle, energy, materialism, and success-seeking, wish nevertheless (when they deal with social policy) that their culture had more of the habits produced by the work ethic.

But need the work ethic be the success ethic? We are coming to a time when that question will press more forcibly upon us.

Should the motive of functioning—working—be the individual's "upward" movement? By its nature that mobility is not a possibility for all, and it distorts the motives and the values of life. Today there is a debate between the older "meritocratic" ideas, of a career open to talent, and equality of opportunity, and the qualification of that, with reference to minority groups, by the so-called "equality of group results." But neither the one nor the other is altogether satisfactory so long as they are built around the metaphor of a race—a race to be won, with some persons (or groups) winning and others losing—one race, all entered, with one measure of the outcome.

The phrase "equality of results" passed by acceptably enough in the swift blur of President Johnson's excellent speech at Howard University in June 1965, but it had a more dubious aspect when one read a more extended presentation of the idea in the famous "Report" on the "Negro Family" written by Daniel Patrick Moynihan.

There it seemed to mean that parity of actual achievement as among ethnic groups should be the conscious object of government policy. "It is increasingly demanded that the distribution of success and failure within one group be roughly comparable to that within other groups," Moynihan wrote. "It is not enough that all individuals start out on even terms, if members of one group almost invariably end up well to the fore, and those of another far to the rear." Surely one must disagree with that. It certainly *would* be "enough" if all individuals "started" on something like "even terms," if we are to persist in this metaphor of "starting" and ending a "race." One objects to the way members of groups "end up" only because, when dealing with large numbers, gross differences indicate that they really *do not* "start" on even terms. The enormous disparities in the outcome of white and Negro life show by inference the disparities in original circumstances.

What was to be achieved in the "next and more profound stage," as Johnson called it—a stage that really has not yet come, with Vietnam and Nixon and economic trouble intervening—was not a new kind of equality, but a deeper understanding of the restrictions on the old equality—the accumulated and environ-mental restrictions on what we still can call by the American slogan "equality of opportunity."

But surely we do not want to have the terrible principle of the balanced ticket spread everywhere throughout the nation's life. Moynihan made one uneasy when he added with apparent ap-proval after the sentences quoted above, "This is what ethnic pol-itics are all about in America." There were two objections to fit-ting the new stage in justice for blacks into the frame of the old ethnic politics of American cities. First, mistreatment of the black American differs from that accorded white minority groups not just in degree but in kind, because of racism, slavery, and legal segregation; and, second, so-called ethnic politics is now a menace to the commonweal. One hopes for the day when it is dead.

Our American hearts still swell when the orator reaches that high moment in which he includes in the great democratic em-brace *all* Americans, "without regard to . . ." Is that bad? In some circumstances it is naïve; in some it is worse than naïve, a rationalization for inaction, the racial equivalent of majestically allowing rich and poor alike to sleep under railroad bridges. Nev-ertheless, this inclusiveness of ours is one of our more desirable popular values, and it often also reflects prudence in practical pol-itics. The presumption should be in its favor; exceptions should bear the burden of proof.

Are there reasons for public policy to single out blacks? Yes, where combating a distinct present-day race-related evil. But the racial discrimination in this new stage of things gets many of its evil effects through the intermediary of the slums and poverty which also affect nonblacks. Income is a more significant correlate of family disorganization than is race.

The government actions that can help "the Negro family" help other families, too; programs in this "next and more profound stage" (when it comes, in truth), as distinguished from the other stages of the black movement, apply also to nonblacks. Nothing in Johnson's phrases at Howard about how "men are shaped by their world" applies exclusively to blacks.

There has been a reversal—quite necessary, but one hopes not

permanent—in the roles of individualism and of group interpretations in the discussion of civil rights. In the old days of "race relations," it was the bigot who thought in group terms, about the
"Negro" this and the "Negro" that, and it was the man of enlightenment—naïvely, no doubt, from our present point of view—who
resisted such a group interpretation and said we must "treat each
man as an individual." Now, with the changes of the years—
mostly progress, partly not—it is the angry white opponents of
busing in the North who say that they resist taking color into account, who speak of *all* children individually and without respect
to race; it is the progressive proponents of black rights who make
group interpretations, who insist that the society and government
cannot be color-blind, that they must take race and color into account in order to overcome the disabilities that accompany them
(for example, in *de facto* segregation of schools and neigh-
borhoods). Counting blacks (counting women!) is now a necessity. But one does not want to see these temporary expedients un-
necessarily expanded, or written into the permanent categories of
the nation.

If we substitute some notion of *group* "success" in a race for the
older notion of the individual's "making it," we will not have
improved the situation. One wants such policies as are necessary
to eliminate categorical barriers, including the environmental
barriers deposited by history. Thus it may be necessary to use
"compensatory" "affirmative action" measures, including, in the
gross instance, a quota (in all-white construction unions in a heavily black city). But these are dangerous instruments, to be used
sparingly and with care, only for the purpose of breaking through
entrenched barriers, of overcoming categorical exclusions.

The fault in the historic American attitude is not only in the
excessively individualist picture of the world, but also in the goals
of living.

I read sometimes to classes of American students these paragraphs from R. H. Tawney, on the capitalist-individualist up-
wardly moving picture of life:

It is possible that intelligent tadpoles reconcile themselves to the inconveniences of their position by reflecting that, though most of them will live and die as tadpoles and nothing more, the more fortunate of the species will one day shed their tails, distend their mouths and stomachs, hop nimbly on to dry land, and croak addresses to their former friends on the virtues by means of which tadpoles of character and capacity can rise to be frogs. This conception of society may be described perhaps, as the Tadpole Philosophy, since the consolation which it offers for social evils consists in the statement that exceptional individuals can succeed in evading them. . . . And what a view of human life such an attitude implies! As though opportunities for talent to rise could be equalized in a society where the circumstances surrounding it from birth are themselves unequal! As though, if they could, it were natural and proper that the position of the mass of mankind should permanently be such that they can attain civilization only by escaping from it! As though the noblest use of exceptional powers were to scramble to shore, undeterred by the thought of drowning companions!

The merit of solid work does not require comparisons, competitions, and invidious and disdainful attitudes. The "success" ethic in fact may be at odds with the work ethic—if it encourages, as a good part of American history since the Civil War suggests that it does, cutting corners, sharp practice, getting your fee while the widow's tears are hot, "business is business." That is not the work ethic; that is something else, an ethic of the jungle. "Getting ahead" and "making it" and "room at the top" and "if you're so smart, why aren't you rich" are the sayings of a society rather different from one that would say: To labor is to pray.

3

Is this all still true, this old familiar picture of the individualistic success-seeking American? Thoughtful students raise their hands in the back of the room and suggest three other views:

1. That we are a nation of "joiners";
2. That we have a strong tradition of social reform and of the politics of social justice; and

3. That recently we have been in danger more of "conformity" than of individualism.

As to the first, our being a nation of "joiners," of many groups and organizations: the student has read Toqueville and so he asks about the many "voluntary associations" that flourished in the nineteenth century in this country and that the visiting Frenchman found impressive. Or he has read Daniel Boorstin and he asks about the American tradition of "philanthropy," not matched elsewhere: the charitable giving to settlements, libraries, hospitals, and foundations. He may quote Gunnar Myrdal: no nation has as many "cheerful givers" as the United States.

The answers to these comments are not hard to extract from the other students who have understood their homework. These references do not contradict the fundamental point, about American individualism, careerism, and preference for the voluntary. Those who have read Niebuhr make a sharp contrast between "charity" (in the slightly debased use we make of that word) and "justice": the former is an overflowing of largesse, reflecting the goodness and the voluntary action of the giver, upon whom the recipient has no claim of right, a "charity" that in conditions of sharp injustice can even be morally putrid. The workers in the cramped berry-picking company towns reject the baskets of food from the wealthy ladies as a kind of insult to their humanity. As the pickets' signs used to say, We want *justice* not charity.

A major section of the American middle classes—let us say, to pick an example not altogether at random, the voters of Grand Rapids—have not characteristically understood this distinction. They have not advanced beyond the voluntary gift-giving charity that leaves the structure of society untouched, and at its worst leaves it reinforced. They do not accept the claims of social justice against some part of the structure itself: the cramped company town, contrasted to the houses on the hill. And the failure to comprehend that distinction is a reflection of the underlying conservative or uncritical individualism, the outlook that takes the given social order completely for granted.

If we are a nation of "joiners," we join clubs and associations and movements voluntarily with various superficial purposes; or if the purpose is social reform (as in the stream of "voluntary associations" flowing out of the free churches in the nineteenth century) then reform is by means of persuasion and exhortion, by change-of-heart one-by-one voluntary means.

Insofar as the United States has in its culture a component of disinterested altruism and social conscience, it ranks high; insofar as its competitive individualism and devotion to the market impedes that altruism, it does not rank so high.

4

It is true, as to the second point, that for all its alleged free-enterprise individualism—the American language that often leaves European observers aghast—the United States has in fact developed a remarkable tradition of social reform and a structure not only of charity and philanthropy but also of social justice. Gunnar Myrdal notes that even American social progressives use the word "freedom" before "equality": but we have, nevertheless, a considerable egalitarian and humanitarian tradition, not only of the "charity" kind, but expressed in law and policy, too. A student with some history may then list the mainstream of American democratic reform: the Jeffersonian movement, surprising the Federalists with the votes of the people and the existence of a party of those out of power; the Jacksonian movement, with the first bold appearance of the common man; the abolition movement, the greatest of our moralistic social crusades; the Populist movement of the late nineteenth century, and the Progressive movement of the early twentieth; and then the New Deal, the Fair Deal, the New Frontier, and the Great Society: a very considerable heritage of political action directed toward social justice. There is this main tradition, conglomerate and variegated though it be, of the more "liberal" or "progressive" or "democratic" side of our political history; there is alongside it, still more conglomerate, sometimes feeding into it and sometimes flowing away, a collection of social movements, crusades, and third parties, "radical" or reformist, that may affect the society in the longer run.

Put these all together and they make a significant part of American history. Therefore: are we so individualistic after all? Yes, on the whole. One may construct a picture of American political history in which the two large traditions compete: the tradition of growing democratic inclusiveness and humane action for social justice—the "tradition" with which, as my choice of words indicates, this book is more sympathetic—and the stronger tradition of competition, free enterprise, individualism, the market. The second is the stronger culturally speaking, despite relatively recent apparent political victories of the first. These victories (of the New Deal and since) have been only partial victories, sharply confined politically (by the conservative combination of Southern Democrats and Republicans in Congress after 1938) and by the comparatively conservative base of these allegedly social-democratic victories. Such social democracy as we have been able to eke out in this country has had an uphill struggle.

As to the rather different third point, students still respond to the popular themes critical of "conformity" and "the Organization Man." In the fifties these familiar themes were appropriated in a way that was not political but personal. They were not a radical attack upon a "system" but a kind of moody middle-class complaint about organized social pressures and an exhortation (perhaps implied) to the individual to preserve his individuality. David Riesman's *The Lonely Crowd* became, in its revised blue-covered Anchor edition, one of those ubiquitous books, like Michael Harrington's *The Other America* in a quite different moment several years later, that stand as the paperback marker for its time. Other-directed discussion groups from coast to coast worried about the degree to which we have become "other-directed." William H. Whyte, Jr., wrote a best seller about *The Organization Man*, and other books, and movies, magazine articles, and television programs dealt with what came to be called "conformity."

This sociological criticism of "conformity" and "bigness" continued and grew in the sixties, but took on a political hue quite different from its coloration in the previous decade. Whereas the fifties' disapproval of the "other-directed" *organization man* had been either nonpolitical or slightly conservative in flavor (it evoked favorable pictures of the "inner-directed" individualist), by the middle of the sixties the political significance of these sociological themes was different. The phrases were given a politically radical turn quite in contrast to their original semiconservative and upper-middle-class flavor. In Herbert Marcuse's *One Dimensional Man*, he rapidly lists books one must read to see what is wrong with technocratic America, and he includes *The Organization Man*. Like everything else, "conformity" was now the fault of the Power Elite.

But in Whyte's book, "conformity" was not the result so much of overt pressure as of an inner attitude. It was not that the organization men were dominated, but that they surrendered. And the surrender was guided by a new ethic or attitude that justified and encouraged their giving up their distinctive individuality to the harmony of the group, avoiding development of their own thought, seeking, above all, "belongingness" and "togetherness," blurring the clarity and blunting the point of their own independence.

But the framework was still the success ethic. Though it was now sought through "antagonistic co-operation" within the organization rather than by the old competitive building of a better mousetrap by oneself, the objective was the same.

The foreshortening of the claims and purposes of living to the tangible and immediate appears not only in the older individualistic concentration upon "success" in a self-made man's economic career, but also in the modern "teamwork" and security ethic that has appeared alongside it. The question must be asked, either of an individualistic or of an organization ethic: toward what claims and purposes is life directed? Among those that have been neglected by an American foreshortening of life is exactly that of political responsibility. We Americans even in the age of organizations remain individualistic in our view of the goals of life (directed toward private career, whether of "success" or of "security") and in our social analysis (what an Individual can do, Moral

Crusades, the Good Man Above Politics). It would be unfortunate if the anticonformist, antiorganization literature, of the older or more recent sort, had the effect of discouraging political responsibility and civic virtue.

The problem is not so much that of "groupism" as of an understanding of human life in depth, against shallowness and triviality. The evils of most of the groupisms described in these books are real enough, but they are not the evils of a search for community itself; they are the evils of a search for it in too superficial, immediate, and perhaps coercive a way, a way that, therefore, endangers, rather than vivifies, the uniqueness and mystery of the self. Part of the fight, no doubt, then and now, is to preserve privacy and elbow room and to minimize the exactions of the Organization and the Group. But the self needs its communities, and the eagerness for "belonging" and "togetherness" was not altogether to be dismissed, however firmly one may set aside that particular way of expressing it. Rather, the corruptions of the need for community are to be attacked in order that the self's true need for a community of warmth, acceptance, and co-operative effort may be more nearly realized. The admission that the self's deepest need for community cannot fully be met by the partial communities seems a condition of the nearer approach to the meeting of it: there must be some openness, some sense of the fragile and fragmentary nature of all communities, some room for purposes and claims that run beyond any that can be put on agendas and referred to committees. It should be the acknowledgment of a more ultimate claim upon the self and the following out of more ultimate purposes that qualifies the individual's response to the Organization, not simply the assertion of individuality. Whyte said "fight" the Organization; but the fight assumes a framework of claims and purposes larger than those of the Organization, within which it is seen that the Organization was made for man, not man for the Organization.

Riesman gave to a collection of his essays the title *Individualism Reconsidered;* but many critics, rightly, in my view, declined to undertake that reconsideration. The problems of our time are not to be solved by reconsidering "individualism." Whyte tried hard to avoid seeming to say that we should return to the old way, but because the indictment of the present ideology was so striking, because the underlying assumption seemed to be that of a kind of pendulum swinging between groupism and individualism, and because the early chapters and the jacket contrasted an older individualism with present trends, the resulting picture was that of a better individualistic past and a worse collectivist present. Riesman insisted in *The Lonely Crowd* that he just described, not preferring one of his types of character to another, but of course the effect of the book was to disparage "other-direction" and to recommend in its place, not Riesman's "autonomy," but an older "inner-direction." It surely was not helpful if what these books created is a kind of nostalgia for a nineteenth-century individualism, or a kind of rebellious eagerness to be eccentric, "radical," and unco-operative for their own sakes.

Beyond the individualism and groupiness of the world, and also beyond radicalisms and conservatisms, there is the dimension that no organization and no political movement can fully represent. It is in the awareness of such a dimension, and not in individual assertiveness, that collective claims of the world may be limited and given place and meaning without being either overextended or overthrown.

I said that American individualism represents a warped or faulty view. Measured by what standard? By the standard of Western humanism at least—religious and secular humanism—if not also by the standard more universal than the West—the standard of the essental nature of the human person.

One may take, as a convenient benchmark for this "humanism" on this topic, this paragraph from Jacques Maritain's small book *The Person and the Common Good.*

The end of society is . . . neither the individual good nor the collection of the individual goods of each of the persons who constitute it. Such a conception would dissolve society as such to the advantage of its parts,

and would amount to either a frankly anarchistic conception, or the old
disguised anarchistic conception of individualistic materialism. . . .

The New Left of the late sixties often approached a "frankly
anarchistic conception" (Bakunin's name is still sandblasted into
the sidewalk on the campus where this is written); Maritain's
phrase "individualist materialism" we may take to be another
name for the American individualism and the competitive success
ethic I have been describing. Maritain says further that according
to this later view "the whole function of the body politic is to
safeguard the liberty of each, thereby giving the strong freedom
to oppress the weak." One is reminded, reading that last phrase,
of another item from R. H. Tawney, his pungent remark on
"freedom" under conditions of gross economic inequality: "freedom for the pike is death for the minnows."

Social justice—which would include enough equalizing of economic power to make the minnows also "free," and perhaps no
longer minnows—is of course one value insufficiently realized in
American life, as a result in part of our "individualism." Another,
increasingly important, is what Maritain would call the "common
good." "The end of society is the good of the community, the
good of the social body."

Maritain goes on to say, implicitly against the reaction of many
that the "common good" is a "totalitarian" or "authoritarian" or
"collectivist" idea:

If the good of the social body is not understood to be a common good of
human persons, just as the social body itself is a whole of human persons,
this conception would lead in its turn to other errors of a totalitarian
type. The common good of the body politic is neither the mere collection
of private goods, nor the good of a whole which, like the species with respect to its individuals or the hive with respect to its bees, draws the
parts of itself alone and sacrifices them to itself. It is the good *human* life
of the multitude, of a multitude of persons; it is their communion in good
living. It is therefore common *to the whole and to the parts;* it flows back to
the parts, and the parts must benefit from it.

He makes the distinction, as others have done, between an "individual," defined by his separation from the community and

exclusion of others, and the "person," open to the needing "community" as part of his own selfhood.

The problem of the future is not so much the individualistic success ethic as the reductionistic antihumanism of some versions of science and most of technology—in shorthand, the outlook of B. F. Skinner. Manipulated scientism, with its technology of behavior, is an enemy, probably *the* enemy, of our future. But the false individualism out of our past is still an important barrier to our thinking well and acting well in the future, in part because one reaction against it increases the menace of a manipulated mass society in the hands of human engineers. The point is not to go "beyond" freedom and dignity but to try under more difficult conditions to achieve and maintain it—to achieve that liberty that does not see community as its opposite, but as its foundation.

12

On Justice and Mercy
for Presidents

On Sunday the eighth of September 1974, a row of black limousines rolled up authoritatively in front of St. John's Church in Washington, just across Lafayette Park from the White House. The car doors popped open at once, as in a Keystone Comedy, disgorging a troop of Secret Service men and photographers. These functionaries remained outside the church while the thirty-eighth president of the United States alone went inside and startled a clutch of worshipers (early-rising Episcopalians in midtown Washington on a Sunday: not a large population group) by attending the short eight o'clock service of Holy Communion. No Secret Service agent accompanied him, as, in his worried fantasy, one of the pastors had pictured it, when the president came forward with a random group of people to receive communion. Back in the White House at eleven o'clock that morning, Gerald Ford startled a much larger public by issuing his proclamation pardoning his predecessor.

An editorial writer who received the news at midday, as he was taking a Sunday walk with his young son, was furious not only at the act itself, but also at the day of the week the president had chosen to do it. Why couldn't he have done it between nine and five on a weekday? These presidents, he said, never consider that the rest of us might have a life of our own, and want to spend Sunday with our families. One almost felt for a moment that the newspaper's editorial the next morning might deal with that interesting but rather subordinate point.

Presumably, though, the president's choice of Sunday morning was not accidental. A chief executive's pardoning power has ancient roots in religion, as is indicated both by the language used to describe it ("an act of grace"; "blots out guilt") and by the older practice of granting pardons on holy days. Ford, the most consistent and religiously best instructed prepresidential churchgoer of modern presidents, no doubt connected the thought-world of Sunday with his "act of mercy."

However, he was thereupon abruptly shown how delicate a task it is to domesticate within our earthly existence that highest layer of religious ideas (about "grace," "mercy," and "love"—Ford had made a point of using the word "love" in his first speech as president to Congress), from which the practice of the royal pardon is borrowed. The reactions and problems that followed represented a pure and explicit case study, such as one had never expected actually to see in a major political event, of the relationship one used to discuss abstractly back in graduate school between Love and Justice.

The layer of ideas represented by the word "love" or "grace" may "rise above" the strict moral logic of justice, of comparison and equality (Aristotle: the Just is a form of the Equal), of reward for merit, of punishment fitting the crime and each man receiving what he deserves. But it may also "fall below" that level.

Love or mercy can be morally higher than justice. It can complete or crown or go beyond justice—as when a man forgives his enemy. Less dramatically, grace can appropriately loosen the often excessively tight moral logic of justice. Ask yourself why Mr. Justice Holmes is quoted as having said—what seems at first glance to have been a strange remark—"I *hate* 'justice.' " But think then of all the fury he had to bear under the self-interested arguments over who gets what and exactly what is mine and what thine, over who deserves this and who merits that. Life requires some grace, some forgiveness and forbearance, some letting go and overlooking and putting all that aside, some forgetting and willingness not to keep score. Both the Christian religion—especially, perhaps, as formulated by Martin Luther—and segments of the psychoanalytic tradition have in their different ways seen the value of relaxing the moral tension, of softening the conscience and the ego when they join in defense of the Law and the Right. The human show cannot be run with the absolutely strict accounting and calculation—what's *mine*, what's *fair*, what I *de-*

serve and he *deserves*—that justice requires. We all in our egotism overestimate what we ourselves deserve, and misjudge what our "enemies" deserve; that egotism is compounded in the collective egotism of groups. It needs the softening and loosening and seasoning of love.

But this grace or love—which in Christianity is, in the first instance, not man's but God's—requires for its application to human affairs the utmost care. Whole sections of Western civilization have confined its ethical or human application to the islands of the monastery, or of the family, or of strictly individual relations. A variety of monastic orders of the Christian past expected of monks a behavior level higher than that of ordinary citizens, let alone of magistrates acting in behalf of the state. In the Lutheran world it is regularly said that there were "two realms," in only one of which, that of the family, the church, and individual relationships, did grace apply—love and forgiveness. Out there in the other realm—the state—everything was to be law and justice. Some of the defects of the politics of Lutheran churches and of Lutheran influences, particularly in Germany, are said to come from the sharpness of this separation.

Even in the family there may be a conflict of unequal love, which overlooks "merit," and equal justice, with its insistence on merit: the law-abiding and righteous Elder Brothers do not like the Father's loving forgiveness of Prodigal Sons.

As extended into the collective realm of the state and great public affairs, grace is even more problematical: if I may in turn be pardoned the metaphor in this religious context, it introduces a wild card into the game of public order, into the Square Deal of Justice, and it is in danger of upsetting the rules of the game altogether.

Ford announced the pardon at eleven o'clock. By noon the word had spread throughout Northwest Washington, and that whole section of the city rose from the ground in fury. One man went about his neighborhood crying "Impeach! Impeach!" Cynicism and conspiracy theories bloomed on the instant on both sides of Connecticut Avenue. The mildest cynical interpretation had Ford acting for political reasons, to anchor his right wing after several actions—nominating Nelson Rockefeller for vice president, proposing a limited amnesty for Vietnam draft evaders, initiating conversations with the black caucus—that were not pleasing to that group. More sinister theories noted that this Sunday, September 8, was exactly thirty days to the day after Nixon's resignation on August 8, and they drew dark inferences therefrom. Even sophisticated followers of public affairs entertained the belief that there had been an arrangement between Nixon and Ford at the time of the former's resignation. Back in Indiana, a young Democratic mayor volunteered his assumption that the deal had been part of Ford's nomination for the vice presidency the previous autumn.

My own reaction did not include belief in any of these cynical ideas or conspiracy theories, but it did include an unhappiness that Ford had acted in such a way as to revive them. This was an action that, in contrast to the open and candid and consultative procedures he had started with in his first days, was taken suddenly and without warning, after little consultation (only four persons, it was later to be reported, knew about the impending pardon; these included Nixon holdover General Haig but did not include the press secretary, Jerry terHorst). As editorials were quick to point out in the days that followed, the action contradicted both what Ford had said in the confirmation hearings before the Senate Rules Committee—that "the public wouldn't stand for it"—and his statement in his first press conference citing the special prosecutor's obligation to take action against "any and all individuals" and stating that it would be "untimely" for him to make commitments before any formal charges or any action had been taken in the courts. An angry friend in New York saw in these ingredients of secrecy, of surprise, of reversal of previous statements a return by Ford to "the Nixon pattern." It was unfortunate that the President acted in such a way as to encourage this view. That was one of the two chief undesirable effects of the timing and the manner of his pardon.

The other, of course, had to do with the relation of this "act of mercy" to both the moral and the legal systems of Equal Justice. This is a matter not only of substance but also of appearance: how the public interprets the deed and draws inferences from it for other situations. One could see springing up on every side the natural inclination to examine what is just and unjust by making comparisons. An angry liberal Democrat, assimilating the news on that Sunday, said that John Dean told the truth and sits in jail; Nixon lied and sits in the sun selling his memoirs for 2 million dollars. The conversation about American politics in the days that followed asked the obvious questions about justice: If Nixon was pardoned, how could one convict Haldeman, Ehrlichman, Mitchell, *et al.*, who were carrying out his orders? How could one recompense Krogh, Magruder, Segretti, Liddy, Chapin, and the others who had served or were serving sentences? Most of all, how could one do justice to Barker and Martinez, Gonzalez and Sturgis, who went to jail because they were small fry loyally carrying out orders?

It did not take much of a leap to extend the logic of a healing mercy, overriding the legal system's justice, from Watergate to Vietnam. One aspect of the unfortunate cynicism was that the conditional amnesty Ford had already said that he would grant to the draft evaders was now soured: was that only a calculated preparation for the pardon of Nixon? And if the draft evaders were granted the same "full, free, and absolute" pardon (instead of a conditional one), how then could one recompense the dead and wounded from Vietnam? Or hold the law in force next time? When Ford floated a trial balloon on the Tuesday after the pardon—that he was considering pardoning the entire Watergate group, forty-eight in all—the reaction was instant, fierce, and negative. The national network TV news on CBS that night went down the row of men in a California court arrested on assorted minor offenses and telecast their colorful indignation at sweeping pardons for the mighty.

Ford said in his statement of pardon that "I, not as President but as a humble servant of God, will receive justice without mercy if I fail to show mercy." His legal adviser Philip Buchen kept insisting that this was an act of *mercy*, *not* of justice. But one could reply that it is exactly the central rule for a presidential pardon that the former should not violate the latter, and that Ford need not have faced himself with the stark choice between them had he waited. Mercy could have followed justice.

No doubt the fury along Connecticut Avenue was tinctured with a vindictiveness toward Nixon which those tempted to it should have overcome. If Alger Hiss had gone to church and emerged forgiving Richard Nixon in his heart, that would have been grace indeed, as would it have been if Helen Gahagan Douglas had reached out in some merciful act to a broken man in San Clemente. But Gerald Ford's situation differed from these others in two ways:

First, he was a long-time friend and supporter, and a recent beneficiary, of Richard Nixon: do not even Publicans the same? For Ford, the true personal moral test would have been to extend that sweepingly "full, free, and absolute" pardon, not a "conditional" pardon, to those protesters in Canada who were his ideological enemies.

Second, his "mercy" is not confined to the heart or to individual moral relations; it is a formal constitutional power injected into the legal system. On the other hand, as chief executive he has an overriding responsibility to uphold the system of justice and to serve the public good. Compared to a private citizen, his mercy is at once more powerful and more confined.

The rule for him should have been this: in granting a formal pardon, "love" should not undercut "justice." It should not short-circuit the law, or leave a necessary political drama incomplete, or affront the public sense of fairness. Mercy can and should season justice, and earthly power, as Portia said, doth then show likest God's; but mercy cannot violate justice, or else, like the dubious pardonings of Chaucer's pardoner, it stinks.

Had Nixon's case become finally separable, as a distinctly individual matter—clear public knowledge of his broken health would have been one way for that to happen—then mercy alone would be appropriate. But so long as it had weighty political significance and legal and moral analogies, the president should have attended to its public effects in a different way than he did. He should have waited until mercy could follow the just treatment and completed the historical record of the fully functioning legal system.

As in the days that followed there were reports that Ford had been motivated by the former president's failing health, one felt that if that was the reason, it should have been explicitly stated to the public as the justification for the pardon, and established clearly and not by hints. And terHorst should have been told.

A pardon, the president halfway said at a press conference and Buchen did say repeatedly, implies guilt: something to be pardoned for. So it is in theology, morals, and logic, but not necessarily, as it turns out, in law. Technically, legally, Nixon was "innocent": an important point. He had not through due process of law been found guilty of specified charges. A full confession by him would have brought his pardon within the just requirements of the state. In religious terms, it is indeed the established guilt, and the contrition for it, that makes an act of pardon—a "nevertheless"—a gracious act; as John Bunyan's title put it, Grace Abounding to the Chief of Sinners. The Chief of Sinners in the present case was playing golf with Walter Annenberg in Palm Springs, California, when presidential grace abounded unto him, and the statement issued in his name was many miles short of honest contrition or a manly confession of guilt.

It was altogether too clear that Nixon not only would not admit his guilt but also would rouse his constituency to assert his innocence.

Trial in the courts would have been the other way unequivocally to bring the pardoning of Nixon within the frame of justice: had the law been allowed to run its course, and had he been convicted, or had the full record been made clear and public, then a pardon for him would have been appropriate. But as it was, two requirements of public order were not met:

First, the Nixonian myths were not quite decisively punctured in the further reaches of (let us say) David Dennis' constituency in Indiana (no impeachment; no confession; no conviction; too rapid an untelevised denouement August 5–9). As Kissinger and Nixon used to say about the slow withdrawal from Vietnam, it is important that it be done so as to leave no wound to fester in the psyche of the silent majority.

In retrospect it would appear that impeachment would have been the best way properly to have concluded the Nixon matter, because that process would have separated from merely individual crimes the offense against the state, the abuse of power, which is the historically significant evil in Watergate and the Nixon scandals. One wishes the House Judiciary Committee proceedings, the worthiest feature of the whole story, could have been followed by the vote on impeachment in the House and the trial in the Senate, both televised and (one may as patriot wish) as dignified and excellent as the work of the House committee. That would have accomplished the education of the public, the establishment of the historical precedent, and the vindication of the instrument of impeachment that the situation required.

The other public requirement was that the equity of the nation's legal machinery be upheld or restored. But it was not. Rather, the opposite. The gracious king issued his Sunday pardon not to the wretched in their prisons, but to another king—to block his trial. Neither of these kings had distinguished himself for understanding another way that love may relate to justice, that is, by leading to *social* justice: to the humane insight into the impact of the social arrangements on the lives of men.

The word "compassion" is now used too much, as was true also of the word "love"; from flabby overuse, these words, too, lose their edge, and because of their borderline with sentimentality they decay into a sickly-sweet sugary stuff. Nevertheless, the moral point of beginning is love, the affirming of the other; as St. Augustine said, "I want you to be." And the affirmation of the person that these words describe, when linked to a modern understanding of society, or to social imagination in any age, leads to social justice, mentioned before in these pages: toward a more inclusive and egalitarian and personalistic perception of justice; toward a perception of the fairness and unfairness—mostly the latter—in the social order itself. So it was with Jane Addams in Chicago, and with Walter Rauschenbusch as a young pastor in Hell's Kitchen, with Reinhold Niebuhr in Detroit while the auto industry was growing, with Eugene Debs in fighting the railroads, and Norman Thomas in New York. So it has been with the thousands of whites, particularly in the South, back to the abolition movement of the eighteen-thirties and before. "I want you to be" can lead to a widening of the circle to whom equal justice applies, and among whom the comparisons of merit are made. It can lead to a repudiation of conventional social injustices, as in Sarah Cleghorn's poem about the golf links being so near the mill that the children at work can see the men at play, or in James Baldwin's anger at the German prisoners of war being served in the front of the restaurant while American Negro soldiers had to go around to the back, or a host of examples about women's "place" right now. Over the centuries the poor man and the criminal and the child and the black man and the woman have come to be included in new ways in judgments about what is fair in the arrangements of society. Although many of the contemporary applications of the enlarging of social justice by love must be more subtle than those called forth by the blatant injustice of the past, the work of such humane social criticism has certainly not completed its work. It never will.

In the days of the Great Society legislation and of riots, Ford attacked the "soft social theory" that the man who throws a rock through your window is a victim of the environment. And he backed his views with votes. Not much of grace and mercy there. And there was an unconscious identification with those who own the windows. Compassion for Richard Nixon is Christian mercy; compassion for a black teen-ager is "soft." A Michigan Democrat said that Jerry Ford would give a hungry child his own lunch— but vote against a systematic free lunch program.

As for Nixon: in his case, bad examples abound, for this point of view. Perhaps the moral nadir on the present issue was his message on treating criminals "without pity."

I believe Ford and Buchen greatly underestimated how it would appear when this king prematurely pardoned the other king. A judge in North Dakota opened the jail doors, and another declined to sentence the offenders before him. Applications for pardon multiplied. Cynical remarks about "the system" became again the fashion. A sense of *social* injustice welled up from common people everywhere, not only in Northwest Washington but also wherever a man without money or connections has to stand trial for his deeds.

I was not as angry at Ford as my host in Northwest Washington and his friends, liberal Democrats, including a writer of fierce intelligent anti-Nixon editorials, who was on the phone in ferocious long-distance conversations about the cynicism and favoritism of this decision. I was surprised and disappointed that Ford had done it prematurely, and worried about what that decision meant about his good sense. I had watched his first press conference as president, during the month of euphoria, with a sinking feeling. The major points of doubt were his social conscience and his intellectual force. It is Eisenhower again, I said to myself. A decent man, with a simplicity and an individual moral earnestness that make it doubly difficult to bring the public to see the defects in his *social* morality, or in his social intelligence. It was, once again, the combination we knew in Ike. To paraphrase Mark Twain, Ford was a decent man in the worst sense of the word.

On the Sunday of the pardon, a ministerial friend asked, as I was packing, "Well, which is winning out, your liberal Democratic opinions or your Christian charity?" "No contest," I answered.

Neither seat mate on the late-afternoon flight had heard of the pardon, or wanted to hear about it, or had opinions about it. The pilot did, however, announce a news item. It seemed that someone with the improbable name Evel Knievel had jumped or flown or dived or been shot or something over a canyon in the West. The passengers did have opinions on that subject.

Gerald Ford, the honest man from Grand Rapids, was grossly romanticized in the honeymoon period in August of 1974 through no fault of his own. The public and the press, desperate from the long Nixonian drought for a leader upon whom to rain their patriotic affection, poured out upon his very breakfast muffins a cloudburst of dammed-up affection. One may still risk believing that he is at least a conscientious man. But one had to conclude that the best theologian or moralist in the new White House in 1974 was not Ford or Buchen, but Mr. Gerald terHorst, who had been Ford's first appointee, as press secretary. He rightly said that when it reaches a presidential level mercy itself must be even-handed. When it was not, he resigned.

13

Three Exaggerations: The Unscrupulous Use of the Crowd, the Exploiting of the Resentments of the Common Man, and the Problem of the Man More Right than His Neighbors

Should an American democrat humbly accept the opinion of "the people" as expressed by the larger number, even though he disagrees with it? Or should he stand bravely alone with his own independent judgment, no matter what the "crowd" may say?

The answer, of course, is that he should do both, each in its own place, and each with the proper recognition of the other. Or the other answer is none of the above: he should do neither, as described in those sentences. He does not necessarily take over the opinion of the "people" as his own, no matter how many vote for it or how many may tell Mr. George Gallup or Mr. Louis Harris their notion about it. Neither, on the other hand, should he shape his own conviction in proud, superior, defiant, and autonomous solitude. The governed continually shape and renew their consent, in a conversation in which he has a voice, and to which also he listens. This is the never-ending ethical dialogue of a free people, which is in fact what it is ideally supposed to be only if the participants are free men—that is, moral agents—whose decent respect for the opinion of mankind informs but does not override their own judgment.

1

Here is an example of what the ethic of democracy does not mean. Robert D. Wood, the president of the CBS Television Network, said, on a television documentary program on September 2, 1974: "I think that probably one of the most democratic institutions in this country is the television industry because, unlike candidates who run every two years or four years or six years, our candidates, that is, our programs, are being voted upon 365 days and nights, every single year." Wood is by no means alone in taking that line; various other television executives and other magnates and defenders of the machinery of modern publicity have promoted a theory—a self-serving theory, in my view—called "cultural democracy," which they use aggressively against the critics of their own decisions and their exercise of power.

One would hope that it would not be necessary to give the full refutation of the position Wood and these others take, but experience suggests some brief negative remarks may be in order.

Turning the knob on a television set is not the same as voting. Voting, which is a constitutionally protected right and a moral duty, is grounded in the theory, which is sometimes true, that the citizen acts responsibly and for the public good. Watching NFL football is not the same thing.

The operator of the television network justifies the material he puts out by saying, "We give the public what it wants." That is only half true, and half a denial of his own responsibility. He helps to determine what the public wants, by what he has accustomed them to want: by what he has selected and designed and promoted. He picks from among the many things the public may want what he wants to give them—often what serves his interest in an intensely competitive battle for the attention of enormous numbers of people.

There is a sense in which the public wants what it gets: having been fed a particular diet, the public develops a taste for it. You and I have many, many *potential* interests and tastes, high and low, in many directions, to which mass communication can appeal, and, by appealing to them, give them a place in the culture.

Executives like the CBS president are not altogether ruled by popular choices. They make choices—moral choices, of importance. No citing of numbers absolves them, or any of us in our comparable decisions.

The aggressive and pseudo-democratic appeal to numbers—there's more of us than of them; we give the public what it wants—is a particular menace to the moral order in America, because in a democratic ethos it is plausible. An American, trained as he is, has a hard time resisting it. But, in all except the proper narrow and institutionally grounded setting in which votes settle the one question—who is to serve in this office? will this bill be enacted into law?—he ought to resist it—resist it exactly in support of a democratic society. And even in that political setting he acquiesces and he learns but he does not necessarily agree; he continues his own moral reflection. Or he should.

When Tocqueville wrote almost a century and a half ago, before there were any Nielsen ratings or public-relations firms, about the "tyranny of the majority," he dealt not only with the overt domination by the sheer numerical force but also with the covert eating away of inner conviction by the majority's moral prestige. "The majority possess a power that is physical and moral at the same time," he wrote. "It acts upon the will as well as upon the actions of men, and it replaces not only all contest, but all controversy." Like the king in other lands, Tocqueville wrote, in this American democracy the majority can do no wrong.

Fifty years after Tocqueville, Lord Bryce discussed Tocqueville's chapter, and added to his discussion a chapter he called the "Fatalism of the Multitude." The distinguishing feature of this phenomenon is not the overt tyranny of the mass, but the *inner disposition* to accept the rule of numbers. Bryce explained how the necessary democratic assumption that the majority must prevail leads to another, "less distinctly admitted, and indeed held rather implicitly than consciously, that the majority is right." If all of those millions voted for Richard M. Nixon, can they have been wrong? Worse, if all of those millions watch Johnny Carson, can he be so bad? But what does it mean, to be wrong or bad? Bryce did not go on to make a further point, more relevant perhaps in our time than in his, that the belief that the majority will choose what is right may modulate into the belief that there is no such thing as "right," except as the majority decides it. Joining this belief is a counterpart conviction that truth and justice make no claim upon one's mind and provide no standard; the only claim is one's own interest or opinion.

Lord Bryce gave as an example the feeling of a voter after his candidate has been defeated in an election. After such a defeat, "the average man will repeat his arguments with less faith, less zeal, more of a secret feeling that he may be wrong." Back when there were students who knew who Harry Truman was, and some even who George Sokolsky was, I used to refer to the posture that the conservative columnist struck in 1948 after Truman, whom he had opposed, was elected president. Someone chided Sokolsky for being "wrong." "I wasn't wrong," he said; "the people were wrong."

The attempt by Nixon and his supporters to use his large victory in 1972 as a plenary indulgence for everything he might subsequently do—a "mandate," invoked for every purpose—relied upon the popular feeling Bryce described and Sokolsky rejected.

The word "democracy" is often used to imply that truth and goodness will come out of the sheer assembling of numbers of people. Tocqueville wrote: "The moral authority of the majority is partly based upon the notion that there is more wisdom in a great number of legislators than in a few; their number is more important than their quality."

Personal responsibility is endangered by that sloppy spirit of democracy; yet that personal responsibility is necessary for democracy itself truly to function. If people individually are not responsible, then the "people" as a whole will not really prevail. The governed will not have given their genuine consent. They will have it "engineered" for them.

The danger of the democratic spirit is that the valuable democratic truth that it is right that the people rule may lead to the populistic half-truth or quarter-truth that the majority ("the people") *will* rule what is right (they will not necessarily); and this, in turn, may lead to the relativistic falsehood that there is no right except what the majority rules—that is, that there really is no such thing as right or good at all, but just desire, opinion, interest.

The Danish religious thinker Sören Kierkegaard was outraged by the irresponsible attacks in a journal of small circulation in Copenhagen in the eighteen-forties, which exploited its relation to "the public" to damage individuals and distort the complex truth. One hesitates to imagine what he would make of Wood and his kind, with the immense power of their instrument and their self-absolving theory of "cultural democracy."

Kierkegaard was not a political thinker at all, being concerned with the "religious" and "ethical" dimension only, and he was not a democrat; he once wrote in his *Journal:* "These democrats are so opposed to monarchy that they even want four-part solos!" Nevertheless, he is one of the more vivid sources for the point one wants to make, about numbers, pseudo democracy, "voting" for programs 365 times a year, and the irresponsible crowd. One of his phrases was "a crowd is the untruth."

There is a view, which conceives that where the crowd is, there also is the truth, and that in truth itself, there is a need of having a crowd on its side. There is another view of life which conceives that wherever there is a crowd, there is untruth, so that (to consider for a moment the extreme case) even if every individual, each for himself in private were to be in possession of the truth yet in case they were all to get together in a crowd, a crowd to which any sort of decisive significance is attributed, a voting, noisy, audible crowd, untruth would at once be in evidence. For a *crowd is the untruth.*

This sounds at first like the socially invidious sort of thing that looks down from some presumed height upon the "crowd culture" of the lower orders, the sort of thing Mencken cheerfully asserted all his life and that one can hear muttered and grumbled fairly often in the places where there are Americans who ought to know better. But a footnote makes it clear that Kierkegaard, whatever one may think of him otherwise, did not hold that snobbish view.

The word crowd is understood in the purely formal sense, not in the sense one commonly attaches to crowd when it means an invidious quali-fication, the distinction which human selfishness irreligiously erects between the crowd and superior persons, etc. Good God, how could a religious man hit upon such an inhuman equality! No, crowd stands for number, the numerical, the number of noblemen, millionaires, high dignitaries, etc. As soon as the numerical is involved, it is the crowd.

The crowd, not this crowd or that, the crowd now living, or the crowd long deceased, the crowd of humble people or superior people, of rich or of poor, etc., a crowd in its very concept is the untruth by reason of the fact that it renders the individual completely impenitent and irresponsible.

One of Kierkegaard's best-known stories makes the point pungently. A tavern keeper who bought drinks at five pennies apiece sold them for three. "How do you make anything?" he was asked. "Oh, it's the volume that does it!"

The point is: no "volume," no number, makes truth or goodness or responsibility, if each individual lacks it. No number of those who are unwise gives wisdom. No number of irresponsible persons gives responsibility. Forty million people turning their TV sets to the Dean Martin Comedy Hour do not make it tasteful, or beneficial, or good in any way, or "democratic" either.

You know how it can sometimes be with a certain kind of "democracy": nobody does it; everybody does it. Everybody blames what happens on everybody else. The crowd as a whole does it; no individual himself takes the responsibility for what happens.

This perennial problem of democracy is given new dimensions by these modern instruments of communication like television, and by the practical technicians of public relations and advertising. An ethos stretches across the consumer economy, and the popular culture, and spreads into politics with the PR men, the engineers of consent, the Southern California advertising men of the Nixon White House.

It is not unsupported in the public at large. I was struck, back in the fifties, by the response evoked by articles critical of "positive thinking" and official Washington piety. Three arguments were consistently reiterated: the *sincerity* of the individuals whom the articles had criticized; the *numbers* of people who had responded favorably to those persons' appeal; and the allegedly "constructive" or "positive" nature of the material under attack, in contrast to the alleged "negative" outlook of the critic. The arguments recurred so often as to tell the recipient something about his culture. And there was an air of utter finality in the way they were given, as though they answered all doubts and no other questions could be asked. The evocation of the *numbers* who respond to these popular messages was to say to the critic: "Well, now, if all these vast millions like it, just *who* are *you* to say it's no good?"

The emphasis on "sincerity" was noted by the analysts of *The Lonely Crowd* back in the fifties. They saw the desire for "sincere" entertainers and "sincere" presidential candidates as part of what they called the "other-direction" of our time. They noted the inclination of the modern public to prefer "sincerity"—with which it can identify—to talent or skill, with which it cannot. (Mencken made that point, too—not with sociology, but with a snort.) The *The Lonely Crowd* sociologists did not say clearly enough that "sincerity" may also take the place of truth and of value. Just as the defenders of "positive thinking" and the like do not entertain the possibility that something millions endorse can nevertheless be wrong, inadequate, or dreadful, so they also ignore the possibility that one can be "sincere" and at the same time be very mistaken.

I remarked in the previous chapter that much of the criticism of "conformity" seemed not quite on the point, for it implicitly or explicitly recommended "individualism" or "autonomy" against the "crowd." But "individual" "autonomous" opinion and desire, with no objective moral and intellectual referent is, when compounded, the stuff of which lonely crowds, with their "conformity," are made. The problem is not exclusively the individual's refusal to oppose the "crowd"; it is the lack of serious standards, with or without popular support. Lonely individuals can be as "wrong," and as "irresponsible," as the lonely crowd.

For Bryce, the American democrat's inner aquiescence to the rule of numbers was reluctant and fatalistic: men regard "the voice of the multitude as the voice of fate." But there is another kind of an appeal one may make to numbers and to the "people" and to the majority that is not at all reluctant and fatalistic, against one's inclination, but, rather, is an eagerly adopted weapon, in line with one's desire. When we Americans have, or plausibly can claim to have, numbers on our side, we use that aggressively to vindicate our position, as with Nixon's mandate, Agnew's unsilent majority, Johnson in the early days of his presidency whipping out of his pocket the polls that showed the enormous numbers of Americans who supported him (later he was silent about polls).

There is an example more repellent still than that of the television executive, and it makes again the more general point: in a democratic ethos one can use numbers falsely and irresponsibly as an instrument of power. In the middle of a fight over busing for racial balance, in a city only 25% black, white citizens would cry out often, "A *minority* is trying to push a *majority* around . . ." and if one were to try, in that overheated setting, to explain why that position is the opposite of democratic—that the only "majority" with moral dignity is one formed by discussion, choice, and voting, and that its authority is limited—one would not have got very far. *Voting* alone, without reason, limited power, and a sense of justice, does not make the dignity of the majority either. One of the devices angry antibusing whites used, where they had the numbers but the reformers opposed to them were more articulate, was to pack meetings and call for a VOTE so the MAJORITY could rule—a vote, a count of hands, as a way to shut off all the talking, as an instrument of *power*.

2

There is another theme, much like that of majority and of numbers but distinguishable from it, that has appeared in a rather new aspect. This is the theme of the aggressive and resentful common man, belligerently asserting his ordinariness—now often in behalf of quasi-conservative positions.

Surely it was a curious development in the short but turbulent history of the industrial proletariat when in spring of 1970 large numbers of construction workers marched through the greatest financial district of the world's leading capitalist power with signs reading not only "God Bless Nixon" and "God Bless Agnew" but also "God Bless the Establishment." No doubt in the past many millions of industrial workers were more deferential to authority, and a great deal more patriotic, than either Marx or Robert Owen would have had them be, but this American thing in 1970 had a quite different quality from past exhibitions of servility and deference. "God Bless the Establishment," on a flag-festooned sign in the New York City streets in 1970, had a very different ring from "God Save the Queen" in London in years past. It was not at all deferential or submissive. There wasn't any forelock-pulling in it; there was, rather, something nearer to the brandishing of a club. The antagonism of the slogans was not directed against the historic enemies of the working class; quite the contrary. Bankers and brokers in the office buildings cheered the marching workers and showered them with confetti. Here were angry and aggressive members of the "working class" marching through Wall Street *attacking* the disturbers of the peace, and supporting and being supported by what "Wall Street" symbolizes to the world. They covered themselves, almost literally, with the symbols of order and of national unity and of the status quo of their capitalist country, not just sentimentally and deferentially, but aggressively and angrily.

They were quite evidently a great deal more passionate in their hatred than in their positive endorsements. The immediate objects of their anger were the student protesters against the war. The word "establishment" obviously was borrowed from the students and their sympathizers, in order exactly to make a riposte: You say, Down with the "establishment" !, then we say, God bless the "establishment" ! Beyond the student protesters in the field of antagonists were all the other critics and disturbers and protesters of recent times. This was an aggressive workers' march in behalf of authority, order, and a kind of cultural vested interest.

Historians of Populism as an actual historical movement object when one calls this common-man theme, in its conservative form, "populistic conservatism." They believe that Richard Hofstadter and other historians, and, still worse, some sociological writers, have overstated the elements of xenophobia, anti-Semitism, racism, and nativism in the actual Populist movement of the eighteen-eighties and nineties, and have mistakenly linked that movement to later phenomena with strength in the same geographical area, like isolationism before World War II and McCarthyism in the early fifties. But whatever the historical case may be, we need a word—lower case, no historical reference intended—for a persistent phenomenon, evident in other countries, especially strong in the United States: "populist" presents itself. It means the asserting of one's ordinariness, one's being "jes' common" (words of praise), as the farmers' wives say in Winnebago, Nebraska, as a value. It may indeed be a value; that depends. "God must have loved the common people because he made so many of them." So far, so good. But this theme turns into something else, something undesirable, when it entails an explicit and defensive attack on what is *not* "common," ordinary, of the people.

Ortega's no doubt too aristocratic and disdainful picture of the "mass man" (whom he assumed to be completely dominant in the United States) has nevertheless its portion of truth: "The characteristic of the hour is that the commonplace mind . . . has the assurance to proclaim the rights of the commonplace and to impose them wherever it will." If one removes the condescension and distance from the phrase "commonplace mind," one must admit that there is continual evidence of this phenomenon in American democratic society.

I said in an earlier chapter that in a forced choice one should take Walt Whitman over Mencken; one should choose Whitman over Ortega, too, if forced to choose. But it is not necessary to make so stark a choice, or to ignore the partial truth the critics of democracy, particularly American democracy, identify. The ordinary American (whoever he is), the "man in the street," the "common man," is a mythical figure in whom we may find many characteristics, only one of which is the temptation to a resentful and aggressive assertion of his ordinariness as normative. But that is certainly one theme discoverable in some of the people some of the time, and it can be fed and exploited by leaders of a certain stripe. George Wallace's version of it is: "There's more of us than of them." The unlamented Agnew was explicit in his resentful attacks upon "elitists," and the Nixon White House had many variants on the theme.

I have found a brief comment on the aggressive-defensive "commonness" that seems to me more satisfactory than many more well-known discussions of "mass society" and the like. This brief comment appears in *The Ethics of Power*, written by an English philosopher named Philip Leon and published in 1935. His book is really a study of many forms of human egotism, and his paragraphs on the "democratic" egotism are better than Ortega's, and far better than Mencken's, because they are not patronizing and because they are included alongside the other displays of egotism—probably worse—that appear under other social-political conditions. Thus, though Leon writes (as Mencken might have done) that ". . . democracies . . . have owed both their hold over men and their vices to the egotism of the average man," he adds (as Mencken would *not* have done) that "none the less, perfect democracy may very well be the ideal condition. Autocracy, its opposite, is also based upon egotism; it satisfies the tyrannic egotism of a few and the servile egotism of the many." So Leon is no antidemocrat; he is, rather, a realistic and critical democrat.

Here is what he wrote about "democratic egotism," long before the speeches of Spiro Agnew and George Wallace:

The ordinary egotist is . . . concerned with not being inferior or with not having anyone or certain ones above him . . . the situation of affairs which best accords with the egotistic self-love—that is, with the conceit and ambition—of the average man (who is the average egotist) . . . is democracy, in which none can be above him unless placed there by himself, so that it is he who is after all the patron. Hence, though latently conceit and ambition are present too, in the generality of men the egotism in evidence is that of *envy* and *jealousy* (*resentment* at the superiority of others). Commoner even than these is the desire to 'hold one's own' or to keep whatever one has come to consider one's proper position. . . . Any impairment of this position, still more any assault upon it, rouses indignation, anger, resentment, hatred, vindictiveness. . . . We shall find one who in all outward things is of the crowd and who either boastfully or with apparent humility proclaims that he is 'just an ordinary plain man, none of your highbrow artist fellows, poets and philosphers;' and in the very tone, not merely of his boasting, but even of his apparent self depreciation, we hear the conviction not only that of course to be plain is to be sane, and to be ordinary is to be supreme ('to be it'), but also that his own ordinariness is more ordinary than that of others, something unique, in fact something extraordinary!

This assertion of an extraordinary ordinariness, a proud un-common commonness, has no doubt a long history in American politics, but the aftermath of the sixties, plus the economic situa-tion of the enlarged middle class—now including much of the blue-collar world—makes for a newly conservative expression of it. The American audience for resentful attacks on alleged elites now itself has wealth and position. The resentment toward those who seem to claim some distinction or eminence still has some-thing of the same geographical direction ("the East" and the "Eastern Establishment" still evoke negative responses, as in Bryan's day), but the political-economic configuration is almost reversed: now it is populistic resentment against an Eastern upper crust, against the city and its leading people, against intellectuals with their pointy heads and "theorists" with their briefcases, against "effete snobs"—for their politically *progressive* views—at least implicitly, for their alliance with the black under class. In Bryan's day, it was otherwise. The present configuration may not be altogether unique, but it has a strength that cannot quite have been duplicated before: so wealthy a country, with so explicit a democratic ethos, with so advanced a mass-technological develop-ment, therefore such a strong theme of a populistic, as distin-guished from an aristocratic, conservatism.

This democracy has a demos that is comparatively comfortable, half "privileged" and half still hurting with grievances, asserting its claims of numbers, of ordinariness, and of self-interest simulta-neously against both "lower" and "upper" groups of people. Let us dramatize a little: the world's first *privileged* demos, a "people" with a minority under class "beneath" it to neglect, avoid, forget, fear, or disdain, and a poverty-stricken majority occupying the same planet.

This American populace has world-wide power, and the temp-tations of the national egotism in the exercise of that power.

There are "undemocratic" (or inhumane) deeds such a people may do, and situations that such an electorate may steadfastly and "democratically" refuse to correct. This is not an imaginary picture: a white, comfortable, and suburban majority consistently declining to respond to the needs of black, poor, central-city minorities, and of other "minorities" of disadvantaged folk, and, at the same time, asserting its own democratic common-man-ish rights against the upper crust.

"Democracy," whether it mean numbers or the merit of the ordinary man or individual freedoms, does not necessarily solve the problem in a case of that kind. It may even exacerbate it. We can see that now. It has historically been true on issues of race, in this country with a 90% majority subordinating a 10% minority. We may now see a similar configuration with respect to the remaining American poor—the world's first *minority* poor, as we have often been told recently.

Perhaps even more of a portent for the future, there is the appeal to numbers in the vast apparatus of popular culture and the consumer economy.

There is a middling demos, insisting that its taste prevail, in television, movies, and books, in stores, even in schools and universities.

And there is the still more portentous threat of the collective egotism built on mass feeling of this comparatively new world power.

In these new situations the perennial requirement of democracy takes on a new force: that the people who rule in their name not be devoid altogether of the capacity to recognize a justice beyond their own interest, and a good beyond what any moment's crowd may respond to.

The forces making modern skepticism and cynicism include a wide range of intellectual and social developments—if not science and modern technology themselves, then at least the positivistic philosophical outlooks that are thought to be associated with them. But the nature of democracy itself—of the free society—cannot be completely absolved. Democracy-as-a-fact, freedom-as-a-fact, may add to these powerful moral undercurrents, which in the end mean the destruction of a free society. Freedom requires a certain openness and toleration, but this openness may become an emptiness. Since we do not know what is going to be *done* until the votes are counted, we may come to believe that no one knows what is *good* or *true* until the votes are counted. Because all positions are equally free to present themselves, there is an inclination to believe that all positions are equally valuable and true. One man's opinion seems as good as the next, and implications to the contrary appear to be undemocratic. The initial relativism that the free society requires may turn into a thoroughgoing and debilitating relativism by which a free society will be undercut. The line between them, not easy to draw, divides a healthy respect for other positions from the unhealthy assumption that all positions are alike, and do not matter one way or another, or that they are wholly matters of taste and opinion and background without any basis in reason or in reality.

Americans are quick to condemn anybody who thinks he knows what is just or good or right, or valuable or excellent in any way: who are you to say? The television executive belligerently cites his Nielsen ratings against such a person, and the demagogic politician rouses the reverse snobbery of the crowd: such a person is an effete snob, an "elitist," and undemocratic. But great swatches of the educated classes also have their own kind of resistance to that sort of presumption, at least as it applies to ethical foundations; they respond predictably and on cue, with clouds of relativism and doubt, and instant accusations against anyone who might seem to think that he might "know what's good for you." The suspicion is planted deep; and grows everywhere.

Nevertheless, there is something alongside it, also planted deep: the picture of the brave and lonely opponent of the crowd, standing with his profile in courage etched against the sky. That picture is planted in our minds, to be sure, by perennial human experience recorded in our history and our literature; it grows in this particularly individualistic and morally heroic way in the

United States because of our soil, and because of the other theme against which it reacts.

A crowd "democracy"? Against that there stands as the alternative a lone, persecuted figure, an "Enemy of the People," who has truth and goodness firmly in his solitary grip. Certainly that sort of image is appealing to young American idealists, disturbed by the ills of their society, when they realize how many of these ills have popular support. I suggest that this construction of our duty, also, is askew.

I suppose the most significant American symbol of the lonely moral prophet is Henry David Thoreau. (He is significant, although it is amusing to read that Justice Oliver Wendell Holmes wrote, at age ninety, to Harold Laski, "I can't see why they seem to take the author of *Walden*—I forget his name—so seriously.") Thoreau may be taken as a central American symbol of the man more right than his neighbors—what is good about that posture, and also what isn't.

Thoreau's essay now called "On Civil Disobedience," ubiquitous in the later sixties, is not really about civil disobedience so much as it is about this responsibility of a citizen. It is a noble, inspiriting, but partly wrongheaded document that states one-half of that responsibility in sentences that have rung a bell around the world. Its influence on Gandhi is known to everybody. Martin Luther King, Jr., read it first as a freshman in Morehouse, and, according to a biographer, it "stirred him more deeply and permanently than any other classroom encounter of the period." It would be a stonyhearted American indeed who would not be a little moved by the memory of the scene, in Montgomery, Alabama, in 1955, of the young Baptist minister coming home from the meeting at which he had been asked to lead the bus boycott, soberly discussing it with his wife and referring to his reading of Thoreau. That essay meant much to him, and his actions in turn meant much to his country. Thoreau's ideas became part of the moral and theoretical justification of that remarkable event the Montgomery bus boycott. But why go on? Justice Holmes to the contrary notwithstanding, we all know that Thoreau has made himself one of the more powerful political symbols of the modern world.

Some of the best students, not only in the days of activism but also before that and afterward, vibrated in a moving way in tune with that essay. A college teacher does remember the readings that some students voluntarily tell him have meant something to them and have been appropriated as something more than an assignment. There can be no doubt that Thoreau's essay ranks high in memories of that kind.

Cost what it may! Thoreau dramatizes the unequivocal and personal moral claim in a way that stirs youthful idealism, and even some not-so-youthful idealism. "If I have unjustly wrestled a plank from a drowning man, I must restore it, though I drown myself." "This people must cease to hold slaves, and to make war on Mexico, though it cost them their existence as a people." Professors of political science, not to mention secretaries of state, do not ordinarily talk that way. "Do justice to the slave and to Mexico, *cost what it may*." One hundred and twenty years later, young people, with their references to "bodies" on the "line," fastened onto sentences like these, and applied them to another war and to the aftermath of slavery in what they came to call "racism." Against the empty go-alongism of the crowd Thoreau represented both the "whiplash of the absolute" (as Kierkegaard put it) and the taking of full personal responsibility upon oneself that democracy both requires and endangers.

He wrote, "The mass of men serve the state . . . not as men mainly, but as machines. . . . In most cases there is no free exercise whatever of the judgment or the moral sense." Though he was in this sentence, and in general, too disdainful of his fellow citizens, he was right about what was required.

He said, "There are nine hundred and ninety-nine patrons of virtue to one virtuous man." One would not share the numerical estimate, or make so sharp a separation among men, but one would share the seriousness of the distinction.

He wrote, with much truth (the sort of thing a radical should write), "Statesmen and legislators, standing so completely within the institution, never distinctly and nakedly behold it. They speak of moving society, but have no resting place without it." (That is the criticism to be made perhaps of the conclusion of the influential political book *The Real Majority*, by Richard Scammon and Ben Wattenberg: "To move the moving center." To move one center, one must have a leverage point.)

But alongside all that is valuable and moving in Thoreau's essay there is something else, not moving and not valuable, although also not easy to separate from the other. This is the combination of a quasi anarchism with a self-righteous insistence on his own moral autonomy. In this regard he anticipates the negative qualities of the idealistic young of 1965–70, and represents the danger to us all of a reaction against those demagogues, those terrible television people and public-relations men—the menace of publicity. Certain of his own rightness, Thoreau does not take with sufficient seriousness the claims of the state, of institutions, of democratic processes, and, also, of the majority—of the people.

Dozens of quotations from Thoreau's short piece illustrate the point one wants to reject. "I think we should be men first—and subjects afterward." But to be a "subject" is an essential part of what it is to be a man, living as men do in a society of other men. One might say that Thoreau here touches a fundamental philosophical error of Americans, that pristine individualism that pictures the lone individual existing outside and before his social relations, about which social relations he may in his own sweet time make his own pure decision. It is not so. We are born in a company of men, with given obligations.

"I am as desirous of being a good neighbor as I am of being a bad subject." Why a "bad" subject? And can you really be the first if you are the second?

"It is not desirable to cultivate a respect for the law, so much as for the right." And yet a respect for the law is part of a respect for the right, and in a body politic must often serve as its main aspect.

"Law never made men a whit more just" (yes it has, every day, in their behavior), "and by means of their respect for it, even the well-disposed are daily made the agents of injustice." Sometimes that does happen, but not "daily"; the point is to distinguish and to discriminate, and Thoreau's attitude no more helps to make the discrimination than does that of the wholly conventional uncritical man.

"I cannot for an instant recognize that political organization as *my* government which is the *slave's* government also." Is that not the voice of pride? An unrealistic, individualist pride? It is *your* government, which fact gives a shape to your effort to make it *not* be a slave's government. It is our government that did the terror bombing of Hanoi December 18–30, 1972, and that dropped atomic bombs on Hiroshima and on Nagasaki in 1945, and that arbitrarily put American citizens of Japanese ancestry behind barbed wire on racial grounds in 1941, and that has done many other reprehensible deeds, joined with still more sins of omission. It is precisely *our* government that does these things, plus many others that are desirable and necessary, in a mixture that a responsible democratic man strives continually to assess and affect.

"I, Henry Thoreau, do not wish to be regarded as a member of any incorporated society which I have not joined." More pride. Henry Thoreau was born into one—into several, really. This, like many others of the sentences in that essay, is the sort of proud utopian personal thing one copies into one's notebook when one is a young American, along with Eugene Debs's address to the judge and sentences from Walt Whitman. Indeed, the whole essay, perhaps the whole lifework of Thoreau, partakes of that proud lonely adolescent idealistic spirit. It is one half of the truth, and in the right circumstance one part of a political education, but taken whole not sound doctrine for a mature citizen.

". . . Any man more right than his neighbors constitutes a majority of one already." It is not possible to build the comity a viable republic requires on that sentiment. It is one of Thoreau's answers to the idea that he should wait upon the majority, try to persuade the majority of Massachusetts citizens to his view. Thoreau says he hasn't time to do that—life isn't long enough. He has other things to do. In the sixties many college instructors and students and "activists" and radicals talked and acted on something like Thoreau's principle, to the damage of their several causes and to our common life.

When the news came that John Brown had raided Harpers Ferry, Thoreau, according to C. Vann Woodward, "never hesitated a moment." On the day after Brown's capture, he compared the hero's inevitable execution with the crucifixion of Christ. Harpers Ferry was "the best news that America ever had"; Brown, "the bravest and humanest man in all the country."

"Thoreau," wrote Woodward further, "carried intolerance to the point of moral snobbery. When a noble deed is done, who is likely to appreciate it? They who are noble themselves. . . ."

I was not surprised that certain of my neighbors spoke of John Brown as an ordinary felon, for who are they? They have either much flesh, or much office, or much coarseness of some kind. They are not ethereal natures in any sense. The dark qualities predominate in them. . . . For the children of the light to contend with them is as if there should be a contest between eagles and owls. . . .

Thoreau's reply to attacks upon John Brown's methods was: "The method is nothing; the spirit is all." This was the Transcendentalist way of saying that means are justified by the ends. According to this doctrine, if the end is sufficiently noble—as noble as the emancipation of the slave—any means used to attain the end is justified.

But what of those who clung to the democratic principle that differences should be settled by ballots and that the will of the majority should prevail? Thoreau asked, "When were the good and the brave ever in a majority?" Not often perhaps; never, if you raise the test of "good" and "brave" to a sufficient height. Nevertheless, a democrat does not dismiss the majority in that arrogant way. He has, instead, a lover's quarrel with the many majorities his people form and re-form and change.

So one can err in one way and another, and, as I said many pages ago, this democratic thing is not so very easy.

Mencken and his betters, assorted European writers, have said that democracy would destroy standards, values, excellence, quality. American democracy, the critics said, would be (or already has become) not only culturally vulgar but also morally corrupt.

Susan Sontag and others of the recent indigenous left pick up the old Menckenesque criticism of the American boob ("John Wayne chawing spareribs in the White House") but now it is no joke: the tone is not one of amused disdain, but of outrage.

We democrats reject the aristocrat's appraisal, partly because we see that the American democratic picture on this count is in fact not as dismal as they say; partly because we are convinced that however bad democracy turns out to be, as in the familiar quotation from Winston Churchill, every alternative is worse; but, most important, because for us no other "value" outranks that of the person, whom, if all its subtle institutions are in place, "democracy" protects.

14

On the Overwhelming
Importance of Purpose
Over Technique

(with an Eminence as a Source)

One of the more interesting discourses on American leadership—interesting in its own right, doubly interesting now because
of the man who wrote it—appeared in *The Reporter* of March 5,
1959. This was a long essay on the relation between the bureau-
crat, the policy maker, and the intellectual, which was spread
across many columns of that publication after much editorial
wrestling with the editor, Max Ascoli. It was written by a
younger foreign-policy expert, a naturalized citizen then teaching
at Harvard and giving advice to Nelson Rockefeller. He represented an even more significant contribution of Germanic civilization to the United States than H. L. Mencken, although he was
not ordinarily as amusing. In 1959 he was already well known in
foreign-policy circles but his fame had not reached the remoter
regions of the English and biology departments. When this essay
appeared, faculty members at the tables in Yale colleges asked,
"Who is this Henry Kissinger?"

Kissinger's point was the "stagnation" that results in high public policy from the unreflective and merely administrative approach that our society encourages in its ablest people (his focus,
characteristically, I think, was rather exclusively on the "ablest
people").

I want to use that essay for the purpose of this chapter and the
one that follows by a mammoth extrapolation, extending Kissinger's point to a far wider territory than he had covered: beyond

foreign policy to public policy in general, or "social" policy in general, and beyond that to the ethical foundations of policy; beyond the "ablest people" (the "executives" and "intellectuals" and "policy makers" in positions of eminence) out to the citizenry at large. In addition, I want to make even more explicit than Kissinger did the reciprocal relationship between the attitudes he describes and bureaucracy as a social form. Finally, I suggest that they both be seen as reciprocally related to modern technology and to its intellectual underpinnings. Let us give this combination a name in its own tongue: the "operational" complex. That means modern technology plus bureaucracy plus functional reasoning. It is important to see that the last is very much included in the phenomenon: habits of mind, attitudes, and ideas. The habits of mind are the central moral difficulty in modern-day America.

My extensions reach so far, perhaps, as to transform what Kissinger was saying into something else, and something he might not accept. He had written elsewhere, more or less offhandedly, back in those younger days, that one cannot go against the genius of a country. I remember asking myself, why not? Perhaps that is true for a budding diplomatist, being groomed by himself and his Harvard professors for the highest circles of foreign-policy leadership: he must take the characteristics of the national culture as given, and work within them. But what about other persons, who were not set upon this earth to be secretary of state? One way a conscientious citizen might shape his role is exactly to lean away from "the genius"—the prevailing attitudes—of his nation.

1

Kissinger had criticized the "administrative stagnation" that results from the way American leaders are trained. Why stop with leaders? And why stop, or start, with administrative stagnation? Kissinger wanted and wants purpose and policy to rule and guide administration, overcoming that stagnation. But policy, in turn, rests on an ethical foundation. One wants his criticism extended to the moral inertia that results from the way modern Americans, whether "leaders" or not, are trained.

I quote a paragraph now from Kissinger's essay, as printed in the last chapter of his book *The Necessity for Choice*. One may notice that he, too, in his academic manifestation was strong on paradox.

One of the paradoxes of an increasingly specialized, bureaucratized society, is that the qualities rewarded in the rise to eminence are less and less the qualities required once eminence is reached. . . . Administration is concerned with execution. Policy making must address itself also to developing a sense of direction . . . in the rise through the administrative hierarchy, the executive is shaped by a style of life that inhibits reflectiveness.

Bureaucracy and specialization, plus certain unreflective characteristics of American life, shape habits of mind inappropriate for the higher levels of policy making. Or, to put it the other way around, "eminence" requires a way of thinking—marked by creativity, purpose, and breadth—that the route to eminence up through the bureaucracy inhibits. The administrative hierarchy is marked by caution, routine, and playing it safe. But the policy maker must occasionally transcend routine with "purpose" (an important word for Kissinger). "One of the challenges of the contemporary situation is to demonstrate the overwhelming importance of purpose over technique."

Kissinger evidently had in mind, in these remarks, the men from business and finance who would come into the realm of high foreign policy. The entire world of young Henry Kissinger seemed to consist of presidents of the United States, actual and potential; top business executives who may join the cabinets of such presidents; and Harvard professors who give advice to these two sorts of people. Perhaps, indeed, it was about like that for him, and perhaps it still is.

He did respect these business leaders more than most Ivy League professors, from ignorance and stereotype as well perhaps as from other reasons, were inclined to do. Sitting in a comfortable chair in a living room in Princeton, back in the middle fifties, he mused about the attitudes of his fellow professors toward the big businessmen he was then meeting at the Council on Foreign Relations, in the circle around Nelson Rockefeller, in the commissions of the Rockefeller Brothers Fund: they (the intellectuals, the professors) think they *could* have accomplished the same things (as the successful businessman) had they chosen to, but most of them couldn't. Kissinger revealed a greater respect for the executive capacity, and a sharper awareness of the distinction between the intellectual virtues of the academician and the practical virtues of the executives, than most of his fellow professors, especially at his age, would have been able to muster. This awareness was reflected also in his essay. In it he recognized the limitations of the intellectual's role (a role he himself was then playing) in relation to policy making in a way that not all "intellectuals" were inclined to do: "ultimately the problem is not the intellectuals alone or even primarily. There is no substitute for greater insight on the part of our executives, in or out of government." He recommended that more of our highest executives-to-be have experience earlier than they now ordinarily do.

. . . it is essential that our most eminent men in all fields overcome the approach to national issues as an extracurricular activity that does not touch the core of their concerns. . . . A way must be found to enable our ablest people to deal with problems of policy and to perform national service in their formative years.

Bureaucratic and specialized routine leaves its mark not only on the "eminent" and "the ablest," but also on the uneminent and the not-necessarily-ablest. They, too, require a greater exposure to national problems; they, too, could benefit while young from the performance of national service; they, too, should learn to treat public life as more than an extracurricular pursuit. One must adapt this idea in order to apply it to the great body of citizens who are not likely to be secretaries of state, or even advisers to a secretary of state, but simply voters who will choose the presidents who select secretaries of state—citizens who will shape the body of opinion for which these leaders must have a decent respect. Nevertheless, it does apply.

The specialization of which he speaks plainly is not confined to rising business executives. As a primary mark of a modern society it extends to virtually every level, every activity, every adult person. The great principle of the Division of Labor has run riot across the face of civilized life, leaving us all now prisoners of our occupational identities. If you ask us who we are, we answer, as your expect us to answer, with our job or our occupational specialty: that is our identity.

And throughout the body politic the habits of mind developed in the routine of that specialty are as deleterious to the public good as Kissinger found them to be in the eminent.

Kissinger pictured a businessman or corporation lawyer projected into high-level public policy making as unsuited to his task because his life has been busy; his criteria for action unexamined, simplified ("briefings," charts, one-page summaries); his appreciation for genuine creativity stifled; his acquaintance with public policy extracurricular at best; the atmosphere out of which he comes unreflective. He has to be "briefed" on everything; he can rarely benefit from the "strong will" that often is his outstanding trait; in the unfamiliar environment of public affairs this strong will becomes mere "arbitrariness."

What part of this does not describe the ordinary citizen? Obviously there is a difference between this ordinary man and the eminent policy maker, but I suggest that the difference has been overdrawn in some quarters. New leaders continually arise from this body of citizens. Our "leaders" do not spring to eminence full accoutered from the brow of Zeus, or from a seminar at Harvard, but work their way up from a haberdashery in Kansas City. Or from the "Progressive party" at South High School in Grand Rapids. At least sometimes they do.

Kissinger said, "A democracy cannot function without a leadership group which has assurance in relation to the issues confronting it. We face, in short, a test of attitudes even more than of policies."

Exactly so. Indeed we do face such a test, and not only in the field of foreign policy. I move two perfecting amendments to Kissinger's first sentence. Drop the word "group" and leave those leaders standing each one on his own two feet ("leadership group" sounds too much a periphrasis for that unfortunate and widespread import "elite"). And then add the citizenry to the same sentence. They and the leaders both need the "assurance" of which Kissinger wrote.

I move another amendment: the needed assurance should rest at last not alone on either expert mastery, or strength of will, but, rather, on civic virtue.

$\mathscr{2}$

Is there something particularly "American" about the society that yields the defects that Kissinger identified? Much of the world says yes. While moving eagerly toward it, the world still blames America for the faults of the machinery and the attitudes of the operational society. And no doubt there are at least affinities with this particular culture: with our practicality and with "equality-of-condition" or democracy. Because these are or can be our virtues, no easy condemnation is allowable.

The most obvious temptation of American democracy is to be unduly hospitable to technology as a result of our overwhelming overemphasis on the practical, the immediate, the useful. The American wants to embody in actual life the goals of living that otherwise are only abstractly celebrated, contemplated, and proclaimed; he wants to realize the goods of life in *practice*. This is a good, for men have a striking capacity to make their theories, not guides and standards actually employed to criticize life, and make life good, and live it well, but, rather, illusions, rationalizations, and substitutes for reality. There is a connection between this practicality and democracy: we, the people, live lives that are very daily, made up of daily practices in the shop, the store, the kitchen, the office, the cab. Where the man of past civilizations stood on the banks of the river contemplating, speculating about, admiring, and praying over the wonders on the other side, the American is the one who set to work and built a bridge.

One can find in the amiable history by Daniel Boorstin an ample and favorable picture of the democratic practicality of the American people, among whom knowledge has come in small and useful parcels—in the inventions and gadgets and layman's experience of the multitudes of common people, relying upon no a priori theory and no permanent elite.

To make these actual changes in concrete life one must be concerned about *technique;* one must ask not only *why* and *what* but also *how.* One must pay attention to the *means.* By attention to the *means,* we Americans have felt, you learn some of the meaning of the final things. (Ends and means cannot be that neatly separated, as the quite American thinker John Dewey would say.) One learns something important about the truth, beauty, goodness, et cetera, of trees and rivers by actually using the techniques of bridge-building. This practical inclination plainly has its merits, and a clear association with democracy. Nevertheless, at least when the modern operational world picks it up, it becomes a source of our predicament.

Kissinger wrote that those business executives who turn up in the field of foreign policy are affected by some deep-seated, though usually not articulated, philosophical attitudes. "Two generations of Americans," he wrote, have been shaped by the "pragmatic" conviction that "inadequate performance is somehow the result of a failure to understand an 'objective' environment properly." (He need hardly have limited it to two generations; long before John Dewey, the practicality of the Connecticut Yankee was a legend.) This attitude tends to "identify a policy issue with the search for empirical data." There is "a greater concern with the collection of facts than with their significance." Get all the facts before deciding—or instead of deciding. Or, rather: the facts *do* the deciding. Facts, data, information, the objective environment: know them and the decision is made. There is no dimension of judgment and evaluation—of moral interpretation—beyond the reach of fact, shaping and selecting fact.

The problem then is magnified by what Kissinger calls "one of the most attractive American traits," a "personal humility": "most Americans are convinced that no one is ever entirely 'right,' or, as the saying goes, that if there is disagreement each party is probably a little in error. The fear of dogmatism pervades the American scene." I believe there is more to this than personal humility, more than what Kissinger calls a psychological bias: there is another philosophical doctrine, allied to pragmatism, a modern relativism or skepticism that some "democratic" attitudes reinforce.

Finally, there are the committees. In Kissinger's 1959 complaint about his discoveries on the foreign-policy circuit he notes the love of committees. Since pragmatically "experience" is the ultimate source of knowledge, the more "experience" the merrier (*i.e.*, the more people around the table with "experience"). Committees proliferate, and consensus becomes the test. One can read between the lines a certain exasperation on the part of the young Henry Kissinger with the circuit of foreign-policy togetherness in the late fifties. He wrote in passing a concessionary criticism of the personalizing of his office by Secretary of State John Foster Dulles ("whose technical virtuosity could not obscure the underlying stagnation") that certainly is fraught with historical interest, the way things have turned out. One would guess that his heart was not in it.

This is not to say that committees are inherently pernicious or that policy should be conducted on the basis of personal intuition. Most contemporary problems are so complex that the interaction of many minds is necessary. . . . Any attempt to conduct policy on a personal basis inhibits creative approaches just as surely as does the purely administrative approach. . . .

It is conceivable that men in the current State Department would read that quotation, from that source, with a certain bemusement.

Each of these American traits requires an antecedent and controlling "purpose," and a moral substance informing that purpose, in order to be beneficial.

The empiricism—the devotion to facts and to the hardness of objective reality—is distinctly worth while if, but only if, the concepts that guide the search for facts, that shape and evaluate them, are grounded in a moral order; otherwise one has immoral curiosity experimenting on prisoners, the amoral love of facts of the merely knowledgeable scientist. The facts do "speak," but they do not quite speak for themselves. Not about the nature of the good, which must be the subject of an endless human quest and conversation.

The pragmatism, similarly, has merit as, and only as, it is subordinated to directing moral reason: only as it is addressed to pragmatic matters, which though of indispensable importance are nevertheless secondary: how to do something and how it works are subordinate questions to what is to be done and why.

And that "democratic" reliance upon the sharing of opinions, upon compromise, adjustment, and committee meetings, has value, but only so far as the participants bring something to the exchange beyond their own reflection of the group opinion.

These American traits have value, but only, so to speak, in their properly subordinate place. We might formulate the point into a near paradox of our own: the operational society makes increased demands upon the moral understanding of citizens, which its own nature inhibits them from achieving.

3

If a modern American democrat is wary about conservatisms, old or new, and too appreciative of the continuity and the complexity of social life to be what is called a radical, what then may be his view of the realm that technique rules, the overarching realm of the modern world, giant organizations and elaborate modern technology? It is here most of all that one refers to the slogan that the direction in which to move is not to the right or to the left, but deeper.

On the one side there is American conservatism (a long way from Edmund Burke) not only complacently endorsing the depredations of modern industry but also itself much dominated by the uncritical ask-no-questions can-do mentality. And there more or less on the same side is the vast consuming public, wheeling carts chock full o' downright goodness, as the ads might say, through the aisles of supermarkets; munching potato frizzlies in front of color TV sets; roaring down monstrous Interstate highways in monstrous station wagons to see monstrous drive-in movies.

On the other side there is the sweeping reaction against all of that reflected in the monstrous sentence I have just written. There are thousands of such sentences, phrases, ballads, songs, and slogans. There are our modern counterparts of the Luddites and the Romantics, reacting today against the technological society as these antecedents did against the industrial society. The youth revolt of the late sixties was, verbally and superficially at least, sweepingly antitechnological: the drug culture, the commune, the return to the land, the dropping out of the "rat race," a faddish popular existentialism, the rejection of the "plastic" society, the spread of assorted irrational cults and fancies out of the East and out of more primitive cultures. There were efforts to construct a world view, or, in the language of this world of thought itself, a "life style," exactly out of the ingredients of the universe the technological society was thought to suppress: spontaneity, mystery, irrationality, the unique and the absurd. The "Fugs" practiced their exorcism in the Pentagon parking lot (the Bureaucracy won that round when some wit gave them permission to lift it no more than five feet). A literary weathervane explained (with whatever measure of seriousness) that in order to understand women he must believe in witchcraft. "Revolution" was deliberately brainless: "revolution without ideology"; revolutions for the hell of it. Students explained to you on the first day of class that the "intellectual" approach had been tried and had failed, so that it was now necessary to take instead the "emotional" approach. The Consumer Economy encourages neurotic anxiety about normal body odors; the radical young opponents typically seemed to say in response: Abolish deodorant; let stink abound.

The holistic attack on modern technology was by no means confined to the wildest and youngest and most bearded and most foolish. There is of course a long literary tradition of unhappiness with machine civilization, and there is also a recent European tradition of existentialism; these found themselves now thrust to the center of the modern stage. A "counterculture" was to be made in the Greened America. The most thoroughgoing of the serious attacks known to me was that of Jacques Ellul, the French philosopher-lawyer-theologian, who published a relentless denunciation of "La Technique"—omnipresent, self-augmenting, international, irreversible. Ellul's powerful book, *The Technological Society*, was being translated in Santa Barbara in 1960–61 by an American sympathizer whose eyes would go cold and steely when he spoke of the physicists, chemists, and technocrats he had once known, with their cold and steely eyes, marching like robots on the modern world with their inhuman science and their inhuman technology. Ellul's book is rather like that translator: a bit extreme.

And so are those radical antitechnology people in general, whether of the popular or the serious kind. What they do is to draw the line against everything that technology is taken to represent, perhaps even that science is taken to represent, and to affirm whatever is on the nether side of that line: let stink abound. Ellul's relentless book offers only this against the terrible omnipresence of technique: spontaneity. One might almost say he rejects every deliberate and rational and purposeful human action, because it already thereby (in being less—or more—than spontaneous) partakes of the evil-thing technique.

I said "rational," and that of course is another section of the battlefield. A student in the late sixties' classroom who said that the rational-intellectual way had been tried and had failed (had led to nuclear weapons and the war in Vietnam) and that it should therefore now be superseded by the "emotional" way was by no means exceptional. All around him then there were the anti-intellectual spooks and dragons of the counterculture, embraced with a particular passion by the young but not by the young alone. "Reason" meant only our modern and empirical reason and the "functional rationality": reason that investigates, tests, and tells how things work; reason that manages, arranges, "operates." That there was an older and deeper role for human reason, not the same as this "reason" of the Dow Chemical Company, these students did not know, and their pied pipers did not tell them. Against all those countercultural people one wants to say, the response to the debased "reason" of technological society is not irrationality, but a moral reason that should control technical reason.

Spontaneity, irrationality, mystery spooks and dragons: that is one direction in which to move, in protest against the modern world. But it is not the direction recommended here. The operational society requires a more severe criticism than it ordinarily receives in popular American thought, but of a different kind from the radicals'.

Discriminate judgment, founded in "true humanism" and the moral substance of the Western tradition: that is the place to begin.

4

The operational society is not simply the land of elaborate machinery; is is also the land of the bureaucracies that produce and control the technological marvels, and which produce the habits of mind Kissinger criticized.

Bureaucracy, as in ancient Alexandria, I suppose, antedates the modern technological world but is closely linked to it all the same, "efficiency" and "rationality" in the one and the other reciprocally related: where would our giant world bureaucracies be without the invention of the telephone? The causes and effects no doubt run back and forth in intricate reciprocity between the organizational and the technological "revolutions," "rationality" in the one encouraging and requiring "rationality" in the other, and both at bottom serving that same purpose, "rationality" in the limited and perhaps debased sense, the sense in which Mannheim could write "the rationalization of society is the derationalization of man." "Rationality" here means, in the first case, what a kind of social scientist means by it, which is virtually identical with the meaning of "efficiency": the least cost for the benefit, the good, the goal or end to be achieved. It is "irrational" to give up more that is of value—time, resources of this sort or that—than is required to obtain the value sought. So says the modern technological and also bureaucratic world. After a cost-benefit "rationality" session of an honors class in politics and economics a very bright Yale undergraduate was asked by his professor, hoping to dramatize a point while they stood on the corner of York and Elm Streets, whether he thought that way about his girl friend. "Absolutely," he responded instantly. Benefit, so much; cost, so much; calculation; clickety-click. Hello, Margorie. His professor walked away depressed.

Bureaucracy has the same principle at root: it is "efficiency" connected to human organization. At bottom there is that great discovery the division of labor: you are the floor sweeper, so you sweep the floor. Built upon that specialized foundation—you do this, you do that, and each of you keep doing it, and we get the whole job done more efficiently—there is the perhaps somewhat less justifiable principle of hierarchy, of subordination and superordination, of who's in charge here?, and the vice president for this division, with a larger office than the associates who have larger offices than the assistants who are grouped together with larger desks than the secretaries. The layers of authority in an army were the purest model for the bureaucracy of Max Weber's classic picture; now those layers, of course, are everywhere. Command—Obey. And the office is separated from the man: unlike primitive and "charismatic" leadership, the authority of the vice president in charge of sales goes with that office, without regard to the characteristics of the man who fills it. "The presidency," as we have had recently all too much chance to learn, is an impersonal "institution," with powers and prerogatives independent of the changing persons, with their differing attributes, who sit in (as we say) "the Oval Office."

The point of these characteristics of bureaucracy is efficiency, however comical that statement may seem to anyone who has served in one or dealt with one. The reason for dividing labor and specializing and having somebody in charge and "rationalizing" the social arrangement is to make it like a machine, a functioning purpose-achieving cost-minimizing operation of human beings related to each other in such a way as to achieve maximum value from the effort . . . as with the machinery the word "technology" originally connotes.

Behind the computers, the Polaris missiles, the plastic organs, and satellite and cable-television sets of modern technology, there is a way of thinking about the world; behind the giant bureaucracies, there is that same way of thinking: "technical and sophisticated"; Maritain and Tillich's "technical reason"; Mannheim's "functional rationality"; the reasoning that asks "*how.*"

But then came this reaction, out of the young, out of the peace movement, out of European intellectual circles. Ellul and his steely-eyed friends went too far; Charles Reich and his beads went too far. They represented the reverse of the antagonist, and therefore, perversely, not a real criticism of it. As the young man sings his antitechnological songs to an electric guitar, as the young radical posts bond, after his arrest for his protest against "the System," with his American Express credit card, so a great deal of the kicking and screaming as we are dragged into the twenty-first century is phony. Much is such mindless protesting, so anti-intellectual, and therefore immediately assimilable in shape, as itself to become a functioning and salable part of the culture against which it is alleged to be in protest. So "the Greening of America" becomes a big money-maker, as did the somewhat better book *The Organization Man* in an earlier decade: eagerly read and discussed by Consciousness II people in organizations. Even the much more serious book to which I have referred—Ellul's *The Technological Society*—is so sweeping, so unqualified, as to make every proposal (governmental action, for an obvious one) that might mitigate that society's effects itself reflect the technique that is the evil, so he has you coming and going: what Ellul wrote is what Samuel Hoffenstein might call a "Poem of Fairly Utter Despair," but omit the Fairly.

"Technique," however, is not an evil in itself, but one expression of essential humanity: man is maker, doer, even an artist. Neither is technical reason an unequivocal evil, nor, certainly, the division of labor or modern science. The line to take is not technical reason unbounded, or irrationality in protest, but the older moral reason controlling technical reason. The overriding point is that the operational society requires an explicit and discriminating moral education, and a self-conscious and continuing ethical criticism, of a sort that is, rather, in the opposite direction from the one generally taken by modern men bewitched by science and technology. To put it another way: technology's remarkable combination of immensely powerful low-level purposefulness with purposeless inertia at higher levels requires more conscious deliberation about human purposes than has hitherto been called for. Toward the end of the long and curiously variegated intellectual career of Walter Lippmann he came in that rather tentative and somewhat disdained book (disdained in the social science departments of universities, at any rate) to recommend a version of natural law which he called a "public philosophy." Let us, though we sympathize, not go so far: an *ethos* would do, rather than so formal and so unified a matter as one public "philosophy." Or a shared moral-political territory in which men with values of many sorts join in a conversation, at least in talking the same language, about the public life of a free people.

Henry Kissinger wrote in 1959 that "few if any of the recent crises of U.S. policy have been caused by the unavailability of data. Our policy makers do not lack advice; they are in many respects overwhelmed by it. They do lack criteria on which to base judgments. And in the absence of commonly understood and meaningful standards, all advice tends to become equivalent."

They lack "criteria" and "commonly understood and meaningful standards," and fall back on "data" and "techniques."

5

Let me in conclusion introduce another manuscript, quite different from any Kissinger product, in the interests of this point: specialization on the one side breeds inept treatment of general ideas on the other, which then drives men back to the satisfying "hardness" of the speciality, of technical knowledge.

We may say this time that the document was found among the unread but coffee-stained discussion papers of a conferee home from a gathering of a sort that some readers may find familiar.

Confessions of a Conference Goer

IF WE ARE NOW to use the word "research" as a verb ("I will research it"), we ought to go all the way. We should stretch the word to cover the inverted and reflexive arrangement in which the man does not seek the data but the data fling themselves upon the man—often to his considerable annoyance. Perhaps we could say something like "It has researched itself upon me." At any rate, the young scholar who pictures himself as having the initiative, choosing his subject and going after it, is in for a nasty surprise. In life, subjects reach up and grab you, pulling you far from your intention, and researching you into becoming a halfhearted semiexpert in some unlikely area, quite against your will.

On the Importance of Purpose Over Technique

I live at the intersection of several do-goodish operations—religious, educational, reforming, and political—and therefore have become, inadvertently, along with what must now be thousands of others, a semiexpert in the consultation, conference, symposium, institute, seminar, round table, or center: its nature and failings.

The kind of gathering I mean is the extramural and voluntary one, sponsored by some foundation, university, or association, that brings together men from widely scattered fields to deal with some broad question. In the mail comes a letterhead with a strange device, and the request that one turn up in Hot Springs or State College or Washington to discuss, with assorted experts from business, labor, government, the universities, the churches, "mass communications," etc., the great question of "Our National Flimflam." Quickly the eye runs down the page to find the paragraph in which the honorarium is given; then one muses, "Our national flimflam: yes, that is truly a significant question," and off one goes. Such conferences—on the increase, I believe, in recent years— are to be distinguished from narrower, intramural meetings of men in one line of work, in which the delegates may be presumed to know what they are talking about.

What I really do in what we may laughingly call my working time at such gatherings is not to think about the subject to which the conference, seminar, etc., itself is addressed (these subjects, in my experience, range from immense to gigantic, and from fluid to gaseous), but, instead, to think, or, rather, mostly to talk, about what is wrong with the symposium, consultation, etc., itself.

I quickly learn, in the hotel rooms and on the mountain trails or the beaches, that this is what most of the other consultants, conferees, seminarians, or delegates are doing, too, insofar as they have any spiritual connection whatever with the meeting to which their bodies, at great expense, have been brought. And it is not only in the more pleasant and unofficial discussions that the feeding hand is bitten; often the formal sessions of the conference itself will be addressed, in effect, whatever the nominal topic may be, to the same great subject, namely, "What is wrong with this conference?"

It is not unknown for a consultation to spend its entire time exactly on that matter. The very first discussant may observe that the topic, fraught with significance though of course it is, really needs another approach, or a redefinition; the second will agree, but offer a contradictory approach, or a different redefinition; another, possibly alone in having looked at the material sent to the delegates beforehand, will add that this material, excellent though it is, does not quite get to the heart of the matter. Others will join in, politely agreeing that though of course this is a magnificent conference on a vastly important subject, with outstanding speakers and good materials, still we really should have a slightly different subject, other speakers, new materials, and possibly also a different time and place.

The agreement among the delegates covers only the one negative point, that the meeting should be other than it is; from there on they divide. Certainly there will be a session, or two or three or more, devoted to the procedure of the sessions themselves, at every level: "I suggest, Mr. Chairman, that it would be better if we proceed from the general to the particular, rather than the other way around." "On the contrary, Mr. Chairman, I think we should take a concrete case, something we can get our teeth into, and avoid these generalities." "Couldn't we have all the speeches simultaneously the first thing in the morning, and get them over with?" "Are we going to have a report? And to whom should it be addressed?" "Can't we have a personal stenographer in every buzz group?" In this way, many happy, high-paid hours are spent.

Now, from having been researched by many of these gatherings, what great conclusions do we draw? What, indeed, was wrong with those meetings?

Much can always be said, of course, against the Conference Man. He is dumber, sleepier, greedier, more confused, and generally less likable than individual man. He is late to meetings. He can bear any amount of nonsense so long as he is fed well and paid well and has the afternoons free for horseback riding and golf. He likes to associate with eminence and to pretend to importance, so long as it does not involve much actual work. So much for him.

Much could also be said against what social philosophers doubtless would call Collective Man—that monument of selfishness who is convinced that he is to be excused any amount of outrageous behavior simply because he represents some worthy and respected pressure group. Logrolling and back scratching are his exercises; *Quid pro quo* and *Cui bono?* are his mottoes; his own interest is all he really cares about.

A good deal would also have to be said, in this connection, about Democratic Man, at least as he appears in the United States. He seems to think that democracy requires much unprepared talking and still more talking, many meetings and still more meetings, and the spontaneous expression of opinions by everyone. If numbers of people meet and talk, and talk and meet, he seems to feel, wisdom thereby arises. He lives by the terrible principle of representativeness. Men are brought to these conferences, regularly, in a sort of balanced ticket: one Jew, one Catholic, one Protestant; one labor leader to every businessman; one Republican to every Democrat; very carefully, a Negro and a woman; an economist with the Economist's View, a psychoanalyst with the Psychoanalytical View, a philosopher with the Standpoint of Philosophy. In my earliest conference-going days I myself was a College Student, attending as representative decoration at conferences composed mainly of older people. Invariably there would come a golden moment when—since I then had sense enough to keep my mouth shut and would not have spoken—the chairman would pounce: "But let us hear from the Student Mind"; or "And how does this sound to Young People?"

THE RUINOUS PRINCIPLE of representativeness and the fierce self-interest of Collective Man tie in with a still greater source of defective consultations and institutes: in the society they draw upon, the great principle of the division of labor has run riot. Men now wrap their minds and souls, and also their egos, around the technical rigor, or anyway the jargon and the outlook, of their own line; they lose, if they ever had it, the ability to treat general and public questions with anything approaching the disciplined intelligence they give, at their best, to their specialty.

A broadly mixed conference, therefore, is something of a battle between competing occupational ideologies. The men of action, flexing their muscles, citing the payrolls they have met, resolutely apply only a practical test to any question: what would you do if you were secretary of state? The men of thought counter this with their prearranged categories and with ever more refined distinctions: just when a nonthinker thinks he has caught on, the thinker has yet another distinction to keep himself in the lead. The fact people cite studies and still more empirical studies, the conclusion of which is that we need yet more studies before any conclusions can be drawn; the idea people, managing to convey the impression that it is beneath the dignity of thinkers to deal in information, jump instead to first principles and to the absolute priority of the philosophical underpinnings. The national people insist on the over-all view; the local people insist that you have to know how it is at the grass roots. The academic intellectuals find the "insights" of the nonacademic intellectuals random and undisciplined, partaking of shallow journalism; the nonacademic intellectuals find the school people's book-dropping stuffy and timid.

And all this barely scratches the surface of a much more intricate pattern of defensiveness and disrespect, among all sorts of highly refined varieties, from metaphysics to business psychology (it has not been researched unto me that this last actually exists, but it must; it is a natural).

Some common thread is needed to bind all these contending varieties together, but we haven't got it.

I spoke of the way data press themselves, unbidden, upon the researcher (or researchee); conclusions do the same. By examining the fault in the conference, I am brought, much to my surprise, to a conclusion about the subject I was avoiding, the very one to which the conference ordinarily is addressed: What is missing in our national purpose, image, democracy, mass communication, morality, commitment, character, education, free society, and will? What is missing is the shared intellectual frame that would make for a fruitful conference.

15

The Moral Comedy of
an Operational Society

The world that has been created by technical reason is, in the phrase of the sociologist Robert K. Merton, "a complex of standardized means to predetermined ends." I adopt its own orderly and numerical manner, to make a little list:

1. It isolates certain ends—the "predetermined" ends—to be served, and sets others aside.

2. It standardizes the means to attain them.

3. It selects certain kinds of ends that fit well with "technique," and neglects others that do not.

4. It gradually leads men's affections away from the ends to be served to the means for attaining them; men come to have an attachment to the means for their own sake.

5. It resists the questioning and revising of the ends or the means, once they have been stamped into their predetermined and standardized tracks.

6. It generates a momentum of its own, rolling down these tracks with a powerful inertia. Ironically, beginning at its best with exceptional and concentrated purposiveness, it ends at its worst with purposeless repetition.

7. Eventually therefore, pursued uncritically, it violates important values, sometimes including in ironic and poetic self-contradiction even those values it was intended to serve. One remembers that American officer in Vietnam who was reported soberly to have explained that it was necessary to destroy this village in order to save it.

8. It produces far-reaching unintended side effects, and not the side effects of one operation only but of another and another and another, and these side effects accumulate and form a culture.

Not, precisely, the culture we are living in, which is a mixture of these with other tendencies. One does not make this list under the impression that it describes reality—not the whole reality. The picture of the modern world that this list evokes is a cautionary negative model, a warning, an indication of very powerful inclinations. It is not our intention to present this complex as some kind of technological determinism, throwing in the towel of one's humanity in the face of an ineluctable wave of the future. That is exactly what one resists, since a great need in such a world is more precisely to underline the character of man as a free and responsible actor, and of the future as real, undetermined, awaiting the exercise of his moral judgment and his action.

The reason for this examination therefore is not to encourage despair, fairly utter or total. The purpose, rather, is moral and political. This society—"technological," "technotronic," "operational"—is shot through with purpose, or with failed purpose: in other words, with what should be, in the broader and older usage, morals. It starts with the proper subject matter of morals: human purposes, ends, or values. It does—or it does not. I may try to deal with human objectives resolutely excluding such considerations, which, then, is an equally appropriate occasion for asserting distinct ethical priorities. Each of the points in that list casts its own warning, and its own instruction about the particular moral sensitivity the modern world requires.

1. The genius of modern technology begins with the clarity and precision with which an end to be sought is identified and isolated. There is an implied analysis of human purposes and wants: a sorting, a separation, a simplification of goals. Men want to eat, we give them food; fat men want *not* to eat, we give them Metrecal; men want speedy movement from place to place, we give them in place of a horse the railroad, the automobile, the airplane, the jet. They want a warm house, we give them central heating; they want a cool house, we give them air conditioning. They want bread, we give them lots of it although with more nutrition in the wrapper than in the bread. They want the nutrition back, we put in something and call it "enriched." They want it to taste better, we put in some additional mass-produced ingredient

and call the result "Mom's Own Homemade Vitamin-enriched Stone-ground Sho'nuff *Bread.*"

In order to make efficient use of the means, one must "predetermine" the end: fix and identify it. When Lewis Mumford distinguishes a tool (a knife) from a machine (a lathe) he notes the multiple uses of the former, as an extension of human powers, and the comparatively limited and confined use of the latter, as a potentially independent instrument. Therein lies the beginning of the technological society: its genius and its danger. By fixing the goal, by honing the definition of it and the means to it, the machine man attains that goal beyond the dreams of merely tool-making man; there follow all the wonders and comforts of the modern world. But if in the original analysis and identifying of his purposes he left something out, or if it is in the nature of higher values not to be separable from other values, or if it is in their nature to change and to blend, then the machine age is in trouble. As indeed it is.

The modern "rigorous" sorting of purposes plainly is not confined to the machine shop. An American philosopher said about training in the law: It sharpens the mind by narrowing it. One could observe, and even discern in oneself, these two effects when thrust for a time into a modern law school. Where, one asked, is that fundamental course in jurisprudence that explores the meaning of law itself? Where do the budding attorneys learn the moral underpinnings of the law? Where indeed? Well, we all do a little of that. There are a couple of fellows up on the third floor who work with that stuff—analyze those terms.

It was a world that was very impressive, very sharp, very narrow. One of the small number of other quotations about the law known to me is Justice Holmes's phrase "To Live Largely in the Law." Recent events and one's experience tempt the observation that many in that field seem to accomplish the opposite.

Not to pick on lawyers: we all live smally in our domains, it may be, in part because the culture shapes us to do so. The culture shapes us to do so because its social machinery is built upon analysis, and upon clarity and "hardness" of purpose. Not only as practical men but also as moral men we seek the exclusions that support and direct the will. The human will moving toward decision and action, whether for lower or higher purposes, wants to simplify, to exclude complicating mixtures. But those exclusions the other considerations shut out for the time being cannot be shut out forever. In war there is no substitute for Victory! said General MacArthur. No doubt in the moment of battle a general needs to think that way, and perhaps a soldier does, too; but a president cannot do that, and even a general cannot do that forever and under all circumstances, changed circumstances. There are not only a Yalu River and a Chinese intervention and a Geneva Convention, but also the political purposes for which the victory is sought, which in turn fit within a larger frame of policy, and eventually of fundamentals about life.

There is, or there should be, a continual dialectic between the simplified purposefulness of the deciding will and the "higher" and more complex understanding and moral insight of reason and conscience, perceiving its obligation to affirm the other man, the human person in every man. The machine world pounds ahead, powerfully, with its single purposes; such a world, then, is doubly and continually needful of that controlling humane understanding—inexact, difficult, shifting—that it does not like to hear about.

Suppose in that isolation of an end efficiently to be served something important was already left out back at the start? Suppose the analysis of goals, separating them, already had destroyed something—the "wholeness of personal being," say—that cannot be restored by further techniques?

The deeper human values are subtle, nuanced, subject to change under changed conditions, intertwined with other values. The insistent technician's analysis, destroying the original wholeness, removes for efficiency the delicate ambience of other values, which finally in some consternation men try to recover.

2. The isolated objective is pursued by standardized means. "Technical reason" is the reasoning that seeks the One Best Way to accomplish the desired result: the efficient way, the way with the least cost for the most benefit. Having found it, it repeats it, and repeats it, and builds the repetition into the sorts of institutions that are its representatives: the assembly line; the giant of-

fice; the "repetitious emphasis" of advertising jingles, dinning the brand name into your head whether you want to know it or not; the stereotypes of the Western film, the afternoon TV drama, and the quiz show, with their formulas.

Labor is divided so that the parts of it may be done repeatedly, and therefore presumably more efficiently: Charlie Chaplin bending and bending his wrist. Of course modern industry is vastly different from the picture, itself a stereotype, in Chaplin's "Modern Times"; decades now of "human relations in industry" have tried to ameliorate the troubles of work in the factory and office. These efforts themselves, however, may partake at their level yet again of the stereotype. The operational society, a mammoth and intricate structure with many, many layers, may show its characteristics once more in more new ways at each level. But repetition, standardization, and stereotype will persist, in particular at the lower levels; they must to some degree, because they are part of the genius of this kind of a society. They are essential to its many benefits: multiple Mustangs, multiple Kinney shoes, multiple McDonald's hamburgers, multiple Boeing 707's, multiple pay checks from the payroll bureaucracy.

And multiple memos with multiples of technical terms, or pieces of jargon. Technological society is not only machinery but also language, habits of thought, ways of looking at the world. Why does any bureaucracy inevitably produce its own kind of gobbledygook? The standardizing quickly goes beyond the level of properly useful activity, where shorthands and exactitudes are routine, to other levels, where such language is habitual, lazy, and distasteful. Technical language in its proper place, like technique of all kinds—skill of all kinds—has its gentle satisfaction for the human spirit: it is a pleasure to understand well and speak properly, exactly, about the art and practice of some interesting human activity: running pass formations, marking up a bill, trading stocks, or editing a manuscript. But that standard language, the exact language, properly used in its narrow domain, is flattened and extended and added to and ruined, as Pierre found out about the principles of military science. Then the words are not pleasing: jargon and gobbledygook go with the modern world, and there is a reason.

This is the picture that popular sociology holds before our eyes, and also not without reason: that men, talking interchangeable formulas, dressed in interchangeable gray flannel suits, drive interchangeable station wagons from interchangeable ranch houses to take interchangeable commuter trains to do interchangeable jobs in interchangeable offices, writing interchangeable memos about interchangeable television programs about men dressed in interchangeable gray flannel suits who drive interchangeable station wagons . . . The question arises whether they became interchangeable men.

3. The operational society is not simply neutral as among the purposes its powerful instruments shall fulfill. It has a potent bias. It selects and favors certain ends—those that fit its bias well—and it neglects others that do not. Modern society creates a mighty undercurrent running toward those objects of human striving that are easiest to predetermine, served by means that are easiest to standardize. A society built around machinelike techniques encourages attention to the more immediate and tangible objects in life: those that a machine can deal with. It chooses the machinelike means, in the arrangements of society, of language, and of thinking. It tends to select those objectives that are most easily dealt with by routine and technique: those that are recurrent, that are shared by all men, that involve no imponderable or unpredictable element, usually those that involve the material basis of life. Thus in the end the ethical, esthetic, intellectual, and religious claims—those, that is, that are qualitative—are threatened by the disproportionate place given to technique. Fundamental purpose and meaning are not examined, and after a time one begins even to forget what they were. Having efficiently built the bridge and crossed to the other side, the American may now be asking, in some puzzlement, just why was it he wanted to be here.

As a man, or society, makes practice and efficient performance a major value in itself, he implicitly also makes other important assumptions. He takes for granted that the goals the techniques "efficiently" serve are worth while: thus the overemphasis on the practical in the long run has a debasing effect. The stress on the operational is not simply neutral as among the goals the operation may serve; it has a built-in bias. It tends to encourage the more immediate and short-run objects in life.

It is no secret that the technological society has provided marvelous improvements in shelter and food and transportation and clothing and entertainment and medical care and a material base of existence. These marvels, however much we may grumble about particular limitations, are something almost all men yearn for. Most of us who criticize this society do so in the comfort, leisure, convenience, and safety it provides. Men, given a choice, go where technology has brought a higher material base for living. In those third worlds and fourth worlds outside the circle of the triumph of the machine, they yearn and strive to come within it.

But the wise men of these so-called underdeveloped countries are right to be wary about the culture that technology brings with it: technology, creator and destroyer.

When he has shaped the field of values so that the tangible and immediate predominate, modern man may then try to extend his technical apparatus back into the realms he has neglected. One finds the effort to be "efficient," to reduce problems to those of technique, to eliminate the imponderable, mysterious, and evaluative, extended even to matters of a "philosophy of life," and of personal relations, religion, and morality, and of politics and social philosophy. In politics, for example, one discovers a kind of American who assumes that government is only a matter of clearcut administration, and of knowledge of fact and technical skill; he does not grasp the irreducible element of value and interest and of risk and of the unknown; he does not see why "businesslike government" is neither possible nor desirable. One finds the techniques of "salesmanship" and "selling" everlastingly extended out from the field of the marketing of products to the fields of political campaigning, winning "the minds of men."

Dwight Macdonald once wrote an amusing long article in *The New Yorker* on "How-To-ism": on books that begin with the words "How To." He discovered, as one would expect, that there were many decent books with that sort of title dealing with *tangible* objectives—how to bake a cake, to build a boat, to save on your plumber's bill—but that the literature turned gooey and terrible when it dealt with larger, more complex, less tangible objectives—how to live with yourself, to find love and happiness, to find a satisfying faith, to rebuild America. The books assumed that the three easy simple steps of baking a cake apply also to these other realms.

There is B. F. Skinner worrying about how his shriveled picture of man as a thing applies to the creative artist: one last little loophole he has to close.

One finds a civilization trying to deal with the whole mysterious reality of the forest and the river from the point of view of the practice of bridgemaking.

A professor of Italian literature stands by the university elevator with computer print-outs under his arm. Computer printouts? Dante? Machiavelli? Silone? Particular words in poems and prose are to be counted. The computer is an immense help in the counting: without the computer it could not be done. But should it be done? Yes, I think it tells something. Should you be doing that instead of what you would otherwise be doing, if the computer were not available, and the pressure to use it in the atmosphere, and even a certain prestige for carrying print-outs under your arm into the Department of Romance Languages and Literatures? In other words, that technique and its social apparatus have influenced your decision about what to study and how to study it: to count words.

4. The "ends" and the "means" are not as easily separated in life as they are in thought. "Means," so called, do not retain their subordinate place. Human beings who devote their energies to presumably instrumental activities make them an end in themselves: the army, the business corporation, the processing of data by computer. Our affections follow our attention. The operation itself takes on an independent value. There is a gradual withdrawal of attention and positive feeling from the original purpose and a transfer to the means. This is true both of the machinery and of human proficiency. No one who knew this country at the height of its love affair with the automobile would believe that the primary focus of devotion was simply convenient movement from

one place to another. The automobile people had a revealing, very subordinate and dismissive, category of plainer vehicles kept in the rear of showrooms for old-maid schoolteachers: "transportation" cars. So much for them. A hi-fi enthusiast plays Mozart so that he can fiddle with the dials to perfect the sound of his set: the G Minor symphony becomes the means to the end of fine tuning. In one nice moment in the motion picture "Dr. Strangelove," the American general played by George C. Scott rejoices in the proficiency of the American bombing force, even though the result will be to blow up the world.

"Efficiency" and "practicality" are regularly listed as "values" characteristically held by Americans, independently of what one may be efficient or practically doing, rather in the way that "success" is admired, to the astonishment of a foreign observer like Charles Dickens, without regard to the field or activity in which this success is achieved.

The practicality of the American is of course a standard item in all characterizations of him: he is the nonspeculative doer and activist concerned with practice and result. It is not quite as standard an item to observe that this practical man has a characteristic way of relating to general ideas by jumping on them unawares, by leaping to them—as was said of Andrew Carnegie writing his book—"without fear and without research." That is to say, without much reading, practice, vocabulary, or supporting culture.

Tocqueville, along with many others, noted the inclination of the American, even before the full flowering of technological culture, to practical rather than theoretical science. "Those who cultivate the sciences among a democratic people are always afraid of losing their way in visionary speculation. They mistrust systems; they adhere closely to facts and study facts with their own senses."

We all experience having our own minds altered by a long-term change of focus. The man who has been in the executive branch, disdainful of the dilatoriness and compromising in Congress, watches in wonderment as his mind slowly alters its chemistry to include a greater sympathy for representative government when he goes to work on the Hill. The hard-news shoe-leather reporter who rejects the "punditry" of the "deep-think" armchair columnists finds, if he is given a column or editorials to write, that this other activity is harder and worthier than he thought. His mind shifts: a man's mind is shaped by what he actually spends his days doing, and by the value those around him place on it.

There is an old saying that a pickpocket who looks at a saint sees his pockets: there is a selectivity of observation, an exclusion and inclusion and focus. So it is also with a society, in which men reinforce each other's focus upon the pockets of the saint. The capacity to observe anything else, finally even the awareness that there is anything else to observe, atrophies. What else is there to observe about a man, after all, except his pockets?

Well, there is—something more, but a conscientious lifelong pickpocket has a hard time describing what it might be. And of course he is much more interesting and knowledgeable talking about pockets and how one picks them than about these other aspects of human life, whatever they may be.

A reduced, excessive, and narrow concentration upon particular limited objects diminishes the capacity to deal with the broad unreduced remainder of human existence. The pickpocket is so boring when he tries to talk about sainthood that one is eager to get him back on the subject of pockets and picking them. That Dante scholar is not going to be nearly as interesting on the subject of Paradise and the Inferno as he is on computers and counting words.

5. The "operator" resists questioning and criticism if it falls outside the domain to which his operation commits him. The human will, having resolved its questions, reached a decision, and moved to action, does not welcome the reopening of original questions. That is true of all of us, in our practical activities, including moral practice: after a certain point, and with reference to a certain set of activities, the decision is made; the questions are evaded. Decision and action require that such a closure be reached. And that characteristic of purposive human action is institutionalized in the techniques and the organizations of the operational society. As I said earlier, a cobbler cannot achieve technically excellent cobbling if he keeps asking himself whether it might be better if people went barefoot. Similarly, in a shoe fac-

tory the man on the line who puts in the laces depends upon the man who punches the holes: the latter is not expected to be exploring new values in sandals, throwing off the assembly line.

To move abruptly from shoes to foreign policy: in the latter field, too, men who carry out policy want it to stay put and men who initiate it do not really want inconveniently fundamental criticisms and questions about it. The writings about the United States's involvement in Vietnam indicate that the presidents making decisions, for all their talking about diversity of advice, did not really seek it or want it or get it. Fairlie says this of John Kennedy, and David Halberstam says it of both Kennedy and Johnson. A key to the whole complicated story is to be found in one paragraph by reporter Hedrick Smith in the foreword to *The Pentagon Papers* as published by the New York *Times:*

The Pentagon account and its accompanying documents reveal that once the basic objective of policy was set, the internal debate on Vietnam from 1950 until mid-1967 dealt almost entirely with how to reach those objectives rather than with the basic direction of policy.

Throughout the Vietnam period I kept remembering an argument I had had in 1958 with one of the men who was to be an important figure in those decisions after Kennedy came into office. He was arguing for "rational decision-making," based on objective and, if possible, quantifiable "data," eliminating thus the element of uncertainty, risk, and personal valuation, and especially avoiding any nonsense about tragedy, guilt, or remorse.

"Do you moralists recommend that we make a different decision?" he asked. "What would you *do* differently?"

I could not at that moment name any specific major difference of conviction about policy.

"Then, the only difference between you and me is that you want us to feel remorse for having taken the action. All you do is to add a dimension of guilty feeling with your talk of tragedy and the risk of decision. All you do then is to leave the decision-maker disturbed, remorseful, and upset when he has to face tomorrow's decision because his conscience is torturing him for yesterday's. Is it not better to think clearly and objectively without this overhanging mystical world of indeterminate and unmanageable moral claims—to think in a way that is *rational* and *objective*, to calculate well, to decide on the basis of the calculation, and then to proceed to the next job with a clear conscience?"

I remember this argument not only because I could not meet the challenge in his terms on the spot—to name some specific difference in American foreign policy to which my outlook would lead—but also because the years since have provided, belatedly for purposes of that debate, such examples, including some in which this man himself was a considerable participant.

But that particular form of argument was mistaken, from my point of view, in any case: the significance of an outlook less "rational" (in his sense, not in mine) than this man defended is not to be found in its discrete application, item by item, to separated decisions about policy. It is to be found, rather, in the more fundamental and longer-term interpretation of the nation's role; in the selection, therefore, over a period of time, of the kinds of decisions about policy that the "policy maker" (and the citizen, too) presents to himself; and in the meaning he perceives in the events in which he participates. In the long run, I believe these fundamental perspectives do "make a difference" in specific policy, and that the decade after my conversation, during which he was not only an "option" man but also a man who saw tough-guy romance in guerrilla warfare, fully demonstrated that point. Talk about guilt, remorse, and tragedy drove him up the wall, but there was cause for those words to come into human speech.

6. The *inertia* of technical reason and its organizational instruments is another paradox: starting with the heightened purposefulness, a focus upon an end to be achieved, practically, efficiently, actively, it comes at last to exhibit a momentum that is purposeless, that violates its own original genius. It rolls forward because it resists the questioning, the re-examining, of ends. It has the momentum of means that are standardized and have themselves become the object of affection. And this compound of fixed ends and standard means has been institutionalized in an organization.

I wrote above about the Bay of Pigs, and Sorensen's bafflement that it could not be stopped. The spring before that event there had been another fiasco: an American U-2 spy plane had been shot down over the Soviet Union, destroying a summit meeting. A chief fault of these two affairs, strikingly similar, was an uncritical reliance on technicians, bureaucrats, and operators, on men with "sophisticated and technical judgment." Means determined ends. People who were supposed to carry out policy in effect set policy. A book called *The U-2 Affair,* written by David Wise and Thomas Ross, concludes that the U-2 was sent so near the time for the summit because policy makers had lost control of the U-2 program, and the people running it wanted to get in one more flight before a possible détente:

They were worried not so much that the U-2 might endanger the summit as that the summit might endanger the U-2. By May of 1960, intelligence had come to dominate policy in the U-2 program. Instead of serving as a basis for policy-making, intelligence-gathering had become an end in itself.

Ironically, the "rationality" of technical reason turns irrational by being stuck in grooves. Since it must take static objectives for granted, and static circumstances, it gets caught when conditions change. The know-how people, like French generals in the familiar criticism, are always fighting the last war. The externalized repetitious precision of technical knowledge carried too far fails in part because of its virtues: it is too closely linked to those objects and conditions it has mastered. Tied to those particulars, it falls down when faced with new ones.

The "anti-intellectualism" in the American make-up has a number of sources, and the late Richard Hofstadter wrote a long book exploring them; one major source is the complex discussed in these paragraphs. The momentum of the machinery resists independent, possibly disruptive, ideas. There is this distinction, though: being annoyed by and opposed to a particular group of people, called "intellectuals," effete, nattering, pseudo, and so forth, is one thing; to allow one's own larger capacity of mind to atrophy is another—the capacity to make significant generalizations; to ask fundamental questions about accepted policies, even about accepted institutions; to criticize and evaluate present society from a standpoint outside it; and the like. The sorting out in the modern world of a particular group called "intellectuals" is a sociological phenomenon of some interest, but the encouraging or discouraging of that capacity in a much larger part of the population is a different and more important point. The technological momentum rolling toward the production of an SST, or the bureaucratic momentum rolling toward the U-2 affair, the Bay of Pigs, or the escalation in Vietnam, could quite well be questioned by men who had never heard of the *New York Review of Books.* It is the *separation* of the critical and evaluating faculties from practical action, and the cultural discouragement of the former, that is the important point. The separating of men of thought from men of action follows; it was not that way among the Founding Fathers, but it is that way today, as Henry Kissinger made clear in the essay referred to in the previous chapter. If moral reason is to guide technical reason, it must be otherwise.

7. Too direct and complete a commitment to the technical and practical, and to limited ends, is finally self-defeating, for continuing reference to the larger ends must discipline, direct, and criticize technique. To be "efficient" or "practical" assumes some frame of values within which the "efficient" adoption of means to ends takes place; if there is a mistake about the values, then no amount of practical "know-how" will save the situation. Finally, the practicality will fail to achieve even its own limited ends, for there is a certain interaction between the ends of living so that even the most immediate ones are not wholly divorced from the larger, more intangible ones. One eats in order to live, and not the reverse. One builds a telegraph because one assumes Maine *does* have something to say to Texas. (The familiar challenge from Thoreau—that Maine may not—is quoted in every book about so-called mass communications, including books that make quite clear that they do not get the point of the quotation.)

Again there is the need for that controlling dialectic with the reason and conscience of man, with the good for man, the expression of which in this life is never static. When in 1957 Sputnik jolted American technological self-confidence, there was much scrambling for more education in science. The General Motors man who was secretary of defense at that time, Charles Wilson, was criticized for underrating basic scientific research—for saying, "Basic research is when you don't know what you are doing"—but perhaps the criticism stopped too soon. It is true that if one emphasizes applied *science* to the neglect of basic science, then in the end even applied science will falter; but it is further true that if one emphasizes science to the neglect of the broader humanistic understanding out of which it should arise, then in the end science will be at least inhumane and perhaps also inadequate in its own narrower terms.

After Sputnik we decided to give ourselves a scientific education in a hurry, to catch up with the Russians. The bright young modern celebrity president elected in 1960 promised that we would put a man on the moon (because it is *there*) within the decade, and, after a great deal of sad history had flowed under our American bridge, we did it. But by the time we did it, it did not quite mean as much as it was supposed to, and a few years thereafter the "space program" had become (although people drew back from admitting it) something of a bore. For all the fanfare, it was not an enterprise engaging a sufficiently serious purpose.

In the end, life will insist again on the relevance of the considerations omitted. With too narrow a purpose, the Operation falls into life-defeating and perhaps self-defeating contradictions. A too exclusive concern with the service of immediate aims not only leads to the neglect and distortion of other aims but also at the last may not even produce the efficient accomplishment of the immediate ones that originally was sought. Why is this so?

The first reason is the enormous collection of unintended side effects. Sheer speed of movement is not a subtle objective; yet it is said that rush-hour traffic on a great city boulevard in a horse and buggy averaged six miles an hour, and that (leaving aside the question why one would want to speed down the boulevard anyway) rush-hour traffic after 100 years of technological ingenuity built around the marvels of the internal-combustion engine also averages six miles an hour.

It once again moves at six miles an hour because the more efficient machine attracted millions of drivers. Social invention did not keep up with mechanical invention: multiple cars jammed the roads and eliminated the "efficiency."

The ends of living, though relatively separable in early stages, come together at the last so that the wholesale neglect of some finally is destructive even of those other purposes in the service of which the neglecting was done.

Here is a small and homely, but representative, example of a skirmish on the technological-bureaucratic terrain. Something like it could be brought forward from every section of the American social landscape.

You are administering a program to bring visitors to a college campus to exhibit in the flesh the joys and sorrows of life in American institutions: not necessarily famous people, but articulate ones. The aim is student enlightenment. The speakers are to appear in a formal class followed by informal sitting-on-the-floor conversation: no need to hire a hall, post billboards, wait to see whether anyone shows. From one little bureaucracy (with a self-interest, as one later realizes) there comes a suggestion: dinner at a price, tickets, make these speakers available to Rotarians and Ladies' Aid from the town. Okay. Good idea. Part of our service. The TV people (with their own purpose and organization) say: How about putting it on TV, televise the dinner. Okay. Good idea. Reach more of the public. Part of our duty. A speaker scheduled for the televised dinner has to change dates, so he can be present for the president's State of the Union message. Commitments have been made to dinner guests who have tickets and to the TV people. Something has to be canceled. What? The informal meeting with students, which was the original purpose of the invitation.

Should one then condemn outright and fiercely the bureaucracies and technologies and self-interests that help make for such familiar reversals? I do not think so. Instead, one should return to the original purpose, articulate it, try to recover it, but also reexamine it, adapt, criticize the new possibilities and dangers in its light: moral reason controlling technical reason. A land of petrified purposes requires exactly that more articulate and constant ethical consciousness that its own characteristics tend to destroy.

To a degree, the experience represented in this little example is part of the story of human existence, with or without modern technology: we start out for Jerusalem and end up in south central

Indiana. But immense new organizational-technological power and pervasive and technical thinking augment this eternal human condition. The earnest graduate student goes forth into the intriguing realm of higher journalism, with the intention thereby to elevate the public by an infusion of the wisdom he has soaked up in his seminar. He writes the central paragraphs of his essay, perhaps a bit weighty with abstractions. Therefore, aware of the necessities of the medium, he sprinkles illustration; he devises an anecdote with which to begin, and a concrete topical reference to clinch the ending. The "piece," as the saying goes, comes back from its editorial processing: the illustrations, the anecdote, and the concrete reference remain, but the paragraphs with the abstract ideas, which were the reason the article was written in the first place, have been scratched out.

Life has its disillusionings and its cross-purposes and its instructive encounters with practical realities, no matter how we may arrange it. But the world of technical reason gives this perennial experience a new dimension. The power and the pressure of "mass" communication, with a giant organization, a multitude of regularized techniques, and higher stakes, alters the relation of purpose to practice. Emily Dickinson composing poems in her room in Amherst had to reduce the fire of inspiration to the confines of words on paper—which is limiting and practical already—but she did not have to satisfy an editorial process that in turn was shaped by competitive and commerical realities. She did not face the menace and the opportunity of the Organization that would present millions of readers or viewers to her at once, on condition that she fit its formulas. But that is our dangerous situation, and if we can restore the moral substance, perhaps also our promising situation.

8. That great central principle by which the faults of the technological world are to be identified—the principle of cumulative unintended side effects—applies as much in the realm of values, ideas, and policies as it does in the realm of machinery. Modern technology separates each of the particular ends to be served and devises then an efficient and standardized Best Way—technique— to accomplish them. But the separation, or attempted separation,

Of Thee, Nevertheless, I Sing

of ends to be served, and the concentration on means, and the standardization of the technique, all have unintended side effects. The exclusions and assumptions and selections made have an effect, so small in each particular instance as not to count, that is added and added to the others to result in at least something like the shallowness, impersonality, fragmentation, inhumanity, and standardization with which a hundred thousand sensitive souls have charged the modern world. As with machinery, and bureaucracy, so with technical reason in policy and philosophy.

The unintended side effects of the machinery are important because the original purpose is so narrow—speedy transportation, fast food, whiter-than-white washdays—and therefore so many other aspects of life, and the other effects of the use of the means, are deliberately set aside. Even so dramatic an evil effect as the killing and maiming by the automobile on the highways is not taken into account by the Automobile Operation except in response to the most heroic exertions by public-spirited citizens. And the same with the polluted rivers made by whiter-than-white washdays, and hundreds of other examples suddenly made familiar by concern about the environment.

To be sure, it is not technology alone, but commerce as well, that does all this. The technological principle reinforced by the private-profit principle creates much of the world we live in. Economists have this faintly comic conception of "externalities" or "neighborhood effect," which seems unconsciously to reveal the defect in the economist's methodological individualism—the separated private consumer, the separated producer, economic man "maximizing" his individual satisfactions. "Externalities" are effects on other people that do not appear in one's own "maximizing" calculations: my smoke polluting the air we all breathe, my garbage in the river we all swim in or drink from or look at or smell, my pine trees offering you a view you did not pay for. Because man is a social animal, and his life is interwoven with other lives in community, these so-called externalities—these effects, good and bad, on other people—are omnipresent and of central importance. To an individualistic economics, though, they are tacked on and a bit of an embarrassment, like a humane merchant who would lower his prices because of compassion rather than market forces.

Our society has had that free-market picture at its center, and that fact complicates our coping with the accumulation of the effects of modern technology; but socialist countries in an advanced industrial condition have their problems with that accumulation also.

That accumulation of many technical exclusions and standardizations and narrowings is like the accumulation of many individual decisions described in a memorable article in *The Public Interest* written by Thomas Schelling, "An Ecology of Micro-Motives": each driver on the Interstate, having been delayed in his turn in blocked traffic, speeds by the mattress lying on the highway, although it would take but a moment for one to stop and remove it and ease the traffic jam for everybody.

The field of race is full of examples. Whenever one tries to explain how a society can be "racist" without the individuals in it necessarily being "racist" (the word is used reluctantly), one resorts to examples of accumulated acts which when added have a racially discriminatory effect: for example, of many unions with father-son apprenticeship systems; or of many banks or many real-estate men or many zoning boards whose red-lining and gentlemen's agreements and two-acre-lot requirements have a distinct racial effect even though not intended. As with these matters, so, in a much larger way, with the modern operational complex— including its effect upon human habits, ideas, and attitudes: to look at trees and see lumber; to look at lumber and see a bridge; to look at a bridge and see dollar signs; to look at a saint and see his pockets.

Not only is the operational medium the message; the social construct that circularly makes and is made by that medium is "the message," too. The problem is not only the computer itself (to shift to that other convenient symbol), but also the men who make judgments about what the computer shall do, which judgments—which men, indeed, and the social order of which they are a part—are reciprocally being shaped by the outlook of which the computer is an expression. As one's opponent always says in these arguments, any fault is not in the computer, but in the use that some men may make of it. The computer people always tell you about GIGO: garbage in, garbage out. To be sure. But one must add the other part of the circle. The use that is made of the computer and of all the vast machinery of our modern life is decided upon by men who are shaped by a world of values the computer comes out of and helps to spread. One might almost then say, Garbage out, garbage in.

The philosopher of science with great amusement and self-satisfaction argues at a cocktail party that it would indeed be possible to make a computer with a "conscience" if moral principles could be ordered for programing (Jeremy Bentham, I suppose, would have agreed). One is tempted to throw up one's hands at that, to say what Louis Armstrong said about understanding jazz: There's some folks that if they don't know, you can't tell 'em.

Technology is not the monster it is presented to be by Ellul and others, but neither is it neutral—merely a collection of means to be used whether this way or that way according to free human choice. There is already a bias in the machinery; it is important to see that the bias is also inside the mind of the machinists, and in the machinists' culture.

A resistant awareness of that bias, and an explicit defense of the human person and the human community against it, is a moral requirement of our time.

One may give content to the guiding notion of respect for the human person by this backhanded method: observing the specific threats to it by the operational society.

—Standardization, homogenization: those interchangeable men. "Your name is a number, your number's a case." (Don't punch, fold, or spindle.) Do the young make too much of this threat? In any case, respect for the human person has included the recognition of the uniqueness, the particularity and distinctness, as it used to be put, "soul," of each.

—Shallowness, superficiality, a merely surface relation to other persons and to the many communities of which one is a part— even Henry Thoreau was a part—including the historical communities, like the nation-state, that we appropriate in part by symbols. The self has its proper relations to other human beings in "depth": a metaphor, to be sure, but all the important supratechnical realities are approached by metaphor.

—Fragmented roles and separated functions, "impersonal," fitting the machinery, but unfitting for the wholeness, the unity, of a man or a woman.

—Passivity, powerlessness, a product of overt and covert forces, manipulated by propaganda machinery and determined not only externally but also internally by impersonal social and psychological forces, a cue ball on the billiard table of history, powerless and "behaving," acted upon but not acting: this as over against man as a free "moral agent," as one who genuinely makes decisions, and whose decisions make a difference—a "responsible" being.

—An irrational being, shaped and controlled by subconscious rumblings and pushings and shovings, by childhood and by the past, by society's ineluctable environing power, all apparent reason and conscience reducible to something else: to psychology, sociology, and a grumpy father. Man in an older and better picture was capable, despite all, of reason.

The modern world has its own way of threatening us as human beings, as selves freely joining with others in common human undertakings, and upholding our obligations as much as we may uphold them, and deliberating with each other and changing our minds and persuading others and being persuaded, and doing those things we ought not to have done and leaving undone those things that we ought to have done, but sometimes also *doing* those things that we ought to have done, and making and breaking and keeping promises, and shaping the future to a degree by our own action; it has its way of attacking us, not only with bombs and gases and chemicals and TV sets, but also with the debased notion that we are not what we are: that we are not responsible and occasionally reasonable human beings.

Of Thee,
Nevertheless,
I Sing

During World War II George Orwell, writing in London under bombardment, began an essay about his native country in the following way:

> As I write, highly civilised human beings are flying overhead, trying to kill me.
> They do not feel any enmity against me as an individual, nor I against them. They are only "doing their duty", as the saying goes. Most of them, I have no doubt, are kind-hearted law-abiding men who would never dream of committing murder in private life. On the other hand, if one of them succeeds in blowing me to pieces with a well-placed bomb, he will never sleep any the worse for it. He is serving his country, which has the power to absolve him from evil.

Shortly after that time, and often since then, a great many Americans have been doing their duty, as the saying goes, in that same way, and in other ways analogous to that entirely impersonal effort to kill George Orwell. The moral absolution of which Orwell spoke has for the most part been extended to these later, American activities, both in the consciences of men doing the deeds and in the attitude of their countrymen. We engaged in saturation bombing of cities in World War II, and dropped atomic bombs on two Japanese cities, without great moral revulsion. The My Lai massacres and similar horrors in Vietnam were swept rather quickly out of sight. One absolving justification for the Watergate collection of misdeeds was "national security." An early disappointment with President Ford was his gramophonic and explicit endorsement of covert American interventions in the internal politics of other countries, specifically in Chile.

George Orwell went on to say:

> One cannot see the modern world as it is unless one recognises the overwhelming strength of patriotism, of national loyalty. . . . As a *positive* force there is nothing to set beside it. Christianity and international Socialism are as weak as straw in comparison with it. Hitler and Mussolini rose to power in their own countries very largely because they could grasp this fact and their opponents could not.

American nationalism has the characteristics of other nationalisms, but in different proportions and perhaps with an additional ingredient. National loyalty here as elsewhere catches up our affection for a familiar natural environment, for rocks and rills and templed hills, even though there are equally amber waves of grain in Russia, equally spacious skies in China, and purpler mountain majesties in Canada. The ingredient of blood relation, of tribalism and kinship, is present also, unfortunately, in American nationalism, despite our tremendous ethnic heterogeneity: until very recently, as the struggles over race reveal, the national psychology has held a kind of a hierarchy of increasing Americanism, with WASPs possessing most of it. Our nationalism, like that of other countries, includes the yearning for order and the fear of anarchy: those flags on the windshields and in lapels in 1969–70 had a quite evident link to such emotions, as did the nasty love-it-or-leave-it theme. This last has its xenophobic and reactionary ingredients, too, along with the fear of change and of the different, the desire for order and continuity and security.

But these familiar aspects of nationalism do not tell the whole story of an American's loyalty to his country. There is also, for ill as well as for good, an aspect in which this nation to a peculiar degree is seen to be the bearer of universal ideals.

"Idealism," to be sure, can refer to many different kinds of ideals. During the 1972 presidential campaign, the late Stewart Alsop wrote a *Newsweek* column attacking the lack of "idealism" on both sides in the campaign, citing as an example of a truly idealistic statement, the measuring rod by which he found the "national mood" in 1972 to be defective, John Kennedy's familiar

"Ask not what . . ." sentence from the inaugural address in 1961. The ideal in the Kennedy sentence is Service to Country—"what you can do for your country," as opposed to "what it can do for you." The implication, at least as Alsop was to use the sentence, was that one is to perform this service to his country *as it now is*— unchanged. And, it may be implied, as an absolute, as a final appeal. One is to make a sacrifice to serve the country, following out the policies national leaders have decided upon, without challenge to those policies. That is very much a Washington Establishment notion of idealism. The model for idealism of this kind is the service of a soldier in wartime, in which young men risk their lives, and many die, doing what those in authority say they must do for their country's defense. In the right setting that can be a high and honorable ideal, an ideal that, one could fully agree with Alsop, was not sufficiently appreciated by the young of the period, trained in the atmosphere of disparagement of the nation, rejection of authority, and disapproval of the then current war. But it is only one among many ideals; it is an ideal with a particularly dangerous moral twist in it; and, like all ideals, it has its underside, its limitation, its conflict with other ideals, its misuse, its particular relation more to some social classes than to others.

This patriotic-conservative ideal (Ask what you can do not for humankind or citizens of other places, but for your country, and not to change or improve your country but to "serve" it as it is) was particularly appropriate to World War II, when the country as it was, unchanged, was to be defended in a ferocious struggle, and when to defend the country was also to serve other peoples and to defend the purposes of civilization. At that moment sacrificing for the United States and sacrificing for higher humane ideals coincided. But it is to be doubted that that kind of moral interpretation should have been transferred intact from the forties to the sixties, let alone the seventies.

The reason for the peculiarly dangerous moral twist in this kind of idealism is the enormous amount of egotism in modern nationalism, very much including American nationalism. Reinhold Niebuhr explained that the strength and danger of a collective egotism, of which modern nationalism is by far the strongest, derived from its compounding of individual altruism with individual egotism. "Americanism" gathers together those sacrificial, idealistic, even heroic motives and actions of soldiers and patriots acting in disregard of self in service of their country, with an egotistic identification with what happens to the country, so that in American "honor" and in America's not being a "pitiful helpless giant" there is an extension of each person's touchy ego. These things are compounded, making collective national egotism a notably tricky and dubious force in the world, as much of America's recent history demonstrates. Alsop, and perhaps Kennedy, and certainly a considerable part of modern American liberalism, did not include the larger dimension by which this nationalism could be subjected to criticism on the basis of ideals that transcend the nation.

This country has been a symbol and to a degree the exemplar of such ideals—of elements of a good society, applicable everywhere.

Certainly we have regularly overstated our national importance to mankind, from the notions of special Providence and God's new Israel in the colonies, through "manifest destiny" and "the last, best hope of mankind," and Woodrow Wilson's proclamations, to the picture of ourselves as the epitome as well as the leader of freedom and democracy in the Cold War period. A story that involves both Kennedy's inaugural speech and Lincoln's at Gettysburg will make the point.

Max Ascoli wrote one of the few editorials critical of Kennedy's address. When he was introduced to the President at the White House in the spring of 1961, Kennedy, no man to mince words, immediately said to him that he understood he did not like the inaugural. Ascoli diplomatically replied that the fault was not in the speech but in the genre. How about the Gettysburg Address? Kennedy responded, perhaps characteristically. Yes, that's another example, Ascoli replied, characteristically on his part. There is, he continued, that sentence about "testing whether that nation *or any nation so conceived and so dedicated,* can long endure"— as though mankind's entire history of liberty turned on the experience of this one nation.

No doubt in our speeches we overdo it. Mankind has other

sources of the political good beyond the boundaries of the United States, and could develop that good even if we should fail or vanish. Nevertheless, the United States is important, and its importance does not rest solely with its power; those of us who are citizens of this country, in particular, want its moral role to be fulfilled.

I remember a conversation with a hardheaded foreign-policy expert (they all had hard heads, and hard noses, too) back in the fifties. He was presenting a rigorous operator's attack upon, as he would say, merely idealistic language in the conduct of political affairs. He seized upon a convenient example. Just that morning he had called to find the times for planes to Toronto, and the airline girl had said, "We have Golden Falcon Service at 6:00," and "Golden Falcon deluxe jet service at 8:00" and an "Ambassador" flight at ten—the "Golden Falcon" part is all that I remember exactly, but there was more of this familiar inflated decorative commercial language. The foreign-policy man looked on all the "Golden Falcon" business of the passenger desk and the airline's advertisements as the equivalent of the language of political ideals, and contrasted it unfavorably to the pilot's flight plan. The latter was *real*. It would give the hard and solid facts of the trip that a practitioner would need to know—no nonsense.

But is all our effort to shape and to state our moral understandings in politics the equivalent of the decorative language about "Golden Falcon Service"?

I used in response a counter-illustration, familiar in religious circles, that comes from H. Richard Niebuhr. To explain the difference between what he called "outer" history and "inner" history he contrasted two accounts of the American Revolution.

In the *Cambridge Modern History* it is described this way:

On July 4, 1776, Congress passed the resolution which made the colonies independent communities, issuing at the same time the well-known Declaration of Independence. If we regard the Declaration as the assertion of an abstract political theory, criticism and condemnation are easy. It sets out with a general proposition so vague as to be practically useless. The doctrine of the equality of men, unless it be qualified and conditioned by reference to special circumstance, is either a barren truism or a delusion.

In the Gettysburg Address it is described in this rather different way:

> Four score and seven years ago our fathers brought forth on this continent, a new nation, conceived in Liberty, and dedicated to the proposition that all men are created equal.

Niebuhr went on to say that the former is not more true than the latter, but representative of a different relation of the self to the events. The kind of relationship the second represents—personal, "internal," moral, a relationship to "our fathers" and to the proposition about equality as our own, our own nation's "dedication"—is not, one may argue, to be dismissed as meaningless, decorative, or less "true" than the *Cambridge Modern History*'s deflationary external comment. Lincoln's sentences are a good deal more than language about "Golden Falcon Service," especially to citizens of his own country.

This now not so new nation, despite its particular defects, does have still the continuing possibility of being the kind of society "our fathers" conceived and brought forth on this continent. It has that continuing possibility chiefly for two reasons.

One is that, "conceived in liberty," it does indeed have free institutions under law. Many who shared the rancid anti-Americanism of the Vietnam period came suddenly to appreciate the nation's constitutional foundations when Senator Sam Ervin appeared on the television screen. Our country has a constitutional heritage providing for enough of an "open society" to prevent tyrants from suppressing varieties of conviction, and to allow some freedom for those varieties to express and promote diverse ideas in the conversation of politics. In fact, despite the intermittent excesses of the Cold War period, we are probably, on balance, improving. The society has been open enough and free enough to correct many of its own errors, and to make possible the continuing humane improvement in its social arrangements, if the citizenry decides to do it.

The other reason is that the citizens sometimes have decided to do it. Free institutions are not enough—even if they were freer and better designed than ours have been. The moral and intellec-

tual substance in the populace is at least as important as the shape
of institutions. Free institutions perform well only if free men act
responsibly . . . only if the ethos supports their doing so. The
United States also has the continuing chance to be what it was
"conceived" to be because of the stuff in the people. The choice is
there. The elements in the cultural heritage are there. To refer
again to Gunnar Myrdal, who has looked at us from the point of
view of a foreign social scientist:

Americans of all national origins, classes, regions, creeds, and colors,
have something in common: a social *ethos*, a political creed. It is difficult
to avoid the judgment that this "American Creed" is the cement in the
structure of this great and disparate nation. . . . America, compared to
every other country in Western civilization, large or small, has the *most
explicitly expressed* system of general ideals in reference to human interrela-
tions. This body of ideals is more widely understood and appreciated
than similar ideals anywhere else.

A society like ours requires such a "body of ideals," and insofar as
we have it that is the basis of such national merit as we may
claim. To some degree the "dedication" mentioned by Lincoln
has been passed on to shape the culture of a free society, although
we have not realized how difficult that is to do.

The civic ideal—the "American creed"—despite our neglect of
it, is not altogether lacking. When there is either the instructive
simplification of dramatic events or sufficient time and exposure
for some public education, the American people have responded
well enough—in a pinch—for our society to have avoided the
worst errors and made its way to this point with some continuing
improvement.

Not to go any further back, we were able despite our ideology
to respond to the Depression with a series of social reforms that
mitigated the suffering and partially corrected some major social
injustices. We were able to play our role in the defeat of Nazi
power, despite our earlier determination to remain isolated from
Europe's wars. We were able to construct a world role for ourselves as a center of an alliance of free nations—or of nations
resisting the Communist empire—with perseverance. We did
have the moral resources at last to diminish the structured injus-

tice to the black citizens of this country. We made our way through a dark period of demagoguery—that associated with Joseph McCarthy—without falling into the worst that many feared. By an intricate combination of the integrity of particular individuals, the viability of several institutions, the gradual moral understanding of the public, and luck, we made our way out of the threat to the constitutional system represented by the Nixon scandals.

In the movement from 1948, or 1954, until 1968 to overcome racial injustice, it was the American creed that had to be more fully articulated and applied in the conversation of the culture, in addition to the need for the Supreme Court to make its ruling, and presidents to belatedly offer leadership, and Congress to belatedly act, in order to achieve what was finally achieved.

Politics, said Max Weber, is the slow boring of hard boards. Government in a free society is the same. Democratic politics in particular is like that. What is required is persistence, and civic virtue for a lifetime. One looks around at American democratic society in the seventies and asks: Where is there a serious and explicit effort to develop such civic virtue?

I have expressed sufficiently in these pages an astonishment that so few have attended to the subtle political culture required by our purposes and our situation. The democratic polity is not easy, but difficult. It rests upon a culture that is freely formed out of the values and ideas and interests of the persons who make up the society. It is not automatic. It does not arise out of mechanical historical forces. Its characteristics are the results of choice, which in turn are rooted in the values of the citizens, and in the sharing of those values in the culture. In other words, it is what we make it. It is not determined. It is not the result of ineluctable psychological forces. It is a moral enterprise—that is, an enterprise of choice, of freedom, of evaluation, and of judgment. And this moral enterprise has an intellectual component. In a complicated arena of choice, like politics, one needs the intellectual work of interpretation. And that in turn requires that one generation pass on to the next its effort to understand how justice and the public good are served by the institutions of the society.

Epilogue: Of Thee, Nevertheless, I Sing

. . .

If one is asked to name the universally valuable ideals of which the United States may be one important defender and exemplar to mankind, and by which at the same time our own national faults are tested, the short answer, of course, is "democracy." It is government of the people, by the people, and for the people. Behind the familiar word and phrases there is a more complicated background of ideas, some of which have been sprinkled through this book. There is our semiegalitarianism—our notion of the equality of men both in the last analysis and in certain regards short of the last analysis. There is a certain affirmation of the common man, which Lincoln understood and Mencken did not. There is our contribution to the history of liberty, some safeguards for which we managed to get down on paper. We managed also not only to fit Liberty and Equality together, up to a point, but also to combine them with what has recently been called "participation," and might better be called by an older phrase, "self-government." Self-government is itself a fundamental value—an aspect of man's dignity—and not an instrument to another end. As I have tried to say and to suggest by examples, these combinations are neither easy nor stable. Behind the complex combination one may discern another affirmation: that the human person as such is worthy of respect. We often describe this by phrases like "the dignity of the individual" that may distort our relation to the communities of which we are a part.

The respect for the human being "democracy" is supposed to embody includes his freedom and his being as good as the next fellow and his having, if we can work it out, something like an "equal" chance in life (although that is a long way from reality). It also should include social justice in a greater measure: the unhumiliating treatment of men and women by the arrangements of society. That means, among other things, a considerably greater redistribution of wealth than the mainstream of American ideologies have provided for. It is also obviously going to require more central government and collective action than Americans have been accustomed to, because the needs of a modern economy will force that on us. Both social justice and the common good, as chief values national policy now should serve, require a greater

321

knowledge of our dependence upon the social fabric than Americans typically have had in the past. It will also require a different kind of internationalism—a decent respect not only for the opinions but also for the well-being of mankind, which respect may often be expressed by our restraint rather than by our power. There was the isolationism of the interwar period. There has been the "internationalism" of Alsop, Kennedy, and our generation, the anti-Munich Cold War internationalism of the past thirty years, in which the major ingredient has been American power, America's throwing her weight around. Now there must be a more sensitive and self-restraining awareness of other peoples and of mankind's interdependence.

The United States still has its important role to play. Karl Jaspers, in his sober book *The Future of Mankind*, wrote, no doubt too sweepingly even in the mid-fifties: "Every Westerner has, in a sense, two countries: the country of his heart, his origin, his language, his ancestors, and one sure foundation of his political reality. Those fatherlands are many, but this foundation is today only one: The United States of America." Does an American in the nineteen-seventies accept as heavy a responsibility for the heritage of the West? Probably not. But if he could change a word or two he would accept another sentence from Jaspers: "In America—today the area of decision in the world of political reality—I hope for the old, pious, morally radical forces."

That implies the other part of our moral role. If you read the books about the growth of the world's population, and the limits of the earth's resources, and the dangers of thermonuclear weapons, and the coming biological developments, you are driven, even with the proper discount against the sensational, to a picture of a future full of necessarily *collective* decisions, by corporations, governments, gatherings of governments. What is to be asserted, then, in such a future is the liberty and moral responsibility of the human person—the conception of man as a self, as a moral agent, as a free being who makes decisions which matter and makes and breaks promises and forms the future out of his values and his decisions.

In the last two chapters of this book there are many remarks about functional reason, bureaucracy, the operational society, the technology of the modern world. That gigantic phenomenon is, of course, the center of the moral and of the political problem of our future. The perennial requirement of politics, to moralize power, now takes the form, to moralize *that* power: to build a free and a just society under conditions making for a mass society, and including the possibility of mankind's self-destruction.

The modern American world is a long way from being as bad as the picture given by its extreme antagonists. It is however (and obviously) sufficiently filled with threat to require a conscious and careful attention to the underpinnings.

Intellectually, philosophically, in creed or faith, it requires a more explicit affirmation of the reality of the self—of the human person in freedom and responsibility, in dignity and value, than another age might require. A true humanism is rejected both by some who deplore technological modernity, but who see its mass society nevertheless as the wave of history; and by those who do not deplore but endorse that mass society as a virtue: "the technology of behavior" in a Brave New World. It is as important to disagree with the former as with the latter. The future is real; human freedom is real; tomorrow's history is still to be made; there is no inevitability.

The horrendous and widely held picture of a mass society of cheerful robots, empty and powerless and manipulated by Big Brother, is a cautionary caricature, a negative ideal type, and not the picture of any reality: not any future reality (certainly not any *necessary* future reality), let alone today's real world. Today's real world, for all the evidence you and I and a hundred writers can give of a "mass" culture, is nevertheless a much more mixed and complicated and human world, indeed a world with much more that is good in it, than these negative utopian pictures of a terrible mass-robot world imply.

One may make a reverse application of the old argument with the optimists and progressives, if necessary. Of course one had to join the Niebuhrian attack against the older, simpler nineteenth-century American optimism and progressivism, with its expectation of a brighter world surely coming tomorrow, of mankind's natural goodness progressively revealing itself as the authoritarian restraints of the past were removed. One had to say—sometimes one still has to say—that not only technology but also science itself is not an unambiguous good. We used to argue with the optimist who had read John Dewey and saw science and democracy as virtually identical, both using the experimental method to progress, to move forward, into a brighter day. It was usual in that argument to cite the menace of modern scientific and technical development—the atomic bomb, most obviously. Every "advance" to some putatively higher level of "development" brings with its "progress" a concomitant regress: there may be wonders of nuclear energy awaiting us, but meanwhile there is the actually existing capacity for a destruction we cannot imagine. Against the optimism about man, the naïve picture of progressive enlightenment as the dead hand of the past is lifted from us, and we have the horrendous example of modern totalitarianism—of Nazis, concentration camps, the Holocaust, and the Gulag Archipelago. We have the milder versions of an inhumane or amoral Operation in the United States. "Progress" is not unambiguous, to put it mildly; "science" and modern technology and "liberation" do not necessarily make men good—which is always the issue. There is regress mixed with our "progress." Or, rather: the problem is always the same, and never goes away: man in his egotism and his genius for evil.

One had to argue that way against the "optimistic" folk in earlier decades. But now the reverse side of this truth is often also appropriate, as more men read and write books of a despairing and cynical kind, about the darker side of man.

Moral choice is indeed possible and real, even in the midst of the terrible possibilities of nuclear plenty and the technological-bureaucratic threat to the human person. Every age is equidistant from eternity. The perennial possibilities for human choice among goods and evils present themselves to men in every age—even, the chastened American witness may add, our own.

Acknowledgments

Index

Acknowledgments

The chief debt I owe for this undertaking is to Robert Goldmann, who has read almost every page of it, some several times, and who encouraged and supported me every step of the way. I cannot thank him enough. I also owe a great debt to Mitchell Sviridoff, who was "the first friend of this book." Their generosity and patience made this book come about. But neither of them, nor the Ford Foundation, with which they both are associated, should be blamed for the product: it is not necessarily what they expected, and it certainly is not what the Foundation had been led to expect when, many years ago, it gave me a travel and study award. Individually and collectively they have my gratitude.

The Poynter Center at Indiana University has generously tolerated having its director take time to finish this book, and has strongly supported it in the person of Dora Fortado, the Center's secretary. She typed and retyped these pages with a cheerful efficiency, devotion, and energy for which I am most grateful.

My colleague, chief, and friend William May generously read an early version and made many helpful comments. So did my wife, Betty Horton Miller, who has vetoed as conventional male chauvinism every sentence I drafted trying adequately to thank her, but to whom I am, anyway, once again heavily indebted and affectionately grateful. William B. Goodman has shown a patient, intelligent, and supportive interest going well beyond the call of an editor's duty.

Parts of this book appeared in different form in *The Reporter*, *The Yale Review*, *The New Republic*, *Commonweal*, the *Center* magazine, *Worldview*, and *Christianity and Crisis*. The faults of this book are exclusively mine.

Index